D1481710

Lineberger Memorial

Library

Lutheran Theological Southern Seminary   Columbia, S. C.

THE LOEB CLASSICAL LIBRARY

FOUNDED BY JAMES LOEB 1911

EDITED BY

JEFFREY HENDERSON

EDITOR EMERITUS

G. P. GOOLD

TERENCE

I

LCL 22

S022 07

TERENCE

THE WOMAN OF ANDROS
THE SELF-TORMENTOR
THE EUNUCH

EDITED AND TRANSLATED BY

JOHN BARSBY

HARVARD UNIVERSITY PRESS
CAMBRIDGE, MASSACHUSETTS
LONDON, ENGLAND
2001

Copyright © 2001 by the President and Fellows
of Harvard College
All rights reserved

LOEB CLASSICAL LIBRARY® is a registered trademark
of the President and Fellows of Harvard College

Library of Congress Catalog Card Number 2001016919
CIP data available from the Library of Congress

21.50

ISBN 0-674-99597-X

CONTENTS

INTRODUCTION

Terence and His Background

Most of our information about the life and background of Publius Terentius Afer comes from the biography written by Suetonius in the second century A.D., preserved for us (with an additional paragraph) by the fourth-century commentator Donatus. This tells us that Terence was born at Carthage and became the slave at Rome of the senator Terentius Lucanus, by whom on account of his intelligence and good looks he was given not only a liberal education but also his freedom. He enjoyed the friendship of many of the nobility, especially Scipio Aemilianus and Laelius; he also gained the approval of Caecilius, the leading comic dramatist of the day, to whom he read the script of his first play, *The Woman of Andros,* before it was approved for performance. After writing six comedies, allegedly with the help of his noble friends, Terence left Rome for Greece, still not yet twenty-five years of age, and died on the return journey. He left a daughter, who married into an equestrian family, and a small estate near the temple of Mars.

NOTE. This Introduction is an adapted version of the Introduction to John Barsby (ed.), *Terence: Eunuchus* (Cambridge, 1999), pp. 1–32.

Suetonius, who quotes a number of conflicting sources, is himself unhappy with several of these details; and modern scholars have been even more sceptical. Terence's alleged Carthaginian origin could simply be a false deduction from the cognomen Afer (= the African), and the story of Caecilius reading the script of *Andria* is open to the chronological objection that Caecilius died two years before that play was performed. It may be too neat a coincidence that Terence's departure from Rome at the age of twenty-four in 160 B.C. puts his birth in 184 B.C., which is precisely the year of the death of Plautus; it also means that he was a young man of only eighteen years when his first play was performed in 166.[1] Terence's connections with Scipio and Laelius, though vouched for by several authorities mentioned by Suetonius, may ultimately be a conjecture based on the reference in the prologue of *The Brothers* (15–16) to "the malicious accusation that members of the nobility assist our poet and collaborate with him in his writing" and on the evidence from the Production Notices (*didascaliae*) of *The Brothers* and *The Mother-in-Law* (second performance) that these two plays were put on at the funeral games of Scipio's father Aemilius Paullus.

There is very little about Terence's life that can be asserted as fact; if we reject Suetonius' evidence, we have to admit that we know very little about him at all. But, given Terence's involvement with the funeral games of Aemilius Paullus, it is by no means an implausible assumption that he was an associate of Scipio's and indeed of Laelius and

[1] However, there is an alternative reading in the MSS of Suetonius' biography which would put Terence's birth ten years earlier.

others who shared Scipio's philosophical and literary interests and his predilection for Greek culture. Terence does not in fact deny the allegations that he received help from his noble friends, but "regards it as a great compliment if he finds favour with men who find favour with you all, men whose services have been freely available to everyone in time of need in war, in peace, and in their daily affairs" (*The Brothers* 17–21). This description does not in fact fit Scipio and Laelius, who were young men of Terence's own age, as well as it would fit Scipio's father Aemilius Paullus and men of his generation; but Terence may well be disguising the truth here in order to turn an allegation into a compliment.

The Production Notices which have been transmitted in the MSS together with the texts allow us to date Terence's six plays to the years 166–160 B.C. This puts them at a very interesting period in Rome's social and cultural history. It was a time when Roman contact with the civilisation of mainland Greece was at its height. Only two years before Terence's first play, in 168 B.C., Aemilius Paullus had won the decisive battle of the third Macedonian war and had brought home as part of the booty the library of the defeated king Perseus. The booty also included enough paintings and statues to fill 250 wagons; and, among the huge numbers of slaves, many must have been educated enough to serve as tutors in the houses of wealthy families or execute artistic commissions for their Roman masters.

The hellenisation of Rome was, of course, a lengthy process spread over several centuries, with Greek culture mediated first through the Etruscans and then through the Greek cities of South Italy and Sicily. Its effect is visible in

3

a number of ways long before the days of Terence, for example in the assimilation of Roman gods to their Greek counterparts or in the adoption by the lower classes of Greek colloquial vocabulary, as reflected in the plays of Plautus. But two clear trends are discernible in the second century B.C.: Greek influence is now derived direct from mainland Greece rather than from South Italy and Sicily, and a clear distinction begins to appear between the gradual hellenisation of the populace and the embracing by the aristocracy of the "higher" Greek culture of literature and the arts. And this cultural split between the aristocracy and the lower classes was accompanied by an ever growing economic division, caused by the sheer amount of wealth that foreign wars generated, whether fought in Greece or in Asia or in the west. The number of sumptuary laws passed in this period, attempting to restrict luxury of various kinds, shows both that luxury was widely enjoyed by the upper classes and that there were those among these same classes who thought that its spread should be controlled.

There were also those among the ruling classes who wanted to control the spread of hellenisation because of the threat that it presented to traditional Roman beliefs and ways of life. The evidence is patchy, but there are enough recorded incidents to make it clear that the opposition to the spread of Greek culture had some political strength. The worship of Bacchus was strictly regulated by the *senatus consultum de Bacchanalibus* of 186 B.C.; two Epicurean philosophers were banished from Rome in 173; and there was a general banishment of Greek philosophers and rhetoricians in 161. It would be an oversimplification to talk of a philhellenic party on the one hand, admirers of

Greek art, thought, and literature, and a nationalist party
on the other, opposed to the spread of Greek culture, or
to suppose that Rome's freeing of Greece after the second
Macedonian war and her favourable treatment of Athens
after the third owed more to sentiment than to practi-
cal political and military considerations. But there is no
reason to deny a general polarisation of opinion, which
can conveniently be illustrated by reference to Plutarch's
biographies of Cato and Aemilius Paullus: Cato himself
instructed his son in Roman history and law, whereas
Aemilius employed Greek tutors to extend the educa-
tion of his sons to grammar, logic, rhetoric, sculpture, and
painting.[2]

It would be surprising if the conflict between the two
points of view did not extend to the theatre. Roman drama,
both tragedy and comedy, was closely based on Greek
models, and the morality depicted in it, whether the grand
crimes of tragedy or the private peccadilloes of comedy,
could easily be seen as inimical to the Roman ideals of the
mos maiorum. In 194 B.C. senators were voted special
seats in the theatre on the proposal of the consul Scipio
Africanus, a known philhellenist, which looks like an asser-
tion of the respectability of the theatre as a place for the
ruling classes. On the other hand attempts to build a per-
manent stone theatre at Rome were thwarted on at least
three occasions in the first half of the second century B.C.;[3]
the opposition to the attempt by the censors of 154 was led
by Scipio Nasica, a known upholder of Roman morality.
In fact, there was no permanent theatre at Rome until

[2] Plutarch, *Cato the Elder* 20.3–5, *Aemilus Paullus* 6.4–5.
[3] See for example Livy 40.51.3, 41.27.5.

Pompey built one in 55 B.C., and there must have been other grounds for opposition than the vain hopes of the conservatives to protect public morality or to check the popularity of the drama. Whatever the precise explanation, the general point is clear: Terence was writing at a time when the conflict between Greek ethics and traditional Roman morality was a live issue, and this conflict was bound to be reflected by a dramatist adapting Greek models for a Roman audience.

Theatrical Conditions and Stage Conventions

Dramatic performances (*ludi scaenici*) were part of the regular public festivals (*ludi*) which were held at Rome in an annual season which ran from April to November and also of occasional private games held to celebrate triumphs or funerals. The four public festivals which included *ludi scaenici* in Terence's day were the Ludi Megalenses (in honour of the Magna Mater) in April, the Ludi Apollinares (in honour of Apollo) in July, the Ludi Romani (in honour of Jupiter Optimus Maximus) in September, and the Ludi Plebeii (also in honour of Jupiter) in November. We know from the Production Notices that four of Terence's plays were performed at the Ludi Megalenses, two at the Ludi Romani, and two at the funeral games of Aemilius Paullus.[4]

These festivals, though religious festivals in the names of the various gods, were in spirit very much public holidays, offering various forms of entertainment for the

---

[4] This total (eight) includes the two unsuccessful stagings of *The Mother-in-Law*.

people at large; apart from several days of *ludi scaenici*, the public festivals regularly included one or more days of *ludi circenses* (chariot races), and *munera* (gladiatorial shows) were a common feature of private games. In this atmosphere the comic dramatists were not always sure of their audience, and the plea for a fair hearing in silence which can be found at the end of each of Terence's prologues is no empty convention. The prologue to the third performance of *The Mother-in-Law* (33–42) reveals that the first performance had to be abandoned because of rumours that boxers and tightrope walkers would appear, and the second because a gladiatorial show was announced, and these were not isolated instances; the speaker of this prologue, the veteran producer Lucius Ambivius Turpio, makes it clear that he had had similar trouble in obtaining a hearing for the early plays of Terence's predecessor Caecilius (14–27).

Ambivius Turpio was in fact, according to the Production Notices, the producer of all six of Terence's plays, and it is clear from the prologues of *The Self-Tormentor* and *The Mother-in-Law*, both of which he spoke in person, that he played a significant part in promoting Terence's dramatic career.[5] The producer (or actor-manager) was an important figure in Roman drama. It seems that, like the modern impresario, he acted as the middle man between the dramatist and the magistrates in charge of the festival (normally the aediles but a praetor in the case of the Ludi Apollinares), buying the text from the playwright and con-

---

[5] Ambivius' reputation in antiquity is attested by references in both Cicero (*On Old Age* 48) and Tacitus (*Dialogue on Orators* 20.3).

tracting with the magistrate to mount the performance of the play; this he did with his own company of actors, often taking the leading role himself (*The Self-Tormentor* 35–52). The size of these acting companies at Rome is a matter of speculation; most Roman comedies can be done with six or seven actors doubling parts as necessary and it would have been uneconomic to maintain troupes much larger than this. The actors themselves, it seems, generally belonged to the lower classes, including freedmen and even slaves, and it may be deduced from the fact that very few names have been preserved before the first century B.C. that, unlike their counterparts at Athens, they were not highly regarded in society.

As we have seen, there was no permanent theatre at Rome in Terence's day. Tacitus (*Annals* 14.20) envisages early Roman theatres as consisting of "hastily erected steps (that is, tiers of seats) and a temporary stage" (*subitariis gradibus et scaena in tempus structa*), and Terence's plays must have been performed in some such settings as these. It is uncertain whereabouts in Rome these temporary theatres were set up; the forum was an obvious place, and there is some indication that theatres were erected near the temple of the god to whom the particular festival was dedicated. The actual structures, being wooden, have left no archeological trace, and there is very little, if anything, that we can say with confidence about their size or shape. The external evidence suggests that we can assume a stage building (*scaena*) with three doors in its façade,[6] a platform stage (*proscaenium*) of which the depth and width and height cannot be determined, and

---

[6] For the three-door set see Pollux 4.124, Vitruvius 5.6.8.

an auditorium (*cavea*) consisting of benches (*subsellia*) probably raised in tiers but not necessarily arranged in a semicircle. The texts of the plays confirm the three-door setting, which itself implies a stage of a certain width but little else. The frequency of eavesdropping and asides does not of itself prove that the stage was of great length or equipped with suitable hiding places (such as side alleys or porches); once the eavesdropping convention was established, the audience would accept that characters looking the wrong way or engrossed in their own thoughts would fail to see or hear others onstage.

As for costumes and masks and styles of acting, we again lack contemporary evidence. The name *fabula palliata* or "play in a Greek cloak" (*pallium* is the Latin equivalent of the Greek ἱμάτιον), which the Romans gave to the type of Greek-based comedy written by Plautus and Terence, makes it clear that the costumes, like the locations, were Greek, and it seems highly likely that the *fabula palliata* took over the masks of the Greek tradition together with the costumes.[7] We have a list of 44 masks compiled by the encyclopedist Pollux in the second century A.D., which describes (for example) ten different types of old men's masks and seven different types of slaves' masks (Pollux 4.143–54), but our best guide to the appearance of masks and costumes and indeed to styles of acting is to be found in the artistic tradition (terracottas, reliefs, mosaics, wall paintings, bronzes) which remains surprisingly homogeneous over several centuries throughout the Greek and Roman world. The most striking masks are those of

---

[7] The literary evidence for masks in the early Roman theatre is curiously self-contradictory.

9

the leading *senex* and *servus* with their frowning fore-heads, beetling brows, and trumpet mouths; those of the *adulescens* and the various female characters are rather more lifelike. Pollux (4.118–120) also provides us with a description of costumes, which can be similarly aug-mented by the artistic tradition. Free characters wear a long tunic reaching to the ankles (in the case of males) or to the ground (in the case of females) with a shorter *pallium* on top; slaves tend to wear a knee-length tunic only, with the *pallium* thrown around their shoulders (*pallium collectum*); soldiers wear an elaborate travelling uniform which includes a cloak (*chlamys*), sword (*machaera*), and military cap (*petasus*). Different characters wear different colours, for example red for young men, white for slaves, and green or light blue for old women. As for acting style, we can no doubt assume a lively style with much gesticula-tion (in masked drama seen from a distance the gestures provide a valuable clue to who is speaking); the artistic evidence suggests the brandishing of sticks by old men and the adoption of a particular wide-legged stance by slaves.

Roman comedy inherited a number of stage conven-tions from the Greeks together with the texts. The doors in the façade of the stage building represent neighbouring houses (or sometimes two houses and a shrine), and the stage represents a street. All the dialogue takes place in the street; indoor scenes cannot be portrayed, and more dis-tant action has to be narrated. The two side entrances to the stage have a fixed conventional significance; unfortu-nately our evidence is confused, but the convention seems to have been that the right-hand entrance (from the audi-ence's point of view) leads to the forum and the left-hand one in the opposite direction (that is, to the harbour or the country).[8] Characters approaching from the wings are normally seen and announced by one of the characters on stage before they become visible to the audience; similarly an entry from one of the stage houses is often foreshadowed by a reference to the sound of the doors opening. Characters entering from the houses frequently deliver a final "over the shoulder" remark to complete a conversation which has been going on indoors; this gives the audience some inkling of what has been said inside, and helps to provide some continuity between house and stage. If two characters enter together (whether from the wings or from one of the stage houses), they usually enter in mid-conversation; more often a single character enters, who typically utters a monologue of greater or lesser length.

The monologue is another feature that Roman comedy inherited from Greek. Monologues are used to narrate what has happened offstage, or to offer reflections on the situation, or to deliberate on a course of action; some monologues fulfil more than one of these functions. A few monologues can be regarded as genuine soliloquies, where a character wrestles with some emotional problem, but most are in fact artificial speeches delivered for the audience's benefit, though the so-called "dramatic illusion" is normally preserved whereby the characters are enclosed within the world of the play and do not directly interact

[8] Vitruvius (5.6.8) states for the Roman theatre that one entrance led from the town (*a foro*) and the other from foreign parts (*a peregre*) but does not state which was which; Pollux's account for the Greek theatre (4.125–7) is hopelessly confused.

with the spectators. Monologues chiefly occur at the beginnings or endings of scenes. By far the commonest is the "overheard entrance monologue" at the beginning of a new scene, spoken by an entering character who is unaware of the presence of eavesdroppers onstage; such monologues can be quite lengthy and are often accompanied by asides and terminated by elaborate recognition formulas. Simple entrance monologues (ones delivered on an empty stage) also occur but are not so frequent. Monologues occur also at the end of the scene, where there are two possibilities, the "link monologue," where the speaker stays onstage to lead into the next scene, and the "exit monologue," after which the speaker departs leaving the stage empty.

The "eavesdropping aside" is not the only type of aside that Roman comedy took over from Greek comedy. There is also the "aside in conversation," where a character turns aside to utter a remark that is not meant to be heard by a dialogue partner. Asides of both kinds may be addressed to nobody in particular, or, where there are three characters on stage, to a second character unheard by the third. The object is often to amuse the audience, but the spectators are not normally directly addressed and the dramatic illusion is therefore maintained. The aside convention may seem to us highly artificial, but it is clear that it was readily accepted by both Greek and Roman audiences.

Terence and His Greek Originals

It was inevitable that the Roman dramatists in adapting Greek comedies for the Roman stage would modify them in significant ways. Not only were they writing for a different kind of audience at a different kind of festival in a different kind of theatre. There was bound also to be some influence from traditional Italian forms of popular entertainment, notably the Atellan farce, the phlyax drama of South Italy, and the mime, whose common features seem to have included improvisation and a tendency towards farce, ribaldry, and stock characters.

The extent to which the Roman tradition had diverged from the Greek by the early second century B.C. can be highlighted by contrasting the typical features of Plautus, for whom we have twenty-one surviving plays spanning the years from about 205 to 184 B.C., with those of Menander, who is the only writer of Greek New Comedy whose plays survive to us in significant quantity. There is inevitably still much in common in terms of characters and plot elements, but there is a considerable difference both in tone and in structure. The setting of a Plautine play is formally Greek, but the stage is peopled by characters who, though they wear Greek clothes and are careful to refer to the Romans as "foreigners" (*barbari*), tend to lapse into Roman jokes or allude to Roman topography and laws and customs. The characters are overdrawn rather than realistically portrayed; real-life roles and relationships are inverted; and certain larger-than-life character types predominate, notably the tricky slave, the pimp, the swaggering soldier, the greedy courtesan, the lecherous husband. Intrigue and trickery are the main focus of the plot, and the dénouement turns on the success or failure of the tricksters and their schemes rather than on the resolution of a genuine human problem. The language of the play is no longer natural but artificial and exuberant, with abuse and insults, direct address to the audience, puns and word-

13

plays, extravagant imagery, striking sound effects, rhetorical flourishes. In terms of structure the most obvious difference is the metrical form; in place of a largely spoken drama Plautus has introduced a considerable amount of recitative and even song. Gone are the choral interludes which divided the play into five acts, imposing a certain discipline on the construction of the plot, and also providing time for offstage action; the action is now continuous, plots are in general more loosely constructed with less regard for probability or proportion, and unity of time becomes much harder to maintain. There are also more characters on stage, with Plautus employing four or five or even more speaking actors at once as against Menander's three; there is a corresponding increase in stage business and a general "thickening" of the plot.

This transformation of Greek comedy from a relatively realistic reflection of real life into a much more self-consciously theatrical performance was not something that Plautus achieved single-handed. On the contrary, he seems to have been working in a largely homogeneous tradition which went back at least to Naevius (whose dramatic career began in the 230s) and was carried on after his own death by writers such as Caecilius and Turpilius (who died in 103 B.C.). Terence, however, seems to have stood outside this tradition, rejecting Plautus' linguistic exuberance and delight in trickery for something more akin to the elegance of language and the serious treatment of human problems to be found in Menander. It is tempting to link Terence's preference for a more restrained and philosophical treatment to his association with the young intellectuals of the day; whatever the reason for this approach, it does not seem to have found favour with his audience at large. Indeed, we can ascribe some of the specific changes which Terence made to his Menandrian originals, such as the addition of the characters of the soldier and flatterer to Menander's *Eunouchos* or the addition of a pimp-beating scene from a play by Diphilus to Menander's *Adelphoi,* to a perceived need to add scenes of farce and humour to satisfy the tastes of the spectators. It cannot be mere coincidence that Terence's *Eunuch,* which is generally regarded as his most Plautine play, was also his most successful; according to Suetonius, it was staged twice in a day and won 8,000 sesterces, the highest sum ever paid for a comedy.

Terence did not have only the tastes of the audience to consider; he also faced criticism from another quarter. The prologues of his plays several times refer to a malevolent critic (*malevolus vetus poeta*) whom he never names but whom Donatus identifies for us as Luscius of Lanuvium (a small town some twenty miles southeast of Rome). Luscius, who had been the senior comic dramatist at Rome since the death of Caecilius, mounted a determined opposition to Terence's dramatic career. This was no doubt partly due to personal jealousy, as the older writer saw his eminence threatened by the younger talent, but there was also a principle at stake. Luscius himself stood outside the "Romanising" tradition established by Naevius and Plautus; he believed that Roman writers should instead present a faithful translation of their Greek originals. Terence's prologues give a colourful, if not objective, account of the campaign which Luscius conducted against his younger rival. Luscius made two principal accusations, (i) that Terence "spoiled" his Greek originals (*contaminare*) and (ii) that he committed "plagiarism" or "theft" (*furtum*). By "contamination" Luscius meant the spoiling

15

of one Greek play by the addition of material from another: this was a rather pedantic charge, and Terence freely admits to the practice. By *furtum* Luscius meant repeating material which had already been used in a Latin play (which was in effect to "steal" from the previous Latin author), and Terence treats this point much more seriously: the Roman audience might well feel itself cheated if, instead of a brand new play, it was presented with a further Latin version of a Greek play which had already been adapted for the Roman stage.[9]

The practice of contamination indicates that Terence was not a slavish translator. There were other ways in which he seems to have significantly changed his Greek originals. It is commonly believed that he altered their openings by omitting expository prologues, and that, although he worked into his own opening scenes enough expository material for his plots to be followed, he nonetheless at times deprived the Roman audience of important information which its Greek counterpart had from the beginning. If this belief is correct, it follows that Terence rejected the opportunities for dramatic irony which the Greek audience's superior knowledge provided, but at the same time was able to exploit the Roman audience's uncertainty to create suspense and surprise. All this depends on the assumption that his Greek models did have expository prologues, and this is a matter of conjecture rather than an established fact. But it is certainly true that all the surviving plays of Menander for which we have sufficient evidence do have expository prologues, spoken by

9 See especially *The Woman of Andros* 9–14, *The Self-Tormentor* 16–19, *The Eunuch* 19–34, *The Brothers* 6–14.

divinities or by one of the human characters of the play, and that several plays of Terence's do produce surprise information at a late stage in a manner unparalleled in Menander. One arrangement of which Menander is particularly fond is worth noting, in that it is often assumed to have been used in the Greek originals of Terence's plays. This is the "postponed divine prologue," in which a divinity corrects misapprehensions created by the opening scenes and fills in other details of the background (as in *The Shield* and *The Shorn Girl*).

It is not easy to detect wholesale changes in the central portions of Terence's plays, but it is clear that he did make some. Terence has a fondness for double plots, involving two pairs of young men, fathers, and slaves, but with one exception it is clear that he took these over from his Greek originals rather than doubling up the plot himself; the exception is *The Woman of Andros*, where Donatus tells us that the second pair of lover and slave were not in Menander. We may also suspect structural change in the middle of *The Eunuch*, where the soldier-parasite pair, which Terence tells us in the prologue were imported from Menander's *The Flatterer*, loom relatively large. Apart from this, our best clue to Terentian change is the presence of four speaking actors in a scene, contrary to Menander's practice. This evidence reveals (for example) that Terence created a speaking part for the maid Dorias in the middle of *The Eunuch* by dividing up the role of the other maid Pythias, and that he extended the role of the young man Antipho in *Phormio* by bringing him back in the middle of the play.

There is also a good case for supposing that Terence made changes in the endings of his plays, nearly all of which involve scenes with more than three speaking actors. In two plays at least (*The Eunuch* and *The Brothers*) there is an unexpected twist to the ending which seems to derive from Terence rather than from the Greek original. If this is the case, one explanation may be that Terence was deliberately exploiting the surprise ending for dramatic effect, even at the expense of consistency. In a genre where there are a limited number of plots and the dénouement can generally be predicted, surprise is a useful weapon in the dramatist's armoury. But ethical considerations may also have played a part, granted Terence's interest in social and moral questions and the potential tension between Greek and Roman views; he may have wanted to bring the Greek play more into line with Roman attitudes, and, even where this was not the case, he may still have been trying to provoke the audience to think about the moral of the play by a change of direction at the end.

Language and Style

One of the criticisms which Luscius made of Terence was that his plays were thin in style (*Phormio* 5 *tenui . . . oratione*). Whatever precisely he meant by this, it is certainly true that Terence's language is restrained in comparison with the exuberance of Plautus'. This restraint was no doubt a conscious choice on Terence's part; as in other respects, he was deliberately rejecting the theatricality of the Roman comic tradition for something more akin to the realism of Menander. Early Latin literature is in general marked by vigour rather than by elegance; Terence's contribution was to bring into it something of the refinement of his Greek models. It is noteworthy that, a century after his death, Terence's style earned the commendation of Cicero and Caesar, who were both very much concerned for the purity and elegance (*urbanitas*) of the Latin language. These writers praise Terence's style for its elegance, charm, and purity while at the same time acknowledging his comparative lack of vigour.[10]

In any discussion of Terence's language the contrast with Plautus is instructive. Both create the impression of colloquial dialogue, as appropriate to the everyday characters and situations of comedy. The essential difference is that Plautus deliberately exaggerates the colloquial elements of the language of his characters in order to make a greater impact on his audience, whereas Terence aims at a colloquialism of a more refined or studied kind, such as will not detract from his portrayal of character and theme. Good examples are terms of abuse, terms of endearment, oaths and interjections, Greek words, puns and wordplays, alliteration and assonance, and imagery. In all cases the examples in Plautus are more numerous and more striking. Plautus, for example, uses 285 different terms of abuse, Terence only 76. Terence uses only two terms of endearment in all his plays,[11] Plautus can have four in a single line.[12] The standard oaths by the gods (*pol, edepol, ecastor, mecastor, hercle, mehercle*)[13] are twice as frequent in

[10] Caesar addresses Terence as a "lover of pure diction" (*puri sermonis amator*).

[11] *Mi anime* "my darling" three times and *meum savium* "my kiss" once.

[12] *Meus ocellus, mea rosa, mi anime, mea uoluptas* "my eye, my rose, my darling, my pleasure"(*The Comedy of Asses* 664).

[13] These are oaths by Pollux, Castor, and Hercules respectively.

Plautus as in Terence; on the other hand, the simple exclamations (*ah, au, attat, hem, hui, oh,* etc.) are actually three times as frequent in Terence. Terence is thus choosing the less obtrusive or more naturalistic way of adding a colloquial flavour to the dialogue.

Another respect in which Terence is more restrained than Plautus is in his use of Greek words, particularly of the kind which may be assumed to have invaded popular speech through increasing contact with Greek speakers; for example, the interjection *eu* (well done, bravo) and its variants *euge, eugepae, euax* occur only seven times in Terence as against some 70 examples in Plautus. There is less downright slang in Terence than in Plautus, though the milder colloquial expressions, such as *actum est* (we've had it), *bene facis* (very kind of you), *numquid uis?* (anything else?), *abi* (get away with you), *quid istuc?* (what's up with you?), are freely used. But there is one aspect in which Terence does come nearer than Plautus to real-life conversation and that is in his use of ellipse and of broken sentences in passages of rapid dialogue. Terence can have four or even more separate utterances in a single line of verse, with speakers breaking off or being interrupted in mid-sentence; responses are made in the minimum number of words, leaving the syntax to be inferred from the surrounding context.

If Terence's language lacks the racy colloquialism of Plautus, it also lacks his exuberant rhetoric. It has been claimed that Terence uses more rhetorical figures than Menander, and that may well be the case; it is not difficult to find examples of doublets, tricola, asyndeton, anaphora, antithesis, even chiasmus. The net effect of these figures is to add a certain elegance to Terence's style; they rarely draw attention to themselves in the Plautine manner. Plautus revels in the use of alliteration and assonance, which are constant features of early Latin; Terence uses them much less obtrusively and with due regard for characterisation. On the other hand Terence does make frequent use of rhetorical figures such as rhetorical question and exclamation, presumably as realistic devices belonging to the natural rhetoric of colloquial speech.

One further feature in which Terence's language is plain beside that of Plautus is imagery. In general Plautus' imagery is striking, exaggerated, fantastic, whereas Terence's is closer to what we find in Menander and to what we may imagine was actually found in the everyday speech of the educated public. There are categories of imagery which are common to both Plautus and Terence and are mostly derived from Greek New Comedy, such as fire and storm, heat and cold, sickness and health, teacher and pupil, hunting and fishing, warfare, and the theatre. Plautus not only extends the range of images (he is particularly fertile in images for deceit and trickery) but is much more audacious in their use, displaying a keen eye for the incongruous and indulging in extended analogies, unlikely personifications, and bold identifications of humans with animals or mythological figures. In Terence by contrast the commonest form of imagery is the single-word metaphor, and the vast majority of examples fall within the common categories listed above.

It has sometimes been claimed that all Terence's characters speak the same basic language, the refined language of the educated classes. Even so, careful analysis shows that Terence, following the example of Menander, does attempt some degree of linguistic differentiation. For one thing he distinguishes between male and female speakers. There are various markers of female speech which he is careful to use;[14] there are similar markers of male speech,[15] and in general Terence maintains these linguistic differences between the sexes to a greater degree than Plautus does. Terence also distinguishes between higher and lower character types: it can be shown statistically that his lower characters (defined as slaves, pimps, prostitutes, parasites, soldiers) use Greek words and metaphorical expressions more frequently than his higher characters, and that they tend to use the more colourful terms in both these categories. Among the higher characters there is some differentiation between young and old, with the *senex* showing a greater tendency to old-fashioned or more long-winded diction; and pairs of characters of the same type are often contrasted in their language, for example Demea and Micio in *The Brothers* or Chremes and Menedemus in *The Self-Tormentor*. Individual characters sometimes stand out against their types, for example Chaerea in *The Eunuch,* whose language is much more

---

[14] For example, the oath *pol,* the interjection *au,* the coaxing words *obsecro* and *amabo,* the self-pitying *misera,* and the intimate form of address *mi* or *mea* + vocative; of these *pol* and *amabo* are very largely restricted to women, and females clearly predominate in the use of the others. The effect of female speech markers is further enhanced by their employment in clusters.

[15] The chief male speech markers are the oaths *hercle* and *mehercle,* the exclamation *ei,* and the polite modifiers *quaeso, age, sis,* and *sodes.*

racy than that of the average young man, and Pythias in the same play, who is a much more assertive character than the average maid and employs some male speech habits in addition to the typical coaxing language of the female. Some characters are even given idiosyncratic speech mannerisms: Thais in *The Eunuch* uses the endearment *mi* + vocative so often (seven times) that Donatus is moved to comment (on line 95) that Terence intends this as a mannerism peculiar to her (*vult enim Terentius velut peculiare verbum hoc esse Thaidis*).

A translation cannot hope to reproduce the elegance and versatility of Terence's style. The one in this edition has a more modest aim: to be readable while giving the sense of the Latin as accurately as possible. There is a particular problem with oaths, exclamations, and other sentence modifiers, which tend to sound heavier in English than in Latin; some attempt has been made to reflect Terence's use of individual and gender speech markers, so that, for example, the female *pol* is consistently translated by phrases involving "heaven" (heaven knows, for heaven's sake) and the male *hercle* by phrases involving "god" (god knows, for god's sake).

Metrical and Musical Structure

The Roman dramatists transformed the metrical structure of their Greek originals. The surviving plays of Menander are written very largely in iambic trimeters; this is the standard dialogue meter of Greek and Roman drama, described by Aristotle (*Poetics* 1449a24–26) as the meter nearest to ordinary speech, and is roughly equivalent to

English blank verse but with six feet instead of five. Menander does however also have occasional scenes in longer lines of seven and a half feet in trochaic or iambic rhythm, which seem to have been accompanied by the pipe and declaimed or recited rather than being merely spoken. These "recitative" tetrameters are chiefly used in scenes which are particularly lively or farcical, but not all scenes in recitative are farcical and not all farcical scenes are in recitative. The proportion of recitative varies from play to play: *The Woman of Samos* has something over 30 percent, but *The Bad-Tempered Man* has only 16 percent, and a number of quite well preserved plays (e.g. *The Shield, The Arbitration, The Hated Man*) have none at all in their surviving portions.

In Plautus, by contrast, there is more recitative than spoken verse. Spoken iambic senarii (the Roman equivalent of iambic trimeters) amount to only 38 percent of the whole, being used chiefly for expository narrative, rapid dialogue, and low-key monologues. Almost half of Plautus (48 percent) is in recitative, including lines of eight feet (octonarii) as well as of seven and a half (septenarii) and using anapestic as well as iambic and trochaic meters; this "long verse" is typically used for more animated monologues and more elaborate passages of dialogue. The remaining 14 percent is in various lyric meters designed to be sung; the songs include both monodies, which are generally used for emotional effect, and songs for two or more actors, which have more varied purposes including the enhancement of the comic atmosphere of the play. Song is a new element, virtually unknown to Menander; its introduction to Roman comedy may owe something to the lyrics of contemporary Roman tragedies or to the visits of travelling solo artists from the Hellenistic world or even to an Italian musical tradition derived from Etruria.[16]

In Terence we find something different again. The proportions are 52 percent spoken verse and 48 percent recitative; there are only three songs in the whole corpus amounting to less than thirty lines altogether (*The Woman of Andros* 481–486, 625–638, *The Brothers* 610–617). Terence is thus rejecting the Roman tradition of song, which is attested in Naevius and Caecilius as well as in Plautus; in its place he introduces a new element of his own, namely mixed-meter recitative (called by Donatus *mutatis modis cantica*) with the meter changing from line to line in what are predominantly trochaic systems. This functions in a similar way to song in Plautus, being used mainly to highlight the entry of a new character in an emotional or excited state, but is much less obtrusive; passages in mixed-meter recitative are kept relatively short and account for only about 7 percent of the whole.

A further feature of Terence's handling of meter is his use of variation within a single scene. This practice is already familiar from Plautus, but Terence carries it much further, ringing the changes not only between mixed-meter recitative, straight recitative, and spoken verse but also between the different recitative meters. These changes form an important clue to Terence's intentions in

[16] The terms "recitative" and "song," as used here, should be treated with caution, since we have no real evidence for how the lines were delivered and the modern terminology may be misleading.

terms of tone and tempo, even though it is difficult for us to gauge the precise effects of the individual meters. It is a reasonable assumption that mixed-meter recitative is the most animated form of utterance and iambic senarii the least, with trochaic septenarii, which is the most common recitative meter, somewhere in the middle and the other recitative meters belonging to the more excited end of the scale.

The Production Notices of all of Terence's plays (and of the *Stichus* of Plautus) name the musician, which is some indication of the importance of the musical element. They also name the type of pipe used, which is variously given as "equal," "unequal," and "two right-hand pipes." Greek and Roman pipes were normally played in pairs, one fingered by each hand. The right-hand pipe seems to have been a straight cylinder, whereas the left-hand one was curved at the end with a bell-shaped opening, as in the combination known as Phrygian pipes; the left-hand one was longer and thus lower in pitch. The second pipe may have been used to extend the range of the first or to complement its scale; the two may both have shared the tune or, at times, one may have provided a drone accompaniment.

A Loeb edition is not the place for a detailed exposition of the metrics of Roman comedy. This edition contains a Metrical Analysis at the end of each volume, which sets out the metrical structure of each play contained in the volume; it uses the terms *mutatis modis canticum* for mixed-meter recitative and *canticum lyricum* for sung lyrics. As a further guide to the reader a blank line is left in the Latin text of the plays to indicate the transition from one metrical section to the next.

The Manuscripts

The main manuscripts of Terence are as follows:

A = codex Bembinus (Vat. lat. 3226), 4th–5th c.

Σ= consensus of Calliopian MSS, 9th–11th c.

Γ= consensus of CEFOPY

C = codex Vaticanus (Vat. lat. 3868), 9th c.

E = codex Riccardianus (Flor. 528), 11th c.

F = codex Ambrosianus (Ambr. H.75 inf.) 10th c.

O = codex Dunelmensis (Bodl. Auct. F 2.13), 12th c.

P = codex Parisinus (Par. lat. 7899), 9th c.

Y = codex Parisinus (Par. lat. 7900), 9th c.

Δ= consensus of DGLNp

D = codex Victorianus (Laur. 38.24), 10th–11th c.

G = codex Decurtatus (Vat. lat. 1640), 10th–11th c.

L = codex Lipsiensis (Bibl. munic. Lips. 1.37), 10th c.

N = codex Leidensis Vossianus (Voss. lat. Q.38), 10th c.

p = codex Parisinus (Par. lat. 10304), 10th c.

A^1 = A before correction; A^2 = A as corrected by a later hand

The manuscript tradition has two branches. One branch consists of the only surviving MS from late antiquity, a MS of the fourth or fifth century A.D. now in the Vatican, known as A; this is generally referred to as the Bembinus, because in the fifteenth century it was in the possession of the Bembo family. It is written in rustic capitals; it divides the text accurately into lines of verse; and it presents Terence's plays in the chronological order *Andria, Eunuchus, Hauton, Phormio, Hecyra, Adelphoe.* The other branch is represented by several hundred medieval MSS, the most significant of which are a dozen or so dating from the ninth to the eleventh centuries. These are written in a minuscule script; they present the plays in a different order from that of A; and they tend to show little understanding of meter, several being written out as if in prose. This second branch is known as the Calliopian family, because several of the MSS acknowledge an otherwise unknown scholar Calliopius as their source.[17] The Calliopian MSS are all indirectly descended from a lost common ancestor known as Σ, perhaps of the fourth or fifth century; more directly they are derived from two intermediary lost ancestors known as Γ and Δ, and they can be divided into two subbranches accordingly, though there has been a certain amount of cross-contamination between the two subbranches. A striking difference is that several of the Γ MSS have miniature illustrations to accompany the scene headings, whereas none of the Δ MSS is illustrated.

This edition presents a plain text with a minimal *apparatus criticus*. The text of Terence is generally well established, and it has not been thought necessary to do a fresh examination of the MSS or to report the readings of individual MSS in detail. Variant readings are given only where there are textual problems of particular difficulty or importance, and it has in many cases been considered sufficient to report the reading of the Bembinus (A) and the consensus of the Calliopian MSS (Σ); the phrase *codd. pl.* (= most of the MSS) is used to indicate a majority reading and *cett.* (= the rest) the reading of all the MSS other than those named. Other authors cited as witnesses to the text

[17] By a subscription in the form *Calliopius recensui* or *feliciter Calliopio bono scholastico*.

are the ancient commentators Donatus and Eugraphius (the phrase *Don. in comm.* identifies a reading mentioned by Donatus in his commentary as an alternative to the one given in his own lemma), the grammarian and commentator Servius, the grammarians Priscian and Charisius, and the encyclopedist Festus; there is also an occasional reference to ancient glossaries and to the scholia on the Bembinus. There are very few papyrus fragments of Terence from antiquity: Π^b (P.Oxy.2401) is referred to here twice for the text of *The Woman of Andros*.

The MSS of Roman comedy do not contain the act and scene enumeration which is found in modern editions (including this one). The act divisions in our texts are the work of the renaissance editors, who divided the plays into five acts in order (it seems) to conform to the five-act rule enunciated by Horace (*Art of Poetry* 189–190); the only reason for retaining them is that they provide a convenient framework for the discussion of the plays. The scene divisions on the other hand do appear in the MSS, though it is unlikely that they go back to Terence himself. The criterion for identifying a new scene is the entry of a new speaking character; when this happens, the MSS list at the head of the scene the names and roles of all the characters who will take part in it.

Changes of speaker within the scene are indicated by the MSS in two ways. Most of the medieval MSS insert an abbreviation of the character's name, either in the margin or in mid-line, at the beginning of every new speech. But the Bembinus, followed by a few of the later MSS, uses a curious "algebraic" system, found also in some MSS of Plautus, whereby each character is assigned a Greek letter in the scene heading and these letters are used in the text to denote the changes of speaker. Again, it is unlikely that either system goes back to Terence: our earliest papyri of dramatic texts use marginal dashes (*paragraphoi*) and mid-line double points (*dikola*) to indicate changes of speaker but rarely name the characters. There is obvious room for error in the transcribing of the speaker assignations, and it follows that the indications in our MSS are not altogether trustworthy: hence there are a fair number of alternative assignations in the apparatus of this edition.

The MSS preface the text of each play with a Production Notice, typically giving the festival, the presiding magistrates, the producer, the musician and the type of pipe, the author of the Greek original, and the date by consular year. These Production Notices do not go back to Terence's day and are full of inconsistencies and contradictions, with material possibly incorporated from later revivals. The author of the Greek original in the case of four plays is Menander; in the other two it is the little known Apollodorus whose style seems to have been similar and who is generally regarded as a pupil of Menander's. The MSS also preserve for each play a twelve-line metrical summary written by Gaius Sulpicius Apollinaris in the second century A.D.

The lists of Characters given in this edition are not found in the MSS but are reconstructed from the names and roles given in the scene headings. The stage directions in the translation are also the work of the editor: ancient dramatists indicate the exits and entrances of their characters and any other stage movements, if at all, by writing them into the words of the text. References to right and left are based on the convention that the right-hand entrance (from the audience's point of view) leads to the

forum and the left-hand one to the country or the harbour:
the location of offstage houses is conjectural and designed
principally to enable arriving characters to use the oppo-
site entrance to departing characters (thus avoiding any
suggestion of an unwanted meeting in the wings).

SELECT BIBLIOGRAPHY

Complete Editions of Terence

Bentley, Richard (ed.). *P. Terenti Afri Comoediae*. Cambridge, 1726.

Bianco, Orazio (ed.). *Terenzio: Commedie*. Turin, 1993.

Dziatzko, K. *P. Terenti Afri Comoediae*. Leipzig, 1884.

Fleckeisen, A. *P. Terenti Comoediae*. Leipzig, 2nd edn 1898.

Kauer, Robert, and W. M. Lindsay (eds.). *P. Terenti Afri Comoediae*. Oxford, 1926 (repr. with supplement by Otto Skutsch, 1958).

Marouzeau, J. (ed.). *Térence*. Paris, 3 vols., 1947–49.

Prete, Sesto (ed.). *P. Terenti Afri Comoediae*. Heidelberg, 1952.

Commentaries

Ashmore, S. G. (ed.). *The Comedies of Terence*. New York, 2nd edn 1908.

Wessner, P. (ed.). *Donatus: Commentum Terenti*. Stuttgart, 3 vols., 1902–08.

BIBLIOGRAPHY

Translations

Bovie, Palmer (ed.). *The Complete Comedies of Terence.* New Brunswick, 1974.

Copley, F. O. (tr.). *The Comedies of Terence.* Indianapolis, 1967.

Radice, Betty (tr.). *Terence: The Comedies.* London, 1976.

Concordances

Jenkins, E. B. *Index Verborum Terentianus.* Chapel Hill, 1932.

McGlynn, Patrick. *Lexicon Terentianum.* London and Glasgow, 1963–67.

General Works On Terence and New Comedy

Anderson, W. S. "Love Plots in Menander and His Roman Adapters." *Ramus* 13 (1984): 124–134.

Barsby, John. "Love in Terence," in S. M. Braund and Roland Mayer (eds.), *Love and Latin Literature.* Cambridge, 1999: 5–29.

Brown, P. G. McC. "The Bodmer Codex of Menander and the Endings of Terence's *Eunuchus* and Other Roman Comedies," in Eric Handley and Andre Hurst (eds.), *Relire Ménandre.* Geneva, 1990: 37–61.

——— "Love and Marriage in Greek New Comedy." *Classical Quarterly* 43 (1993): 189–205.

Duckworth, G. E. *The Nature of Roman Comedy.* Princeton, 1952 (repr. with bibliographical appendix by R. L. Hunter. Bristol, 1994).

Fantham, Elaine. "Sex, Status, and Survival in Hellenistic Athens: A Study of Women in New Comedy." *Phoenix* 29 (1975): 44–74.

Forehand, W. E. *Terence*. Boston, 1985.

Fraenkel, Eduard. *Elementi Plautini in Plauto*. Florence, 1960 (translation with addenda of *Plautinisches im Plautus*. Berlin, 1922).

Frank, Tenney. "Terence's Contribution to Plot-construction." *American Journal of Philology* 49 (1928): 309–322.

Gentili, Bruno. *Theatrical Performances in the Ancient World*. Amsterdam, 1979.

Gilula, Dwora. "The Concept of the *bona meretrix*: A Study of Terence's Courtesans." *Rivista di Filologia e di Istruzione Classica* 108 (1980): 142–165.

Goldberg, S. M. *Understanding Terence*. Princeton, 1986.

Gratwick, A. S. "Drama," in E. J. Kenney and W. V. Clausen (eds.), *The Cambridge History of Classical Literature: II. Latin Literature*. Cambridge, 1982: 77–137.

Hunter, R. L. *The New Comedy of Greece and Rome*. Cambridge, 1985.

Konstan, David. *Roman Comedy*. Ithaca, 1983.

——— *Greek Comedy and Ideology*. New York, 1995.

Lefèvre, Eckard. *Die Expositionstechnik in den Komödien des Terenz*. Darmstadt, 1969.

Ludwig, Walther. "The Originality of Terence and His Greek Models." *Greek Roman and Byzantine Studies* 9 (1968): 169–182.

Norwood, Gilbert. *The Art of Terence*. Oxford, 1923.

——— *Plautus and Terence*. New York, 1931.

Pierce, K. F. "The Portrayal of Rape in New Comedy," in S. Deacy and K. Pierce (eds.), *Rape in Antiquity: Sexual*

Violence in the Greek and Roman Worlds. London, 1997: 163–184.

Prescott, H. W. "Link Monologues in Roman Comedy." *Classical Philology* 34 (1939): 1–23, 116–126.

——— "Exit Monologues in Roman Comedy." *Classical Philology* 37 (1942): 1–21.

Saller, Richard. "The Social Dynamics of Consent to Marriage and Social Relations: The Evidence of Roman Comedy," in A. E. Laiou (ed.), *Consent and Coercion to Sex and Marriage in Ancient and Medieval Societies.* Washington D.C., 1993: 83–104.

Sandbach, F. H. *The Comic Theatre of Greece and Rome.* London, 1977.

Wright, John. *Dancing in Chains: the Stylistic Unity of the comoedia palliata.* Rome, 1974.

Theatre and Production

Bader, Bernd. "The ψόφος of the House-door in Greek New Comedy." *Antichthon* 5 (1971): 35–48.

Bain, David. *Actors and Audience: A Study of Asides and Related Conventions in Greek Drama.* Oxford, 1977.

Barsby, J. A. "Actors and Act-divisions: Some Questions of Adaptation in Roman Comedy." *Antichthon* 16 (1982): 77–87.

Beacham, R. C. *The Roman Theatre and Its Audience.* London, 1991.

Beare, William. *The Roman Stage.* London, 3rd edn 1964.

Bieber, Margarete. *The History of the Greek and Roman Theater.* Princeton, 2nd edn 1961.

Garton, Charles. *Personal Aspects of the Roman Theatre.* Toronto, 1972.

Goldberg, S. M. "Plautus on the Palatine." *Journal of Roman Studies* 88 (1998): 1–20.

Hanson, J. A. *Roman Theater-temples*. Princeton, 1959.

Johnston, Mary. *Exits and Entrances in Roman Comedy*. New York, 1933.

Mattingly, H. B. "The Terentian didascaliae." *Athenaeum* 37 (1959): 148–173.

———— "The Chronology of Terence." *Rivista di Cultura Classica e Medioevale* 5 (1963): 12–61.

Neiiendam, Klaus. *The Art of Acting in Antiquity*. Copenhagen, 1992.

Péché, Valérie. "Les *tibiae,* Instruments de la Scène Romaine: l'Exemple de la Comédie et de la Pantomime," in *Instruments, Musiques et Musiciens de l'Antiquité Classique* (= *Ateliers* 4). Lille, 1995: 71–91.

Rambo, E. F. "The Significance of the Wing Entrances in Roman Comedy." *Classical Philology* 10 (1915): 411–431.

Ross Taylor, Lily. "The Opportunities for Dramatic Performances in the Time of Plautus and Terence." *Transactions of the American Philological Association* 68 (1937): 284–304.

Webster, T. B. L. *Monuments Illustrating New Comedy*. 3rd edn, revised and enlarged by J. R. Green and Axel Seeberg, London, 1995.

Language and Style

Adams, J. N. "Female Speech in Latin Comedy." *Antichthon* 18 (1984): 43–77.

Allardice, J. T. *Syntax of Terence*. London, 1929.

BIBLIOGRAPHY

Denzler, Bruno. *Der Monolog bei Terenz*. Zürich, 1968.

Fantham, Elaine. *Comparative Studies in Republican Latin Imagery*. Toronto, 1972.

Haffter, Heinz. *Untersuchungen zur altlateinischen Dichtersprache*. Berlin, 1934.

Hofmann, J. B. *Lateinische Umgangssprache*. Heidelberg, 3rd edn 1951.

Hough, J. N. "Terence's Use of Greek Words." *Classical World* 41 (1947–8): 18–21.

—— "Rapid Repartee in Roman Comedy." *Classical World* 65 (1969–70): 162–167.

Lilja, Saara. *Terms of Abuse in Roman Comedy*. Helsinki, 1965.

Maltby, Robert. "Linguistic Characterization of Old Men in Terence." *Classical Philology* 74 (1979): 136–147.

—— "The Distribution of Greek Loan-words in Terence." *Classical Quarterly* 35 (1985): 110–123.

Otto, A. *Die Sprichwörter und sprichwörtlichen Redensarten der Römer*. Leipzig, 1890.

Palmer, L. R. *The Latin Language*. London, 1954: 74–94.

Preston, Keith. *Studies in the Diction of the sermo amatorius in Roman Comedy*. Diss. Chicago, 1914, repr. New York, 1978.

Meter

Barsby, John (ed.). *Terence: Eunuchus*. Cambridge, 1999: 290–304.

Gratwick, A. S. (ed.). *Terence: The Brothers*. Warminster, 1987: 268–283.

Laidlaw, W. A. *The Prosody of Terence*. London, 1938.

Lindsay, W. M. *Early Latin Verse*. Oxford, 1922.

MacCary, W. T., and M. M. Willcock (eds.). *Plautus: Casina*. Cambridge, 1976: 211–232.

Questa, Cesare. *Introduzione alla Metrica di Plauto*. Bologna, 1967.

Soubiran, Jean. *Essai sur la Versification Dramatique des Romains: Sénaire Iambique et Septénaire Trochaique*. Paris, 1988.

Textual Transmission

Andrieu, Jean. *Le Dialogue Antique*. Paris, 1954: 209–272 (on speaker assignation).

Grant, J. N. *Studies in the Textual Tradition of Terence*. Toronto, 1986.

Jachmann, G. (ed.). *Terentius: codex vaticanus latinus 3868 phototypice editus*. Leipzig, 1929.

Jones, L. W., and C. R. Morey. *The Miniatures of the Manuscripts of Terence Prior to the Thirteenth Century*. Princeton, 1931.

Jory, E. J. "Algebraic Notation in Dramatic Texts." *Bulletin of the Institute of Classical Studies* 10 (1963): 65–78.

Prete, Sesto. *Il codice di Terenzio vaticano latino 3226*. Vatican, 1970.

Reeve, M. D. "Terence," in L. D. Reynolds (ed.), *Texts and Transmission: A Survey of the Latin Classics*. Oxford, 1983: 412–420.

Wahl, K. U. *Sprecherbezeichnungen mit griechischen Buchstaben in den Handschriften des Plautus und Terenz*. Tübingen, 1974.

BIBLIOGRAPHY

Bibliographical Aids

Arnott, W. G. *Menander, Plautus, Terence*. Oxford, 1975.

Cupaiuolo, Giovanni. *Bibliografia Terenziana (1470–1983)*. Naples, 1984.

———— "Supplementum Terentianum." *Bolletino di Studi Latini* 22 (1992): 32–57.

Gaiser, Konrad. "Zur Eigenart der römischen Komödie," in Hildegard Temporini (ed.), *Aufstieg und Niedergang der römischen Welt*, I.2. Berlin, 1972: 1027–1113.

Goldberg, S. M. "Scholarship on Terence and the Fragments of Roman Comedy: 1959–1980." *Classical World* 75 (1981): 77–115.

Lentano, M. "Quindici Anni di Studi Terenziani: Parte Prima: Studi sulle Commedie (1979–1993)." *Bolletino di Studi Latini* 27 (1997): 497–564.

———— "Quindici Anni di Studi Terenziani: Parte Seconda: Tradizione Manoscritta ed Esegesi Antica (1979–1993)." *Bolletino di Studi Latini* 28 (1998): 78–104.

Marti, H. "Terenz 1909–59." *Lustrum* 6 (1961): 114–238, 8 (1963): 5–101, 244–264.

Prete, Sesto. "Scholarship on Terence 1934–58." *Classical World* 54 (1961): 112–122.

THE WOMAN OF ANDROS

INTRODUCTORY NOTE

The Woman of Andros was Terence's first play, written (if we can believe the traditional chronology) when he was only nineteen years old. It already reveals a familiarity with the traditional characters of comedy, notably the angry father, the lovesick son, and the tricky slave, and it foreshadows the interest in father-son relationships which will dominate several of Terence's later plays. It also foreshadows Terence's liking for double plots, involving two contrasting love affairs and contrasting pairs of fathers, sons, and slaves, though in this case the second plot is left relatively undeveloped.

The plot is centred on the love affair between the young Athenian Pamphilus and a young woman from Andros called Glycerium. Pamphilus' father Simo has arranged for his son to marry Philumena, the daughter of his neighbour Chremes. Chremes withdraws his consent on hearing of Pamphilus' affair with Glycerium, but Simo persists in the pretence that the marriage is going ahead in order to test his son's loyalty and in the hope that Chremes will eventually relent. Simo's slave Davus, having deduced from the lack of preparations in either house that the marriage is in fact off, persuades Pamphilus that it is in his long-term interest to pretend to agree to it; this plan misfires badly when Simo persuades Chremes that Pamphilus and Glycerium have quarrelled and the marriage is on again. Meanwhile Glycerium gives birth to Pamphilus' child, which Davus produces in order to convince Chremes that Pamphilus is not a suitable son-in-law. The problems are resolved when Crito, a cousin of Glycerium's dead sister Chrysis, arrives from Andros to claim Chrysis' property. Simo, who is convinced that the baby has been "planted" and that Crito is an impostor, has Davus tied up, disowns Pamphilus, and abuses Crito; however, when Crito explains that Glycerium had been brought to Andros from Athens as a small girl by her uncle Phania, Chremes recognises the name as his brother's and Glycerium as his own long-lost daughter. The way is now clear for Pamphilus to marry Glycerium; and Philumena is free to marry her suitor Charinus, who with his slave Byrria has flitted in and out of the play trying to stake his claim.

The play provides the first example of the practice of "contamination" for which Terence was criticised by his critic Luscius of Lanuvium. Menander had written both a *Woman of Andros* and a *Woman of Perinthos;* Terence admits in his prologue that he has incorporated material from the latter into his own version of the former. The extent of the additions is hard to determine. The commentator Donatus reveals that the dialogue between Simo and his freedman at the beginning of Terence's play is based on *The Woman of Perinthos,* where the old man had a dialogue with his wife, rather than on Menander's *Woman of Andros,* where the old man spoke a monologue. Donatus also declares that Charinus and Byrria were "not in Menander"; critical opinion is divided on whether this means that they were an addition of Terence's own or allows for the possibility that they came from Menander's *Woman of Perinthos*. Whatever the truth of this, the *Woman of Andros* is the least well balanced of Terence's double plots. Charinus and Byrria play too little part, and are too lightly characterised, to provide an effective contrast to Pamphilus and Davus. Charinus does have two scenes of jealous conflict with Pamphilus, but his main function (as Donatus remarks) is to provide someone for Philumena to marry at the end of the play.

Though the solution of the plot depends, as often, on a fantastic coincidence, *The Woman of Andros* does have some effective scenes and some interesting characterisation. Pamphilus makes two romantic declarations of love and loyalty and is probably the most romantic of all lovers in Roman comedy; at the same time he feels a genuine conflict between his love and his duty to his father, and when faced with his father's anger agrees to accept his bidding, even if it means losing his girl. Simo, like many angry fathers, is suspicious of the plotting of his slave on his son's behalf, but he is not as stupid as some of his Plautine counterparts; so far from being easily deceived, he practises a deception of his own, and, by an interesting twist, eventually deceives himself into disbelieving what is in fact the truth. He is introduced as a father who has always wanted to believe the best about his son, and the scene where, through a misunderstanding of the situation, he is finally brought to disown Pamphilus approaches pathos. Davus acts the part of the traditional tricky slave but risks becoming the bungling slave (one of Terence's favourite variations on the character) when his original plan goes wrong; he does however redeem himself in the excellent cross-purpose scene in which he accuses the puzzled Mysis of "planting" the baby in order that her denials may be the more convincing to Chremes' ears.

SELECT BIBLIOGRAPHY

Editions and Commentaries

Posani, M. R. (Bologna, 1990).
Shipp, G. P. (Oxford, 1960).

Criticism

Goldberg, S. M. "The Dramatic Balance of Terence's *Andria.*" *Classica et Mediaevalia* 33 (1981–1982): 135–143.
——— "The *duplex comoedia,*" in *Understanding Terence.* Princeton, 1986: 126–135.
McGarrity, T. "Thematic Unity in Terence's *Andria.*" *Transactions of the American Philological Association* 108 (1978): 103–114.
Steidle, W. "Menander bei Terenz." *Rheinisches Museum* 116 (1973): 303–347.

DIDASCALIA

INCIPIT ANDRIA TERENTI
ACTA LVDIS MEGALENSIBVS M. FVLVIO M'. GLABRIONE
AEDILIBVS CVRVLIBVS
EGERE L. AMBIVIVS TVRPIO L. ATILIVS PRAENESTINVS
MODOS FECIT FLACCVS CLAVDI TIBIIS PARIBVS DEXTRIS VEL
SINISTRIS
GRAECA MENANDRV
FACTA I M. MARCELLO C. SVLPICIO COS.

C. SULPICI APOLLINARIS PERIOCHA

sororem falso creditam meretriculae
genere Andriae Glycerium vitiat Pamphilus,
gravidaque facta dat fidem uxorem sibi
fore hanc. namque aliam pater ei desponderat,
gnatam Chremetis; atque ut amorem comperit,
simulat futuras nuptias, cupiens suus
quid haberet animi filius cognoscere.
Davi suasu non repugnat Pamphilus.
sed ex Glycerio natum ut vidit puerulum
Chremes, recusat nuptias, generum abdicat.
mox filiam Glycerium insperato agnitam
hanc Pamphilo, aliam dat Charino coniugem.

---

[1] The Production Notice, which is preserved in the MSS for Terence's other five plays, is missing for *The Woman of Andros*. The one here given is reconstructed on the same model from information supplied by Donatus.

PRODUCTION NOTICE[1]

Here begins the Woman of Andros of Terence, acted at the Ludi Megalenses[2] in the curule aedileship of M. Fulvius and M'. Glabrio. Produced by L. Ambivius Turpio and L. Atilius of Praeneste.[3] Music composed by Flaccus, slave of Claudius, for equal pipes, left-hand or right-hand. Greek original by Menander. The author's first play, performed in the consulship of M. Marcellus and C. Sulpicius.[4]

SYNOPSIS BY C. SULPICIUS APOLLINARIS

Glycerium, who was wrongly believed to be the sister of a courtesan of Andrian birth, is raped by Pamphilus, who, when she becomes pregnant, promises to make her his wife. But his father had arranged another marriage for him with the daughter of Chremes. When the father discovers the love affair, he pretends that the marriage is going ahead, hoping to find out what the son's real intentions are. On the advice of Davus, Pamphilus offers no objection. However, when Chremes sees the baby born to Glycerium, he cancels the marriage, refusing to have Pamphilus as his son-in-law. In due course Glycerium is unexpectedly recognised as Chremes' daughter. He then marries her to Pamphilus and gives his other daughter to Charinus.

[2] The Ludi Megalenses, founded in 204 B.C. in honour of the Great Mother (Magna Mater), were held in April and were the occasion of four of Terence's six plays.

[3] For Ambivius Turpio see Introduction. Atilius was probably the co-producer, or second actor of Ambivius' troupe, though some have seen him as the producer of later revivals.

[4] That is, in 166 B.C.

PERSONAE

SIMO senex
SOSIA libertus
DAVOS servus
MYSIS ancilla
PAMPHILUS adulescens
CHARINUS adulescens
BYRRIA servus
LESBIA obstetrix
GLYCERIUM virgo
CHREMES senex
CRITO senex
DROMO lorarius

Scaena: Athenis

CHARACTERS

SIMO, an old man, father of Pamphilus
SOSIA, freedman of Simo
DAVUS, slave of Simo
MYSIS, maid of Simo
PAMPHILUS, a young man, son of Simo, lover of Glycerium
CHARINUS, a young man, lover of Philumena
BYRRIA, slave of Charinus
LESBIA, a midwife
GLYCERIUM, a young woman, supposed sister of Chrysis of
   Andros, in fact daughter of Chremes
CHREMES, an old man, father of Philumena and (as it turns
   out) of Glycerium
CRITO, an old man from Andros, cousin of Chrysis
DROMO, slave of Simo

Staging

The stage represents a street in Athens. On it are two houses,
belonging respectively to Simo and Glycerium. The exit on the
audience's right leads to the forum and the house of Chremes,
that on their left leads to the harbour and to the house of
Charinus.[5]

[5] The locations of the offstage houses is conjectural.

ANDRIA

PROLOGUS

poeta quom primum animum ad scribendum appulit,
id sibi negoti credidit solum dari,
populo ut placerent quas fecisset fabulas.
verum aliter evenire multo intellegit.
5 nam in prologis scribundis operam abutitur,
non qui argumentum narret sed qui malevoli
veteris poetae maledictis respondeat.
nunc quam rem vitio dent, quaeso, animum advortite.
Menander fecit Andriam et Perinthiam.
10 qui utramvis recte norit ambas noverit,
non ita dissimili sunt argumento, et tamen
dissimili oratione sunt factae ac stilo.
quae convenere in Andriam ex Perinthia
fatetur transtulisse atque usum pro suis.
15 id isti vituperant factum atque in eo disputant
contaminari non decere fabulas.
faciuntne intellegendo ut nil intellegant?
qui quom hunc accusant, Naevium, Plautum, Ennium
accusant, quos hic noster auctores habet,
20 quorum aemulari exoptat neglegentiam

1-887 *deest A nisi frustula* 787–878

THE WOMAN OF ANDROS

PROLOGUE

When the playwright first turned his mind to writing, he believed that his only problem was to ensure that the plays he had created would win the approval of the public. He now realises that the reality is quite different. He is wasting his time writing prologues, not to explain the plot but to respond to the slanders of a malicious old playwright.[6]

Now please pay attention while I explain the substance of his criticisms. Menander wrote a "Woman of Andros" and a "Woman of Perinthos." If you know one, you know them both, since the plots are not very different, though they are written in a different language and style. Our author confesses that he has transferred anything suitable from the "Woman of Perinthos" to the "Woman of Andros" and made free use of it. His critics abuse him for doing this, arguing that it is not right to contaminate[7] plays in this way. But isn't their cleverness making them obtuse? In criticising our author, they are actually criticising Naevius, Plautus, and Ennius, whom he takes as his models, preferring to imitate their carelessness in this respect rather

[6] The reference is to Luscius of Lanuvium (see Introduction).

[7] On "contamination" see Introduction.

potius quam istorum obscuram diligentiam.
dehinc ut quiescant porro moneo et desinant
maledicere, malefacta ne noscant sua.
favete, adeste aequo animo, et rem cognoscite,
25 ut pernoscatis ecquid spei sit relicuom,
posthac quas faciet de integro comoedias
spectandae an exigendae sint vobis prius.

ACTUS I

I. i: SIMO. SOSIA.

SIM vos istaec intro auferte, abite. Sosia,
ades dum. paucis te volo.

SOS   dictum puta:
30 nempe ut curentur recte haec?

SIM   immo aliud.

SOS   quid est
quod tibi mea ars efficere hoc possit amplius?

SIM nil istac opus est arte ad hanc rem quam paro,
sed eis quas semper in te intellexi sitas,
fide et taciturnitate.

SOS   exspecto quid velis.

35 SIM ego postquam te emi, a parvolo ut semper tibi
apud me iusta et clemens fuerit servitus
scis. feci ex servo ut esses libertus mihi,
propterea quod servibas liberaliter.
quod habui summum pretium persolvi tibi.

40 SOS in memoria habeo.

---

[8] This seems to be a reference to over-literal translation (compare
The Eunuch 6–7).

than the critics' own dreary pedantry.[8] So I am warning them from now on to hold their tongues and stop their slanders, or they will be forced to acknowledge their own shortcomings.

Give us your support, listen with open minds, and come to a decision. It is for you to determine what hope our author has, whether the new comedies he writes in the future are to gain an audience or be driven off the stage without a hearing.

ACT ONE

Enter SIMO *right from the direction of the forum with* SOSIA *and slaves carrying provisions.*

SIM   (*to the slaves*) You take those things inside. Off you go! (*the slaves exit into Simo's house*) Sosia, stay here a moment. I want a few words with you.

SOS   Consider them said. You want me to see the food's properly cooked?

SIM   No, it's something else.

SOS   What else is there on which my art could be better employed?

SIM   It's not your art that's needed for what I have in mind, but qualities which I have always known you to possess, loyalty and discretion.

SOS   I await your instructions.

SIM   (*with a hint of pomposity*) Ever since I bought you, when you were a small child, you know how just and kind I have been to you as a master. You were my slave, but I gave you your freedom, because you served me with the spirit of a free man. I bestowed upon you the highest reward that was in my power.

SOS   I haven't forgotten.

53

	SIM	haud muto factum.
	SOS	gaudeo

SOS   si tibi quid feci aut facio quod placeat, Simo,
et id gratum fuisse advorsum te habeo gratiam.
sed hoc mihi molestumst; nam istaec commemoratio
quasi exprobratiost immemori benefici.

45   quin tu uno verbo dic quid est quod me velis.

SIM   ita faciam. hoc primum in hac re praedico tibi:
quas credis esse has non sunt verae nuptiae.

SOS   quor simulas igitur?

SIM   rem omnem a principio audies.
eo pacto et gnati vitam et consilium meum

50   cognosces et quid facere in hac re te velim.
nam is postquam excessit ex ephebis, Sosia, et
liberius vivendi erat potestas (nam antea
qui scire posses aut ingenium noscere,
dum aetas, metus, magister prohibebant?)—

SOS   itast.

55 SIM   —quod plerique omnes faciunt adulescentuli,
ut animum ad aliquod studium adiungant, aut equos
alere aut canes ad venandum aut ad philosophos,
horum ille nil egregie praeter cetera
studebat et tamen omnia haec mediocriter.

60   gaudebam.

SOS   non iniuria. nam id arbitror
apprime in vita esse utile, ut ne quid nimis.

SIM   sic vita erat: facile omnis perferre ac pati;

---

44 immemori *edd.*, immemoris Σ *Don. Eugr.*

SIM And I don't regret it.

SOS I'm delighted if anything I've done, or do, pleases you, Simo, and I'm grateful that my behaviour has found your favour. But now you disturb me. Your reminder sounds like a reproach for ingratitude. Why don't you tell me in a word what you want me to do?

SIM I will. The first thing I want you to know about the situation is this. The wedding which you believe is taking place is not a real one.

SOS So why pretend it is?

SIM I'll tell you the whole story from the beginning. That way you'll understand my son's behaviour and my own scheme and how I'd like you to help me. After he'd finished his military service[9] and had the opportunity to live with greater freedom—for how could you know him or judge his character before, while he was restrained by age and apprehension and a tutor?—

SOS Quite so.

SIM —he behaved as all young lads tend to do, involving themselves in some pursuit like breeding horses or hounds or studying philosophy. However, he didn't pursue any one of these things in particular but all of them in moderation. I was delighted.

SOS And rightly so. I believe that the best principle in life is nothing in excess.[10]

SIM I'll tell you how he lived his life. He was patient and toler-

_____

[9] Athenians were required to serve as ephebes for two years from the age of eighteen, during which time they underwent military training and performed guard duties on the coast and in the country.

[10] A traditional Greek saying ($\mu\eta\delta\grave{\epsilon}\nu$ $\check{\alpha}\gamma\alpha\nu$), inscribed over the portal of Apollo's temple at Delphi.

cum quibus erat quomque una eis se dedere;
eorum obsequi studiis, advorsus nemini,
65 numquam praeponens se illis; ita ut facillume
sine invidia laudem invenias et amicos pares.
SOS sapienter vitam instituit. namque hoc tempore
obsequium amicos, veritas odium parit.
SIM interea mulier quaedam abhinc triennium
70 ex Andro commigravit huc viciniae,
inopia et cognatorum neglegentia
coacta, egregia forma atque aetate integra.
SOS ei! vereor ne quid Andria apportet mali.
SIM primo haec pudice vitam parce ac duriter
75 agebat, lana et tela victum quaeritans.
sed postquam amans accessit pretium pollicens
unus et item alter, ita ut ingeniumst omnium
hominum ab labore proclive ad lubidinem,
accepit condicionem, dehinc quaestum occipit.
80 qui tum illam amabant forte, ita ut fit, filium
perduxere illuc secum ut una esset meum.
egomet continuo mecum: "certe captus est,
habet." observabam mane illorum servolos
venientis aut abeuntis. rogitabam: "heus, puer,
85 dic sodes, quis heri Chrysidem habuit?"; nam Andriae
illi id erat nomen.
SOS   teneo.
SIM   Phaedrum aut Cliniam
dicebant aut Niceratum; nam hi tres tum simul
amabant. "eho! quid Pamphilus?" "quid? symbolam

---

11 Andros is one of the larger Cyclades islands in the Aegean Sea.

ant with everybody. Whoever his companions were, he
devoted himself to them. He fell in with their pursuits,
opposed nobody, never putting himself first. That's the
way to earn a good name, avoid jealousy, and find good
friends.

SOS (*aside*) He's chosen a wise path. These days obsequious-
ness makes friends, the truth just makes you unpopular.

SIM Meanwhile, about three years ago, a woman moved into
the neighbourhood from Andros,[11] driven here by pov-
erty and the indifference of her family, a most beautiful
woman in the prime of life.

SOS (*aside*) Oh dear! I'm afraid the Andrian woman brings
trouble.

SIM At first she lived a virtuous life, sparing and thrifty, earn-
ing her living by spinning wool. But when a lover ap-
proached her offering money, first one and then another,
human nature being always inclined to prefer pleasure to
toil, she accepted the offers and took up the profession. It
so happened that her lovers of the time, as young men do,
took my son along to keep them company. Straightaway I
thought to myself "He's caught for sure; she's got him." I
took to watching his friends' slaves going to and fro in the
early hours of the morning, and I'd question them: "Hey,
my lad, tell me if you don't mind, who went with Chrysis
yesterday?" That was the name of the Andrian woman.

SOS I see.

SIM They'd say Phaedrus or Clinia or Niceratus—she had
these three as lovers simultaneously. "Oh! What about
Pamphilus?" "Him? He just put up his share[12] and joined

[12] It was a common Greek practice for people to club together for
dinner with each person paying a contribution ($\sigma\upsilon\mu\beta o\lambda\dot{\eta}$).

dedit, cenavit." gaudebam. item alio die
90   quaerebam. comperibam nil ad Pamphilum
quicquam attinere. enimvero spectatum satis
putabam et magnum exemplum continentiae.
nam qui cum ingeniis conflictatur eiusmodi
neque commovetur animus in ea re tamen,
95   scias posse habere iam ipsum suae vitae modum.
quom id mihi placebat tum uno ore omnes omnia
bona dicere et laudare fortunas meas,
qui gnatum haberem tali ingenio praeditum.
quid verbis opus est? hac fama impulsus Chremes
100   ultro ad me venit, unicam gnatam suam
cum dote summa filio uxorem ut daret.
placuit, despondi. hic nuptiis dictust dies.

SOS   quid obstat quor non verae fiant?

SIM   audies.
fere in diebus paucis quibus haec acta sunt
105   Chrysis vicina haec moritur.

SOS   o factum bene!
beasti. ei metui a Chryside.

SIM   ibi tum filius
cum illis qui amabant Chrysidem una aderat frequens.
curabat una funus. tristis interim,
nonnumquam collacrumabat. placuit tum id mihi.
110   sic cogitabam: "hic parvae consuetudinis
causa huius mortem tam fert familiariter:
quid si ipse amasset? quid hic mihi faciet patri?"
haec ego putabam esse omnia humani ingeni
mansuetique animi officia. quid multis moror?
115   egomet quoque eius causa in funus prodeo,
nil suspicans etiam mali.

SOS   hem! quid id est?

them for dinner." I was delighted. I made similar enquiries on another day, and I could find nothing which implicated Pamphilus. I supposed he had come through the test and proved himself a fine model of self-restraint. When a man is involved with characters like that and doesn't fall to temptation, you can be sure that he is now capable of taking control over his own life. This was not only a source of pleasure to me; everyone else with one accord spoke well of him, and they congratulated me on my good fortune in having a son endowed with such a disposition. To cut the story short, Chremes was so impressed with my son's reputation that he came to me of his own accord to offer his only daughter in marriage with a substantial dowry. I accepted the offer and arranged the match, and today is the day fixed for the wedding.

SOS   So why is this not a real wedding?

SIM   I'll tell you. Within a few days of this arrangement our neighbour Chrysis died.

SOS   Good news! I'm a happy man. I was afraid what Chrysis would do to him.

SIM   At this point my son was spending all his time with Chrysis' lovers, helping them with the funeral. He was distressed at times and occasionally joined in their weeping. At the time I was pleased at this. I thought "He's taking her death very personally when he barely knew her. What if he had himself been one of her lovers? What will he do in my case, his own father?" I supposed his behaviour was all due to human feeling and a sympathetic nature. Anyway, I went to the funeral myself for his sake, still not suspecting that anything was amiss.

SOS   Oh! What's this about?

SIM   scies.
        effertur, imus. interea inter mulieres
        quae ibi aderant forte unam aspicio adulescentulam
        forma—

SOS   bona fortasse.

SIM   —et voltu, Sosia,

120   adeo modesto, adeo venusto ut nil supra.
        quae tum mihi lamentari praeter ceteras
        visast et quia erat forma praeter ceteras
        honesta ac liberali, accedo ad pedisequas,
        quae sit rogo. sororem esse aiunt Chrysidis.

125   percussit ilico animum. attat! hoc illud est,
        hinc illae lacrimae, haec illast misericordia.

SOS   quam timeo quorsum evadas!

SIM   funus interim
        procedit. sequimur, ad sepulcrum venimus.
        in ignem impositast, fletur. interea haec soror

130   quam dixi ad flammam accessit imprudentius,
        satis cum periclo. ibi tum exanimatus Pamphilus
        bene dissimulatum amorem et celatum indicat.
        accurrit, mediam mulierem complectitur.
        "mea Glycerium," inquit "quid agis? quor te is perdi-
           tum?"

135   tum illa, ut consuetum facile amorem cerneres,
        reiecit se in eum flens quam familiariter!

SOS   quid ais?

SIM   redeo inde iratus atque aegre ferens.
        nec satis ad obiurgandum causae. diceret:
        "quid feci? quid commerui aut peccavi, pater?

---

121 quae *codd. pl.,* quia *P¹C Don.*

SIM   I'll tell you. The body was carried out, and we went along. Meanwhile among the women who were present I caught sight of one young lass whose looks were—

SOS   Not bad, perhaps.

SIM   —and whose expression, Sosia, was unsurpassably modest and lovely. Her grief seemed to me deeper than the others and her appearance more dignified and ladylike than the others. So I went up to the attendants and asked who she was. They said she was Chrysis' sister. The truth struck me at once. Oh no! This is it; this is the explanation of his tears[13] and distress.

SOS   I dread to think where this is leading.

SIM   Meanwhile the funeral procession continued. We followed and came to the burial ground. The woman was laid on the pyre, and the lamentations began. Meanwhile this sister I was talking about approached the flames with little regard for her own safety and was in real danger. At this point Pamphilus revealed by his alarm the love he'd disguised and hidden so well. He ran forward, grasped the woman round the waist, and said "My dear Glycerium, what are you doing? Why are you risking your life?" She fell into his arms and wept. It was such an intimate scene—you could readily see that they were lovers.

SOS   You don't say!

SIM   I returned home angry and annoyed, but I still hadn't a sufficient reason for reproaching him. He would have said "What have I done? How do I deserve this, father,

[13] The Latin phrase (*hinc illae lacrimae*) became proverbial in the sense "so that's the explanation" (see Cicero, *For Caelius* 61, Horace, *Epistles* 1.19.41).

140 quae sese in ignem inicere voluit, prohibui.
servavi." honesta oratiost.

SOS   recte putas.
nam si illum obiurges vitae qui auxilium tulit,
quid facias illi qui dederit damnum aut malum?

SIM venit Chremes postridie ad me clamitans
145 indignum facinus: comperisse Pamphilum
pro uxore habere hanc peregrinam. ego illud sedulo
negare factum, ille instat factum. denique
ita tum discedo ab illo ut qui se filiam
neget daturum.

SOS   non tu ibi gnatum—?

SIM   ne haec quidem
150 satis vehemens causa ad obiurgandum.

SOS   qui? cedo.

SIM "tute ipse his rebus finem praescripsti, pater.
prope adest quom alieno more vivendumst mihi.
sine nunc meo me vivere interea modo."

SOS qui igitur relictus est obiurgandi locus?

155 SIM si propter amorem uxorem nolet ducere,
ea primum ab illo animum advortenda iniuriast.
et nunc id operam do, ut per falsas nuptias
vera obiurgandi causa sit, si deneget.
simul sceleratus Davos si quid consili
160 habet, ut consumat nunc quom nil obsint doli,
quem ego credo manibus pedibusque obnixe omnia
facturum, magis id adeo mihi ut incommodet
quam ut obsequatur gnato.

SOS   quapropter?

---

[14] The Latin idiom is "with hands and feet."

what's my crime? A woman tried to throw herself on to a pyre; I prevented her. I saved her." It's a fair argument.

SOS You're right. If you reproach a person who's saved somebody's life, what are you going to do to one who's done real harm or damage?

SIM Chremes came to me the next day making a terrible fuss. It was outrageous, he said. He'd discovered that Pamphilus was treating this foreign woman as his wife. I strenuously denied that this was the case. He insisted that it was the case. In the end we parted with the understanding that he was withdrawing his consent to his daughter's marriage.

SOS What about your son? Surely now—

SIM Even this wasn't a strong enough reason for rebuking him.

SOS How so? Tell me.

SIM "You yourself have prescribed an end to all this, father. The time has almost come when I have to adapt my life to suit another's. In the meantime let me live in my own way."

SOS So what grounds does this leave for rebuking him?

SIM If he refuses to marry because of his love, that will be a clear act of disobedience on his part which deserves to be punished. And that's my purpose now with this pretended marriage, to create a valid reason for rebuking him if he refuses. At the same time, that rascal Davus will use up whatever scheme he has now when his tricks can do no harm. I'm sure he'll strive with might and main,[14] doing everything he can—and that more to annoy me than to serve my son's interests.

SOS Why?

SIM   rogas?
     mala mens, malus animus. quem quidem ego, si
     sensero—
165   sed quid opust verbis? sin eveniat quod volo,
     in Pamphilo ut nil sit morae, restat Chremes
     qui mi exorandus est, et spero confore.
     nunc tuomst officium has bene ut assimules nuptias,
     perterrefacias Davom, observes filium
170   quid agat, quid cum illo consili captet.

SOS   sat est,
     curabo.

SIM   eamus nunciam intro. i prae, sequar.
     non dubiumst quin uxorem nolit filius.
     ita Davom modo timere sensi, ubi nuptias
     futuras esse audivit. sed ipse exit foras.

I. ii: DAVOS. SIMO.

175 DAV   mirabar hoc si sic abiret et eri semper lenitas
     verebar quorsum evaderet,
     qui postquam audierat non datum iri filio uxorem suo,
     numquam quoiquam nostrum verbum fecit neque id
        aegre tulit.

SIM   at nunc faciet neque, ut opinor, sine tuo magno malo.

180 DAV   id voluit nos sic necopinantis duci falso gaudio
     sperantis iam amoto metu, interoscitantis opprimi,
     ne esset spatium cogitandi ad disturbandas nuptias:
     astute!

[167] qui mi exorandus Σ *Don. Eugr., Non.*, cui mi expurgandus *Don.
in comm.*
[171] eamus nunciam intro *Simoni dant edd.*, *Sosiae* Σ
[172] *hic novam scaenam (non 175) indicant* Σ *edd.*

SIM Don't ask. Evil mind, evil heart. Indeed, if I find him—
But why waste words? If things turn out as I wish and
Pamphilus offers no resistance, I've only Chremes to
persuade, and I'm confident that can be done. Now, it's
your job to maintain the pretence of the marriage, scare
Davus off, and keep an eye on my son's doings and on any
plan the two of them conceive.

SOS All right. I'll see to it.

SIM Let's go in now. You go first, I'll follow. (*Sosia exits into
Simo's house*) There's no doubt that my son will refuse
the marriage. I noticed Davus was worried just now
when he heard that the wedding was going to take place.
But he's coming out.

Enter DAVUS from Simo's house.

DAV (*to himself*) I was surprised if it could end this way. The
master was so calm, and I've been afraid all the time
where that was leading. Ever since he heard that his son's
wedding was cancelled, he hasn't said a word to any of us
or been at all upset.

SIM (*aside*) Well, he will now, and, if you ask me, it means a
thrashing for you.

DAV He meant to lead us on with false rejoicing, unsuspect-
ing, full of hope, freed from fear, and then to catch us
napping, giving us no time to think up a plan to prevent
the marriage. The cunning old blighter!

SIM   carnufex quae loquitur?

DAV   erus est neque provideram.

SIM Dave!

DAV   hem! quid est?

SIM   ehodum, ad me!

DAV   quid hic volt?

SIM   quid ais?

DAV   qua de re?

SIM   rogas?

185   meum gnatum rumor est amare.

DAV   id populus curat scilicet.

SIM hocine agis an non?

DAV   ego vero istuc.

SIM   sed nunc ea me exquirere
iniqui patris est. nam quod antehac fecit nil ad me atti-
net.
dum tempus ad eam rem tulit, sivi animum ut expleret
suom.
nunc hic dies aliam vitam adfert, alios mores postulat.

190   dehinc postulo, sive aequomst te oro, Dave, ut redeat
iam in viam.
hoc quid sit? omnes qui amant graviter sibi dari uxorem
ferunt.

DAV ita aiunt.

SIM   tum si quis magistrum cepit ad eam rem improbum,
ipsum animum aegrotum ad deteriorem partem ple-
rumque applicat.

DAV non hercle intellego.

---

[15] Literally "the hangman," "the executioner," a colourful term of

SIM   (*aside*) What's the scoundrel[15] saying?

DAV   (*catching sight of Simo*) It's the master. I didn't see him.

SIM   Davus!

DAV   (*aside*) Oh! What's this?

SIM   Here you, look at me.

DAV   (*not looking*) What does he want?

SIM   What have you got to say for yourself?

DAV   (*finally facing Simo*) About what?

SIM   As if you didn't know! There's a rumour that my son's in love.

DAV   (*ironically*) It's a matter of public interest, obviously.

SIM   Are you taking me seriously or not?

DAV   Yes, I am.

SIM   Well, I would be a harsh father to pursue that now. What my son did in the past is not my concern. While the time was appropriate for such things, I allowed him to satisfy his desires. But today brings another life, demands another way of behaving. From now on I expect you or, if I may properly do so, I implore you, Davus, to bring him back to the right path. Let me explain. All lovers resent being given a wife.

DAV   (*cautiously*) So they tell me.

SIM   What's more, if any of them have a reprobate for a teacher, he tends to steer their lovesick hearts in the wrong direction.

DAV   (*with assumed innocence*) For god's sake, I don't understand.

---

abuse, which is used three times of Davus in the play (see lines 651, 852). The hangman's job was considered so vile that he was not even allowed to reside within the city of Rome (Cicero, *For Rabirius on a Charge of Treason* 15).

	SIM	non? hem!
	DAV	non. Davos sum, non Oedipus.
195	SIM	nempe ergo aperte vis quae restant me loqui?
	DAV	sane quidem.

SIM   si sensero hodie quicquam in his te nuptiis
fallaciae conari quo fiant minus,
aut velle in ea re ostendi quam sis callidus,

verberibus caesum te in pistrinum, Dave, dedam usque
    ad necem,

200   ea lege atque omine ut, si te inde exemerim, ego pro te
    molam.

quid? hoc intellexti? an nondum etiam ne hoc quidem?

DAV   immo callide.

ita aperte ipsam rem modo locutu's, nil circumitione usus
    es.

SIM   ubivis facilius passus sim quam in hac re me deludier.

DAV   bona verba, quaeso!

SIM   irrides? nil me fallis. sed dico tibi,

205   ne temere facias, neque tu haud dicas tibi non praedic-
    tum. cave!

---

²⁰⁵ haud *Don.*, hoc Σ

---

¹⁶ Oedipus solved the riddle of the Sphinx and saved the city of
Thebes; he thus became proverbial as a riddle solver. This is one of
Terence's rare allusions to Greek mythology.

SIM   No? Really!

DAV   No. I'm Davus, not Oedipus.[16]

SIM   You mean you want me to say the rest in plain words, then?

DAV   Yes indeed.

SIM   If I find you attempting any trick today to prevent this marriage, or trying to show how clever you are in this situation, I shall whip you to the point of death and send you to the mill, Davus, on the solemn condition that, if I release you from there, I will work the mill myself in your place.[17] Well, have you understood? Or is even that taking time to sink in?

DAV   No, I understand perfectly. You've explained the situation very plainly, no beating about the bush.

SIM   (*half to himself*) I'd rather be tricked in any other matter than in this one.

DAV   (*with feigned concern at these ill-omened words*) Hush, I beg you!

SIM   Mocking, are you? You can't fool me.[18] But I'm warning you not to do anything rash. You can't say you haven't been told. Be careful! (*he exits right in the direction of the forum, leaving Davus onstage alone*)

---

[17] Being sent to the mill is one of the more extreme punishments with which slaves are threatened in comedy. Slaves were evidently chained to their mills, which were simple hand-driven affairs, to prevent them absconding, and flogged if they slackened.

[18] The Latin is a direct translation of the Greek νῦν δ᾽ οὐ λέληθάς με, which is preserved for us by Donatus. This is one of only six places where Donatus gives the text of Menander's *The Woman of Andros*.

I. iii: DAVOS.

DAV enimvero, Dave, nil locist segnitiae neque socordiae,
quantum intellexi modo senis sententiam de nuptiis.
quae si non astu providentur, me aut erum pessum da-
bunt.
nec quid agam certumst, Pamphilumne adiutem an aus-
cultem seni.

210 si illum relinquo, eius vitae timeo; sin opitulor, huius mi-
nas,
quoi verba dare difficilest. primum iam de amore hoc
comperit;
me infensus servat ne quam faciam in nuptiis fallaciam.
si senserit, perii; aut si lubitum fuerit, causam ceperit
quo iure quaque iniuria praecipitem in pistrinum dabit.

215 ad haec mala hoc mi accedit etiam. haec Andria,
si ista uxor sive amicast, gravida e Pamphilost.
audireque eorumst operae pretium audaciam.
nam inceptiost amentium, haud amantium.
quidquid peperisset decreverunt tollere.
220 et fingunt quandam inter se nunc fallaciam
civem Atticam esse hanc. "fuit olim quidam senex
mercator. navem is fregit apud Andrum insulam.
is obiit mortem." ibi tum hanc eiectam Chrysidis
patrem recepisse orbam parvam. fabulae!

225 miquidem hercle non fit veri simile; atque ipsis commen-
tum placet.
sed Mysis ab ea egreditur. at ego hinc me ad forum ut
conveniam Pamphilum ne de hac re pater imprudentem
opprimat.

---

[19] The exposure of unwanted babies is common in New Comedy
and no doubt reflects real-life practice. Female and illegitimate babies

DAV (*to himself*) Well, Davus, there's no room here for idleness or procrastination, if I understood the old man's intention about the marriage just now. If this business isn't managed with some skill, it'll be the ruin either of myself or of my master. I can't decide what to do, whether to help Pamphilus or obey the old man. If I abandon Pamphilus, I fear for his life; if I assist him, I've the old man's threats to fear, and he's a difficult man to deceive. For a start he's already found out about the love affair: he's watching me like an enemy in case I play some trick over the wedding. If he catches me, I'm lost; in any case, if the fancy takes him, he'll find a reason for despatching me headlong to the mill, whether I deserve it or not.

On top of all this there's a further problem. The Andrian woman, whether she's a wife or a mistress, is pregnant by Pamphilus. And you should just listen to their impudence. They're scheming like lunatics rather than lovers. They have decided to raise the baby, whatever it is.[19] And they're now concocting a story between them that the woman is an Athenian citizen. "Once upon a time there was an elderly merchant. He was shipwrecked off the island of Andros and died. The girl was washed ashore and Chrysis' father took the little orphan in." What nonsense! It seems pretty improbable to me, but they're pleased with their fiction. But here comes Mysis from the house. I'll be off to the forum to find Pamphilus, in case his father catches him off guard with the news. (*he exits right in the direction of the forum*)

were particularly at risk. The decision appears to have lain with the father, who could choose whether or not to acknowledge the baby by picking it up; this is the technical sense of the word "raise" here (Latin *tollere*).

I. iv: MYSIS.

MYS audivi, Archylis, iamdudum: Lesbiam adduci iubes.
  sane pol illa temulentast mulier et temeraria
230 nec satis digna quoi committas primo partu mulierem.
  tamen eam adducam. importunitatem spectate aniculae
  quia compotrix eius est. di, date facultatem, obsecro,
  huic pariundi atque illi in aliis potius peccandi locum.

  sed quidnam Pamphilum exanimatum video? vereor
   quid siet.
235 opperiar, ut sciam numquidnam haec turba tristitiae
  afferat.

I. v: PAMPHILUS. MYSIS.

PAM hocinest humanum factu aut inceptu? hocin officium
   patris?
MYS quid illud est?
PAM   pro deum fidem, quid est, si haec non contumeliast?
  uxorem decrerat dare sese mi hodie. nonne oportuit
  praescisse me ante? nonne prius communicatum opor-
   tuit?

240 MYS miseram me! quod verbum audio!
PAM quid? Chremes, qui denegarat se commissurum mihi
  gnatam suam uxorem, id mutavit quia me immutatum
   videt?

 235 num *Don.*, nunc Σ
 236 factu aut inceptu *Don. in comm.*, factum aut inceptum Σ

Enter MYSIS *from Glycerium's house.*

MYS (*speaking back to the housekeeper inside*) I heard you the first time, Archylis; you want me to fetch Lesbia. (*coming forward*) She's a drunken[20] and unreliable woman, for heaven's sake, not the sort to be entrusted with a first confinement. I'll fetch her even so. (*a voice is heard from inside*) See how the old woman nags me, just because the two of them are drinking partners. Ye gods, I beseech you, grant my mistress an easy birth and let the midwife do her mischief somewhere else. (*looking down the street*) But here's Pamphilus. Why is he in such a state? I dread to think what this means. I'll wait and see whether his confusion means bad news. (*she stands aside*)

Enter PAMPHILUS *right from the direction of the forum in a state of agitation.*

PAM (*to himself*) Is this human in deed or thought? Is this how a father should behave?

MYS (*aside*) What's this about?

PAM In heaven's name, if this isn't an outrage, what is? He'd decided to marry me off today. Shouldn't I have been told beforehand? Shouldn't there have been some prior notification?

MYS (*aside*) Oh dear! What am I hearing?

PAM And what about Chremes? Having refused to trust me with his daughter's hand, has he now changed his mind because he sees I haven't changed mine? Is he so deter-

[20] Drunkenness is a standard characteristic of midwives and of older female slaves in general in comedy.

73

itane obstinate operam dat ut me a Glycerio miserum
   abstrahat?
quod si fit pereo funditus.
245 adeon hominem esse invenustum aut infelicem quem-
   quam ut ego sum!
pro deum atque hominum fidem,
nullon ego Chremetis pacto affinitatem effugere potero?
quot modis contemptus, spretus! facta transacta omnia.
   em
repudiatus repetor. quam ob rem? nisi si id est quod sus-
   picor.
aliquid monstri alunt. ea quoniam nemini obtrudi potest,
250 itur ad me.

MYS   oratio haec me miseram exanimavit metu.
PAM nam quid ego dicam de patre? ah!
tantamne rem tam neglegenter agere! praeteriens modo

mi apud forum: "uxor tibi ducendast, Pamphile, hodie"
   inquit. "para,
255 abi domum." id mihi visust dicere: "abi cito ac suspende
   te."
obstipui. censen me verbum potuisse ullum proloqui?
   aut
ullam causam, ineptam saltem, falsam, iniquam? ob-
   mutui.
quod si ego rescissem id prius, quid facerem si quis nunc
   me roget:
aliquid facerem ut hoc ne facerem. sed nunc quid pri-
   mum exsequar?
260 tot me impediunt curae, quae meum animum divorsae
   trahunt:
amor, misericordia huius, nuptiarum sollicitatio,

74

mined to drag me away from Glycerium and condemn
me to misery? If this happens, I'm utterly lost. To think
that a man can be so unlucky in love, so ill-fated as I am!
In the name of gods and men, is there no way I can es-
cape this marriage tie with Chremes? I'm insulted and
scorned at every turn. It's all signed and sealed.[21] Here I
am, the reject recalled. Why? Unless what I suspect is
true, that they've reared a monster, and, since they can't
foist her on anyone else, they come to me.

MYS (aside) Poor me, this speech leaves me fainting with fear.

PAM What can I say about my father? Oh! How can he treat
such an important matter in such an offhand way? He
was passing me in the forum just now, and he said "You're
getting married today, Pamphilus. Go home and get
ready." He might as well have said "Run off and hang
yourself." I was flabbergasted. Do you think I could get
out a word? Or produce any argument, even a silly, un-
true, unreasonable one? I was struck dumb. If anyone
now asked me what I would be doing if I'd known about it
before, (lamely) I would be doing something so as to
avoid doing it. But as it is, what's my best course of ac-
tion? There are so many concerns weighing me down and
pulling my heart in different directions—love, pity for
her, anxiety about this wedding, and on the other side re-

---

[21] According to Donatus the Latin phrase (*facta transacta*) was pro-
verbial.

tum patris pudor, qui me tam leni passus est animo usque
    adhuc
quae meo quomque animo lubitumst facere. eine ego ut
    advorser? ei mihi!
incertumst quid agam.

MYS   misera timeo "incertum" hoc quorsus accidat.

265   sed nunc peropust aut hunc cum ipsa aut de illa aliquid
    me advorsum hunc loqui.
dum in dubiost animus, paullo momento huc vel illuc im-
    pellitur.

PAM quis hic loquitur? Mysis, salve.

MYS   o salve, Pamphile.

PAM   quid agit?

MYS   rogas?
laborat e dolore atque ex hoc misera sollicitast, diem
quia olim in hunc sunt constitutae nuptiae. tum autem
    hoc timet,

270   ne deseras se.

PAM   hem! egone istuc conari queam?
egon propter me illam decipi miseram sinam,
quae mihi suom animum atque omnem vitam credidit,
quam ego animo egregie caram pro uxore habuerim?
bene et pudice eius doctum atque eductum sinam

275   coactum egestate ingenium immutarier?
non faciam.

MYS   haud verear si in te solo sit situm,
sed vim ut queas ferre.

PAM   adeon me ignavom putas,
adeon porro ingratum aut inhumanum aut ferum,
ut neque me consuetudo neque amor neque pudor

280   commoveat neque commoneat ut servem fidem?

spect for my father, who has up to now been so generous
and allowed me to do whatever took my fancy. Oppose
him now? Oh dear! I just don't know what to do.

MYS (*aside*) Poor me, I dread to think where that "don't know"
is leading. But now it's imperative that either he speaks
with her or I say something to him about her. When a
man's wavering, a little thing can influence him one way
or the other.

PAM (*finally aware that there is someone present*) Who's that
speaking? (*recognising Mysis*) Mysis, good day.

MYS Oh, good day, Pamphilus.

PAM How is she?

MYS Well may you ask! The poor girl's in pain from her labour,
and she's anxious because your marriage was originally
fixed for today. On top of that, she's worried that you are
going to abandon her.

PAM What! Could I even think of doing that? Let the poor girl
be betrayed on my account when she has trusted me with
her heart and her whole life, when I have held her so very
dear and treated her as my wife? Let a nature formed and
fashioned in purity and innocence be corrupted by the
demands of poverty? I won't do it.

MYS I wouldn't be afraid if it depended solely on you, but you
may be forced against your will.

PAM Do you think me so base or ungrateful or inhuman or un-
feeling, that neither our intimacy nor love nor my sense
of honour could stir my heart or impel me to keep my
word?

MYS	unum hoc scio, hanc meritam esse ut memor esses sui.
PAM	memor essem? o Mysis, Mysis, etiam nunc mihi
	scripta illa dicta sunt in animo Chrysidis
	de Glycerio. iam ferme moriens me vocat.

285 accessi, vos semotae, nos soli. incipit:
"mi Pamphile, huius formam atque aetatem vides,
nec clam te est quam illi nunc utraeque inutiles
et ad pudicitiam et ad rem tutandam sient.
quod ego per hanc te dexteram et genium tuom,
290 per tuam fidem perque huius solitudinem
te obtestor ne abs te hanc segreges neu deseras.
si te in germani fratris dilexi loco
sive haec te solum semper fecit maxumi
seu tibi morigera fuit in rebus omnibus,
295 te isti virum do, amicum, tutorem, patrem;
bona nostra haec tibi permitto et tuae mando fide."
hanc mi in manum dat. mors continuo ipsam occupat.
accepi, acceptam servabo.

MYS   ita spero quidem.

PAM sed quor tu abis ab illa?

MYS   obstetricem accerso.

PAM   propera. atque audin?

300 verbum unum cave de nuptiis, ne ad morbum hoc etiam—

MYS   teneo.

MYS   All I know is that she doesn't deserve to be forgotten.

PAM   Forgotten? Oh Mysis, Mysis, even now Chrysis' words about Glycerium are engraved on my heart. She summoned me on her death bed, and I went to her. You were all sent away, and we were alone. "My dear Pamphilus," she said "you see her youth and beauty, and you are well aware that both of these are now useless to protect her honour or her property. By this right hand of yours and by your own better self, by your good faith and her lonely state, I beseech you not to turn your back on her or abandon her. If I have cherished you like my own brother, if she has always honoured you above all others, if she has obeyed you in everything, I give you to her to be her husband, friend, protector, father. I entrust these possessions of ours to you; I commit them to your good faith." She put Glycerium into my hands, and at that moment death overcame her. I accepted the charge, and, having accepted it, I will not let her down.

MYS   That is my hope.

PAM   But why have you left her side?

MYS   I'm fetching the midwife.

PAM   Hurry. And listen. Not a word about the wedding, in case on top of her pains—

MYS   I understand. (*she exits right in the direction of the forum*)

ACTUS II

II. i: CHARINUS. BYRRIA. PAMPHILUS.

CHA   quid ais, Byrria? daturne illa Pamphilo hodie nuptum?

BYR   sic est.

CHA   qui scis?

BYR   apud forum modo e Davo audivi.

CHA   vae misero mihi!

ut animus in spe atque in timore usque antehac attentus
    fuit,

ita, postquam adempta spes est, lassus cura confectus
    stupet.

305 BYR   quaeso edepol, Charine, quoniam non potest id fieri
    quod vis,

id velis quod possit.

CHA   nil volo aliud nisi Philumenam.

BYR   ah!

quanto satiust te id dare operam qui istum amorem ex
    animo amoveas,

quam id loqui quo magis lubido frustra incendatur tua!

CHA   facile omnes quom valemus recta consilia aegrotis da-
    mus.

310   tu si hic sis aliter sentias.

BYR   age age, ut lubet.

CHA   sed Pamphilum

video. omnia experiri certumst priusquam pereo.

BYR   quid hic agit?

CHA   ipsum hunc orabo, huic supplicabo, amorem huic narra-
    bo meum.

credo, impetrabo ut aliquot saltem nuptiis prodat dies.

interea fiet aliquid, spero.

ACT TWO

Enter CHARINUS *and* BYRRIA *right from the direction of the forum.*

CHA   What are you saying, Byrria? She's being married to Pamphilus today?

BYR   That's right.

CHA   How do you know?

BYR   I heard it from Davus in the forum just now.

CHA   Oh damn and blast! Up to now my mind has been racked with hope and fear; now all hope is gone, it's sick to death with worry and numbed with exhaustion.

BYR   Please, Charinus, for god's sake, since you can't have what you want, want what you can have.

CHA   The only thing I want is Philumena.

BYR   Oh! How much better to set about banishing that love from your heart than to say things which only inflame your desire to no purpose!

CHA   We can all readily give good advice to the sick when we're well. If you were in my place, you would feel differently.

BYR   All right, all right, as you like.

CHA   (*finally catching sight of Pamphilus, who is standing aside immersed in his problems*) But there's Pamphilus. I'm determined to try everything possible before I'm lost.

BYR   (*aside*) What's he going to do?

CHA   I'll plead with him, I'll go down on my knees, I'll tell him of my love. I'm sure I can persuade him at least to postpone his wedding for a few days. Meanwhile something will turn up, I hope.

BYR   id "aliquid" nil est.

CHA   Byrria,

315   quid tibi videtur? adeon ad eum?

BYR   quidni? si nil impetres,
ut te arbitretur sibi paratum moechum, si illam duxerit.

CHA abin hinc in malam rem cum suspicione istac, scelus?

PAM Charinum video. salve.

CHA   o salve, Pamphile.

ad te advenio spem, salutem, auxilium, consilium expe-
    tens.

320 PAM neque pol consili locum habeo neque ad auxilium co-
    piam.
sed istuc quidnamst?

CHA   hodie uxorem ducis?

PAM   aiunt.

CHA   Pamphile,
si id facis, hodie postremum me vides.

PAM   quid ita?

CHA   ei mihi!
vereor dicere. huic dic, quaeso, Byrria.

BYR   ego dicam.

PAM   quid est?

BYR sponsam hic tuam amat.

PAM   ne iste haud mecum sentit. ehodum, dic mihi:

325   numquidnam amplius tibi cum illa fuit, Charine?

CHA   ah, Pamphile!
nil.

PAM quam vellem!

CHA   nunc te per amicitiam et per amorem obsecro,
principio ut ne ducas.

PAM   dabo equidem operam.

BYR (*aside*) Nothing, more like.

CHA Byrria, what do you think? Shall I approach him?

BYR (*sarcastically*) Why not? If you can't persuade him, you'll give him the idea that you're all set for a spot of adultery after the marriage.

CHA Go to hell, you and your insinuations, you villain!

PAM (*at last seeing them*) It's Charinus. Good day.

CHA Oh, good day, Pamphilus. I am coming to you in need of hope, salvation, help, advice.

PAM Heaven knows I'm in no position to advise and I've no means to help. But what's this about?

CHA Are you getting married today?

PAM (*without enthusiasm*) So I'm told.

CHA (*dramatically*) If you are, Pamphilus, this is the last time you'll see me.

PAM Why so?

CHA Oh dear! I'm afraid to tell you. You tell him please, Byrria.

BYR All right, I will.

PAM What is this?

BYR He's in love with the woman who's engaged to you.

PAM I don't share his feelings, believe me. Hey, tell me, is there anything more between you?

CHA Oh Pamphilus! Nothing.

PAM How I wish there were!

CHA (*dramatically again*) I implore you, in the name of friendship and love, in the first place don't marry her.

PAM I'll do my best not to.

83

CHA   sed si id non potest
aut tibi nuptiae hae sunt cordi—

PAM   cordi?

CHA   —saltem aliquot dies
profer, dum proficiscor aliquo ne videam.

PAM   audi nunciam.

330   ego, Charine, ne utiquam officium liberi esse hominis
         puto,
quom is nil mereat, postulare id gratiae apponi sibi.
nuptias effugere ego istas malo quam tu adipiscier.

CHA reddidisti animum.

PAM   nunc si quid potes aut tu aut hic Byrria,
facite, fingite, invenite, efficite qui detur tibi.

335   ego id agam mihi qui ne detur.

CHA   sat habeo.

PAM   Davom optume
video, quoius consilio fretus sum.

CHA   at tu hercle haud quicquam mihi,
nisi ea quae nil opus sunt scire. fugin hinc?

BYR   ego vero ac lubens.

       II. ii: DAVOS. CHARINUS. PAMPHILUS.

DAV di boni! boni quid porto? sed ubi inveniam Pamphilum,
ut metum in quo nunc est adimam atque expleam ani-
       mum gaudio?

340 CHA laetus est nescioquid.

PAM   nil est. nondum haec rescivit mala.

CHA   But if you can't help it or if you actually desire this wedding—

PAM   Desire it?

CHA   —at least postpone it for a few days, while I go somewhere where I can't see it.

PAM   Now listen. For my part, Charinus, I reckon that it is not at all becoming for a gentleman to expect gratitude when he doesn't deserve it. I am keener to avoid this marriage than you are to achieve it.

CHA   I breathe again.

PAM   Do whatever you can, you and Byrria here, plot, scheme, contrive to have her given to you. I'll do the same to have her not given to me.

CHA   I'm happy with that.

PAM   (*looking down the street*) Excellent! Here's Davus. I rely on his advice.

CHA   (*to Byrria*) But I don't get any from you, god knows, except what I don't want to hear. Make yourself scarce.

BYR   I will, gladly. (*he runs off*)[22]

Enter DAVUS right from the direction of the forum in some excitement.

DAV   (*to himself*) Good gods! What good news I bring! But where shall I find Pamphilus to banish his fears and fill his heart with joy?

CHA   (*to Pamphilus*) Something's making him happy.

PAM   (*to Charinus*) It's nothing. He hasn't found out the bad news yet.

[22] The offstage movements of Byrria are hard to plot. When he next returns (line 412), he is following Simo, who is coming from the forum.

DAV   quem ego nunc credo, si iam audierit sibi paratas nup-
      tias—

CHA   audin tu illum?

DAV   —toto me oppido exanimatum quaerere.
  sed ubi quaeram? quo nunc primum intendam?

CHA   cessas alloqui?

DAV   abeo.

PAM   Dave, ades, resiste.

DAV   quis homost qui me—? o Pamphile,

345   te ipsum quaero. euge, Charine! ambo opportune. vos
  volo.

PAM   Dave, perii!

DAV   quin tu hoc audi.

PAM   interii!

DAV   quid timeas scio.

CHA   mea quidem hercle certe in dubio vitast.

DAV   et quid tu, scio.

PAM   nuptiae mi—

DAV   etsi scio?

PAM   —hodie—

DAV   obtundis, tam etsi intellego?
  id paves ne ducas tu illam, tu autem ut ducas.

CHA   rem tenes.

350 PAM   istuc ipsum.

DAV   atque istuc ipsum nil periclist. me vide.

PAM   obsecro te, quam primum hoc me libera miserum metu.

DAV   em
  libero. uxorem tibi non dat iam Chremes.

PAM   qui scis?

---

344 abeo Σ *Don. in comm.*, habeo *Don.*

DAV If he's now heard his wedding's all arranged, I'm sure—

CHA (*to Pamphilus*) Do you hear him?

DAV —he'll be looking for me all over the town in a panic. But where shall I find him? Where shall I try first?

CHA (*to Pamphilus*) Why don't you speak to him?

DAV I'm off. (*he turns to leave*)

PAM (*to Davus*) Davus, come here, stop.

DAV (*not looking*) Who is this fellow who dares . . . ? (*recognising Pamphilus*) Oh, Pamphilus! I was looking for you. You too, Charinus, splendid! How convenient! Just the two people I want.

PAM Davus, I'm lost!

DAV Just you listen to this.

PAM I'm ruined!

DAV I know what you're afraid of.

CHA *My* life's at risk for sure.

DAV And I know what *you're* afraid of.

PAM My wedding's—

DAV I know.

PAM —today.

DAV Do you have to go on about it, when I understand the situation perfectly? You're in a panic in case you have to marry her, and (*to Charinus*) *you're* in one in case you can't.

CHA You've got it.

PAM Exactly.

DAV But there's exactly no danger. Leave it to me.

PAM I implore you, put me out of my fear and misery, and quickly.

DAV Very well, I will. Chremes has withdrawn his consent to the marriage.

PAM How do you know?

DAV   scio.
tuos pater modo me prehendit. ait tibi uxorem dare
hodie, item alia multa quae nunc non est narrandi locus.

355   continuo ad te properans percurro ad forum ut dicam
        haec tibi.
ubi te non invenio, ibi escendo in quendam excelsum lo-
        cum.
circumspicio: nusquam. forte ibi huius video Byrriam.
rogo: negat vidisse. mihi molestum. quid agam cogito.
redeunti interea ex ipsa re mi incidit suspicio: "hem!

360   paullulum opsoni, ipsus tristis, de improviso nuptiae.
non cohaerent."

PAM   quorsumnam istuc?

DAV   ego me continuo ad Chremem.
quom illo advenio, solitudo ante ostium. iam id gaudeo.

CHA   recte dicis.

PAM   perge.

DAV   maneo. interea introire neminem
video, exire neminem, matronam nullam in aedibus.

365   nil ornati, nil tumulti. accessi, intro aspexi.

PAM   scio:
magnum signum.

DAV   num videntur convenire haec nuptiis?

PAM   non opinor, Dave.

DAV   "opinor" narras? non recte accipis.
certa res est. etiam puerum inde abiens conveni Chremi:

368 Chremi E^1 Don., Chremis Σ Prisc.

DAV   I do. Your father stopped me just now. He said that he was marrying you off today, and a host of other things which there's no time to relate now. I immediately ran to the forum in haste to tell you. When I couldn't find you there, I climbed up on to some high ground and had a look round. You were nowhere to be seen. Then I happened to see your friend's slave Byrria and asked him. He said he hadn't seen you. It was annoying, and I wondered what to do. While I was on my way back, the facts of the situation began to make me suspicious. "Wait a minute. There's not much food; the old man's looking gloomy; the wedding's sudden. It doesn't make sense."

PAM   Where's this leading?

DAV   I went straight to Chremes'. When I got there, there wasn't a soul at the door. That raised my spirits.

CHA   It would do.

PAM   (to Davus) Go on.

DAV   I waited. During this time I saw nobody go inside, nobody come out; not a married woman[23] in the house, no preparations, no bustle. I went up and looked inside.

PAM   I see. That's a pretty clear indication.[24]

DAV   Does this seem to square with a wedding?

PAM   I don't think so, Davus.

DAV   Think? You haven't understood. It's a certainty. What's more, I met one of Chremes' slave boys as I left, carry-

[23] Married women acted as bride's attendants (pronubae) at a Roman wedding.

[24] As this conversation implies, the wedding banquet was normally held at the bride's house; it was followed by a procession to that of the bridegroom.

holera et pisciculos minutos ferre obolo in cenam seni.
370 CHA liberatus sum hodie, Dave, tua opera.
DAV   ac nullus quidem!
CHA quid ita? nempe huic prorsus illam non dat.
DAV   ridiculum caput!
quasi necesse sit, si huic non dat, te illam uxorem ducere,
nisi vides, nisi senis amicos oras, ambis.
CHA   bene mones.
ibo, etsi hercle saepe iam me spes haec frustratast. vale.

II. iii: PAMPHILUS. DAVOS.

375 PAM quid igitur sibi volt pater? quor simulat?
DAV   ego dicam tibi.
si id suscenseat nunc quia non det tibi uxorem Chremes,
ipsus sibi esse iniurius videatur, neque id iniuria,
prius quam tuom ut sese habeat animum ad nuptias pers-
    pexerit.
sed si tu negaris ducere, ibi culpam in te transferet.
380 tum illae turbae fient.
PAM   quidvis patiar.
DAV   pater est, Pamphile:
difficilest. tum haec solast mulier. dictum factum invene-
    rit
aliquam causam quam ob rem eiciat oppido.
PAM   eiciat?
DAV   cito.
PAM cedo igitur quid faciam, Dave?

---

375 *novam scaenam indicat Don. Eugr., non* Σ
381 dictum factum *edd.*, dictum ac factum Σ

---

[25] This is a pretty small amount. At Athens the obol was the smallest

ing an obol's worth[25] of greens and a bit of fish for the old
man's dinner.

CHA I'm a free man today, Davus, thanks to you.

DAV Oh no, you're not.

CHA How so? He's quite obviously not giving her to *him* (*in-dicating Pamphilus*).

DAV Don't be ridiculous. As if it followed that, if he doesn't give her to him, she'll marry *you,* unless you look sharp and canvas the old man's friends for support.

CHA Good advice. I'll go, though, god knows, my hopes have often been dashed before. Goodbye. (*he exits right in the direction of the forum, leaving Pamphilus and Davus on-stage*)

PAM So what's my father up to? Why this pretence?

DAV I'll tell you. If he flew into a rage now at Chremes' refusal to give you his daughter, before having established *your* attitude towards the wedding, he would feel that he was putting himself in the wrong, and rightly so. But if you refuse to marry her, he'll transfer the blame on to you. And then there'll be trouble.

PAM I'll put up with anything.

DAV He's your father, Pamphilus; it's difficult. Besides, Gly-cerium has no one to protect her. He'll find a pretext for driving her out of town, no sooner said than done.

PAM Driving her out?

DAV And quickly.

PAM So tell me, what shall I do, Davus?

silver coin: there were six obols to the drachma, 100 drachmas to the
mina, and 60 minas to the talent. For comparison, the basic wage was
three obols a day.

DAV   dic te ducturum.

PAM   hem!

DAV   quid est?

PAM egon dicam?

DAV   quor non?

PAM   numquam faciam.

DAV   ne nega.

385 PAM suadere noli.

DAV   ex ea re quid fiat vide.

PAM ut ab illa excludar, hoc concludar.

DAV   non itast.

nempe hoc sic esse opinor. dicturum patrem
"ducas volo hodie uxorem;" tu "ducam" inquies.
cedo quid iurgabit tecum? hic reddes omnia
390 quae nunc sunt certa ei consilia incerta ut sient
sine omni periclo. nam hoc haud dubiumst quin
    Chremes
tibi non det gnatam. nec tu ea causa minueris
haec quae facis, ne is mutet suam sententiam.

patri dic velle, ut, quom velit, tibi iure irasci non queat.
395 nam quod tu speres "propulsabo facile uxorem his mori-
    bus;
dabit nemo," inveniet inopem potius quam te corrumpi
    sinat.
sed si te aequo animo ferre accipiet, neglegentem fece-
    ris.
aliam otiosus quaeret. interea aliquid acciderit boni.

PAM itan credis?

DAV   haud dubium id quidemst.

PAM   vide quo me inducas.

DAV   Agree to marry.

PAM   (*startled*) What?

DAV   What's the matter?

PAM   Agree?

DAV   Why not?

PAM   I won't do it, ever.

DAV   Don't you refuse.

PAM   Don't you try to persuade me.

DAV   Consider the advantages.

PAM   I'll be shut out from *her* (*pointing to Glycerium's house*) and shut in *here* (*pointing to Simo's*).

DAV   Not so. This is the situation as I see it. Your father will say "I want you to marry today." You'll say "All right." Tell me, how can he quarrel with that? This way you'll throw all his well-laid plans into confusion and without any danger to yourself: there's no doubting that Chremes will refuse to give you his daughter. But you mustn't for that reason alter your present behaviour or he may change his mind. Tell your father you're willing, so that he can't rightly be angry with you whenever he chooses. As for your hope that "With my character I'll easily avoid marriage; nobody will give me a wife," he'll find you a poor one rather than see you go to the bad. On the other hand, if he hears you're taking this calmly, he won't worry so much. He'll look for another one at his leisure, and meanwhile (*vaguely*) something will turn up.

PAM   Do you believe that?

DAV   There's no doubting it.

PAM   Watch where you're leading me.

---

386 hoc *Don.*, hac Σ *Eugr.*

	DAV	quin taces?
400	PAM	dicam. puerum autem ne resciscat mi esse ex illa cau-tiost.

nam pollicitus sum suscepturum.

	DAV	o facinus audax!
	PAM	hanc fidem

sibi me obsecravit, qui se sciret non deserturum, ut da-
rem.

DAV curabitur. sed pater adest. cave te esse tristem sentiat.

II. iv: SIMO. DAVOS. PAMPHILUS.

SIM reviso quid agant aut quid captent consili.
405 DAV hic nunc non dubitat quin te ducturum neges.
venit meditatus alicunde ex solo loco.
orationem sperat invenisse se
qui differat te. proin tu fac apud te ut sies.
PAM modo ut possim, Dave!

	DAV	crede, inquam, hoc mihi, Pamphile,
410		numquam hodie tecum commutaturum patrem

unum esse verbum, si te dices ducere.

II. v: BYRRIA. SIMO. DAVOS. PAMPHILUS.

BYR erus me relictis rebus iussit Pamphilum
hodie observare ut quid ageret de nuptiis
415 scirem. id propterea nunc hunc venientem sequor.
ipsum adeo praesto video cum Davo. hoc agam.
SIM utrumque adesse video.

DAV Don't worry.

PAM I'll tell him. But we must make sure he doesn't find out I've a child by Glycerium. I've promised to raise it.

DAV That's a rash undertaking!

PAM She implored me to give my word, to be sure I wouldn't abandon her.

DAV We'll see to it. (*looking down the street*) But here's your father. Don't let him see you looking gloomy. (*they withdraw to the far side of the stage*)

Enter SIMO right from the direction of the forum.

SIM (*to himself*) I've come back to see what they're doing, what schemes they're hatching.

DAV (*to Pamphilus*) He's in no doubt now that you'll refuse to marry. He's been to some lonely spot to practise his speech, and he's confident he's found an argument that will confound you. So be sure you keep your wits about you.

PAM If only I could, Davus!

DAV Take my word for it, Pamphilus. I tell you, your father won't have a thing to say to you if you agree to marry.

Enter BYRRIA from the right in pursuit of Simo. He pauses at the side of the stage.

BYR (*to himself*) My master told me to drop everything else and keep an eye on Pamphilus today to find out what he was doing about the marriage. So I followed *him* (*indicating Simo*) on his way here. (*seeing Pamphilus and Davus*) There he is with Davus. I'll listen in.

SIM (*seeing Pamphilus and Davus*) There they are, the pair of them.

DAV	em serva.
SIM	Pamphile!
DAV	quasi de improviso respice ad eum.
PAM	ehem, pater!
DAV	probe.
SIM	hodie uxorem ducas, ut dixi, volo.
BYR	nunc nostrae timeo parti quid hic respondeat.
PAM	neque istic neque alibi tibi erit usquam in me mora.
BYR	hem!
DAV	obmutuit.
BYR	quid dixit?
SIM	facis ut te decet,

420 PAM: neque istic neque alibi tibi erit usquam in me mora.

quom istuc quod postulo impetro cum gratia.

DAV	sum verus?
BYR	erus, quantum audio, uxore excidit.
SIM	i nunciam intro, ne in mora, quom opus sit, sies.
PAM	eo.
BYR	nullane in re esse quoiquam homini fidem!

425 BYR:

verum illud verbumst, volgo quod dici solet,
omnis sibi malle melius esse quam alteri.
ego illam vidi; virginem forma bona
memini videri. quo aequior sum Pamphilo,
430 si se illam in somnis quam illum amplecti maluit.
renuntiabo, ut pro hoc malo mihi det malum.

II. vi: DAVOS. SIMO.

DAV hic nunc me credit aliquam sibi fallaciam
portare et ea me hic restitisse gratia.

---

²⁶ There is a play here on the word *malum* ("trouble"), which in slave talk usually means a thrashing.

DAV   (*to Pamphilus*) Now, be on your guard.

SIM   Pamphilus!

DAV   (*to Pamphilus*) Turn round as if you've only just seen him.

PAM   (*to Simo, with feigned surprise*) Oh hello, father!

DAV   (*to Pamphilus*) Well done!

SIM   As I told you, I want you to marry today.

BYR   (*aside*) I'm dreading his reply on our account.

PAM   Neither in this matter nor in any other will I ever stand in your way.

BYR   (*aside*) What!

DAV   (*to Pamphilus*) That's silenced him.

BYR   (*aside*) What did he say?

SIM   It does you credit that you agree to my request with a good grace.

DAV   (*to Pamphilus*) Didn't I tell you?

BYR   (*aside*) If I can believe my ears, my master has just lost a wife.

SIM   Go inside now, so you won't keep us waiting when we need you.

PAM   I'll go. (*he exits into Simo's house*)

BYR   (*to himself*) You can't trust anyone in anything! It's quite true what they say: every man looks to his own interest rather than his neighbour's. I've seen her, and, as I recall, she's a good-looking girl. So I'm not unsympathetic to Pamphilus if he chooses to sleep with her in his own arms rather than let my master have her. I'll report back; bad news for him means bad news[26] for me. (*he exits right, leaving Davus and Simo onstage*)

DAV   (*aside*) He's sure I've some trick up my sleeve and that's why I'm staying here.

SIM	quid Davos narrat?	
DAV		aeque quicquam nunc quidem.

435 SIM nilne? hem!

DAV nil prorsus.

SIM atqui exspectabam quidem.

DAV praeter spem evenit, sentio. hoc male habet virum.

SIM potin es mihi verum dicere?

DAV nil facilius.

SIM num illi molestae quippiam hae sunt nuptiae
huiusce propter consuetudinem hospitae?

440 DAV nil hercle, aut, si adeo, biduist aut tridui
haec sollicitudo (nosti?), deinde desinet.
etenim ipsus secum id recta reputavit via.

SIM laudo.

DAV dum licitumst ei dumque aetas tulit,
amavit; tum id clam. cavit ne umquam infamiae

445 ea res sibi esset, ut virum fortem decet.
nunc uxore opus est: animum ad uxorem appulit.

SIM subtristis visus est esse aliquantum mihi.

DAV nil propter hanc rem, sed est quod suscenset tibi.

SIM quidnamst?

DAV puerilest.

SIM quid id est?

DAV nil.

SIM quin dic, quid est?

439 *sic edd. metro consulentes*, propter huiusce hospitae consue-
tudinem Σ *Don.*

442 id recta *Fleckeisen*, eam rem recta *codd. pl.*, eam rem *P¹C¹Don.*

---

27 Donatus takes this as a reference to line 185, where Davus re-

SIM   (*approaching him*) What does Davus have to say for himself?

DAV   No more than before.[27]

SIM   Nothing? Really!

DAV   Nothing at all.

SIM   Well, I was expecting something.

DAV   (*aside*) It's taken him by surprise, I can see that. He's not enjoying this.

SIM   Can you tell me the truth?

DAV   Nothing easier.

SIM   Isn't he a little bit annoyed at this wedding in view of his affair with the foreign woman?

DAV   God, no. Or, if he is, he'll only be upset for a day or two, you know, and then he'll get over it. He's been thinking it over himself in his own mind, and he's on the right path.

SIM   Good for him.

DAV   While the licence of youth permitted it, he had a love affair. Even then he kept it quiet, taking care that it should never bring him into disrepute, as an honest man should. Now it's time for a wife, and he has directed his thoughts towards a wife.

SIM   He seemed a little bit subdued to me.

DAV   But not on this account. There's something else which is upsetting him.

SIM   Whatever is it?

DAV   (*with feigned reluctance*) It's childish.

SIM   But what is it?

DAV   Nothing.

SIM   Why don't you tell me? What is it?

fused to be drawn into answering Simo's question about Pamphilus' behaviour.

99

450	DAV	ait nimium parce facere sumptum.
	SIM	mene?
	DAV	te.

       "vix" inquit "drachumis est opsonatum decem.
       non filio videtur uxorem dare.
       quem" inquit "vocabo ad cenam meorum aequalium
       potissumum nunc?" et, quod dicendum hic siet,

455   tu quoque perparce nimium. non laudo.

	SIM	tace!
	DAV	commovi.
	SIM	ego istaec recte ut fiant videro.

       quidnam hoc est rei? quid hic volt veterator sibi?
       nam si hic malist quicquam, em illic est huic rei caput.

ACTUS III

III. i: MYSIS. SIMO. DAVOS. LESBIA. (GLYCERIUM).

	MYS	ita pol quidem res est ut dixti, Lesbia.
460		fidelem haud ferme mulieri invenias virum.
	SIM	ab Andriast ancilla haec? quid narras?
	DAV	itast.
	MYS	sed hic Pamphilus—
	SIM	quid dicit?
	MYS	—firmavit fidem.
	SIM	hem!
	DAV	utinam aut hic surdus aut haec muta facta sit!
	MYS	nam quod peperisset iussit tolli.

461 quid narras? *Simoni continuant* Σ, *Davo dant edd. nonn.*

---

28 For monetary amounts see note 25.

DAV He says you're being too tight-fisted.

SIM Me?

DAV You. "You've scarcely spent ten drachmas[28] on food," he says. "It doesn't look like a wedding for a son. How am I going to choose" he says "which friends to invite to the dinner?" And, if I may say so, you really are being very tight-fisted. I don't approve.

SIM You hold your tongue!

DAV (*aside*) That's stirred him up.

SIM I'll see that it's put right. (*aside*) Whatever's going on here? What's the old rogue up to? If there's any trouble brewing here, look (*indicating Davus*), there's the source of it.

ACT THREE

Enter MYSIS right from the direction of the forum with the mid-wife LESBIA.

MYS Heaven knows you're quite right, Lesbia. You can scarcely find one single man who's loyal to a woman.

SIM (*to Davus*) Is this the Andrian woman's maid? What do you say?

DAV (*to Simo*) Yes, it is.

MYS But our Pamphilus—

SIM (*aside*) What's she saying?

MYS —has proved himself faithful.

SIM (*aside*) What!

DAV (*aside*) How I wish he had lost his hearing or she her tongue!

MYS He's given instructions for her baby to be raised.

101

	SIM	o Iuppiter,
465		quid ego audio? actumst, siquidem haec vera praedicat.
	LES	bonum ingenium narras adulescentis.
	MYS	optumum.

sed sequere me intro, ne in mora illi sis.

	LES	sequor.
	DAV	quod remedium nunc huic malo inveniam?
	SIM	quid hoc?

adeon est demens? ex peregrina? iam scio. ah!

470		vix tandem sensi stolidus.
	DAV	quid hic sensisse ait?
	SIM	haec primum affertur iam mi ab hoc fallacia.

hanc simulant parere, quo Chremetem absterreant.

	GLY	Iuno Lucina, fer opem, serva me, obsecro.
	SIM	hui! tam cito? ridiculum. postquam ante ostium
475		me audivit stare, approperat. non sat commode
		divisa sunt temporibus tibi, Dave, haec.
	DAV	mihin?
	SIM	num immemores discipuli?
	DAV	ego quid narres nescio.
	SIM	hicin me si imparatum in veris nuptiis
		adortus esset, quos mihi ludos redderet!
480		nunc huius periclo fit, ego in portu navigo.

III. ii: LESBIA. SIMO. DAVOS.

	LES	adhuc, Archylis, quae adsolent quaeque oportent
		signa esse ad salutem, omnia huic esse video.

---

[29] Juno Lucina was the Roman goddess of childbirth. Donatus tells us that in Menander's version the appeal was to Artemis.

[30] This is one of only two lyric passages in the play, which would have been sung in the original performance; the other is at line 625. There may be a hint here that Lesbia has been drinking.

SIM   (*aside*) Jupiter! What am I hearing? It's all over, if she's telling the truth!

LES   You make him sound a very nice young man.

MYS   The best. But follow me in. You mustn't keep her waiting.

LES   I'm coming. (*they exit into Glycerium's house*)

DAV   (*aside*) How can I find a way out of this mess?

SIM   (*aside*) What's this? Is he quite out of his mind? A foreign woman's child? (*after a pause*) Now I see. Oh, how stupid! I've only just realised after all this time.

DAV   (*aside*) What does he say he's realised?

SIM   (*aside*) This is the first of the tricks he's planning for me. They're pretending she's having a baby to frighten Chremes off.

GLY   (*from inside the house*) Juno Lucina,[29] help me, save me, I beseech you!

SIM   (*aside*) Wow! So soon? It's ridiculous. As soon as she heard I was standing in front of the door, she speeded it up. (*turning to Davus*) There's something wrong with your timing here, Davus.

DAV   Mine?

SIM   Have your actors forgotten their cues?

DAV   I don't know what you're talking about.

SIM   (*aside*) If this had been a real marriage and he'd caught me off my guard, what a fool he would have made of me! But now he's the one who's in danger: my ship's in harbour.

Enter LESBIA *from Glycerium's house.*

LES   (*to the housekeeper back inside the house, singing*)[30]
     So far, Archylis, all is normal.
     All the proper indications of a safe delivery are present.

103

nunc primum fac ista ut lavet, poste deinde
quod iussi dari bibere et quantum imperavi
485   date; mox ego huc revortor.
per ecastor scitus puer est natus Pamphilo.

deos quaeso ut sit superstes, quandoquidem ipsest inge-
    nio bono,
quomque huic est veritus optumae adulescenti facere
    iniuriam.

SIM   vel hoc quis non credat qui te norit abs te esse ortum?
DAV   quidnam id est?
490 SIM   non imperabat coram quid opus facto esset puerperae,
sed postquam egressast illis quae sunt intus clamat de
    via.
o Dave, itane contemnor abs te? aut itane tandem ido-
    neus
tibi videor esse quem tam aperte fallere incipias dolis?
saltem accurate ut metui videar certe si resciverim.
495 DAV   certe hercle nunc hic se ipsus fallit, haud ego.
SIM   edixin tibi,
interminatus sum ne faceres? num veritu's? quid re tulit?

credon tibi hoc nunc, peperisse hanc e Pamphilo?
DAV   teneo quid erret et quid agam habeo.
SIM   quid taces?

DAV   quid credas? quasi non tibi renuntiata sint haec sic fore.
500 SIM   min quisquam?

---

[31] According to Donatus, the midwife in Menander prescribed the
yolk of four eggs here rather than a drink.

First make sure she has her bath, and after that
Give her the the potion I prescribed in the right dose.[31]
I'll be back soon.

(*to herself, in a more normal voice*) Lord knows that's a
lovely baby Pamphilus has got! I pray the gods it survives.
He's a nice young man and he wasn't going to wrong that
nice young girl. (*she exits right in the direction of the
forum*)

SIM   (*to Davus*) Well, any one who knew you would be sure
this was your doing.

DAV   How do you mean?

SIM   She didn't give her instructions for the needs of the
mother at the bedside, but came out of the house and
shouted them back inside from the street. Do you have so
little respect for me, Davus? Do you think I'm the sort of
person who can be deceived with such obvious tricks? At
least try to make it seem you're afraid of what I'll do if I
find out.

DAV   (*aside*) This time he's deceiving himself, for god's sake.
It's nothing to do with me.

SIM   Didn't I instruct you not to do this? Didn't I threaten
you? Did you hesitate at all? Did it make any difference?
Do you expect me to believe the girl has had a child by
Pamphilus?

DAV   (*aside*) I see the mistake he's making, and how I can use
it.

SIM   Why no reply?

DAV   Expect you to believe what? As if you weren't told that
this would happen!

SIM   Me? By whom?

DAV	eho! an tute intellexti hoc assimulari?
SIM	irrideor.
DAV	renuntiatumst. nam qui istaec tibi incidit suspicio?
SIM	qui? quia te noram.
DAV	quasi tu dicas factum id consilio meo.
SIM	certe enim scio.
DAV	non satis me pernosti etiam qualis sim, Simo.
SIM	egon te?
DAV	sed si quid tibi narrare occepi, continuo dari

505   tibi verba censes.

SIM	falso?
DAV	itaque hercle nil iam muttire audeo.
SIM	hoc ego scio unum, neminem peperisse hic.
DAV	intellexti.

      sed nilo setius referetur mox huc puer ante ostium.
      id ego iam nunc tibi, ere, renuntio futurum, ut sis sciens,
      ne tu hoc posterius dicas Davi factum consilio aut dolis.

510   prorsus a me opinionem hanc tuam esse ego amotam
            volo.

SIM	unde id scis?
DAV	audivi et credo. multa concurrunt simul

      qui coniecturam hanc nunc facio. iam prius haec se e
            Pamphilo
      gravidam dixit esse. inventumst falsum. nunc, postquam
            videt
      nuptias domi apparari, missast ancilla ilico

DAV Hey, did you work it out for yourself that this was a pretence?

SIM (*aside*) I'm being mocked.

DAV Somebody told you. How else did you come to suspect?

SIM How? Because I know you.

DAV You're as good as saying it was all my plan.

SIM I'm quite sure it was.

DAV You don't really know what sort of person I am, Simo.

SIM I don't?

DAV If I ever try to tell you something, you immediately suppose that I'm deceiving you.

SIM And wrongly?

DAV The result is that now I daren't utter a word, for god's sake.

SIM The one thing I do know is that nobody has had a baby here.

DAV You realised! Even so, any moment they'll bring a baby out and put it on the doorstep. I'm telling you this will happen now, master, so that you'll be warned and you can't afterwards say that it was all some plot or trick of Davus'. I want to dispel your prejudice against me once and for all.

SIM How do you know this?

DAV I heard it, and I'm sure it's true. There are a number of things which, if you take them together, point to this conclusion. Some time ago she said that she was pregnant by Pamphilus;[32] this has been shown to be false. Now, when she sees wedding preparations being made at home, she immediately sends her maid to summon the midwife and

---

[32] There has been no precise reference to this in the play.

515   obstetricem accersitum ad eam et puerum ut afferret
         simul.
     hoc nisi fit, puerum ut tu videas, nil moventur nuptiae.

SIM   quid ais? quom intellexeras
     id consilium capere, quor non dixti extemplo Pamphilo?

DAV   quis igitur eum ab illa abstraxit nisi ego? nam omnes nos
         quidem

520   scimus quam misere hanc amarit. nunc sibi uxorem ex-
         petit.
     postremo id mi da negoti. tu tamen idem has nuptias
     perge facere ita ut facis, et id spero adiuturos deos.

SIM   immo abi intro. ibi me opperire et quod parato opus est
         para.

     non impulit me haec nunc omnino ut crederem.

525   atque haud scio an quae dixit sint vera omnia.
     sed parvi pendo. illud mi multo maxumumst
     quod mi pollicitust ipsus gnatus. nunc Chremem
     conveniam, orabo gnato uxorem. si impetro,
     quid alias malim quam hodie has fieri nuptias?

530   nam gnatus quod pollicitust, haud dubiumst mihi, id
     si nolit, quin eum merito possim cogere.
     atque adeo in ipso tempore eccum ipsum obviam.

III. iii: SIMO. CHREMES.

SIM   iubeo Chremetem—
CHR   o te ipsum quaerebam.
SIM   et ego te. optato advenis.

bring in a baby at the same time.[33] If she can't get you to see the baby, there's no stopping the wedding.

SIM Tell me then, when you realised that was her plan, why didn't you inform Pamphilus at once?

DAV (*with feigned indignation*) Who was it but me who dragged him away from her? We all know how desperately he was in love with her; now he wants to take a wife. In short, let me look after this. Meanwhile you go on with the wedding as you're doing, and I hope the gods will give us their blessing.

SIM No, you go inside. Wait for me there, and prepare everything we need. (*Davus exits into Simo's house*) (*to himself*) He hasn't altogether convinced me; yet, for all I know, everything he says may be true. But I don't care very much. By far the most important thing to me is the promise my son gave me. I'll go and find Chremes now and ask for his daughter in marriage. If he agrees, what better day for the wedding than today? If my son tries to go back on his promise, there's no doubt I'll have every right to compel him. But here comes Chremes, just at the right moment.

Enter CHREMES right from the direction of the forum in some agitation.

SIM Chremes, please accept—

CHR Oh! I was looking for you.

SIM And I for you. I'm glad you've come.

[33] The bringing in of suppositious babies to ensnare their supposed fathers or otherwise precipitate a marriage is a traditional feature of the life depicted in comedy (see *The Eunuch* 39, Plautus, *The Threepenny Bit* 391–411).

CHR aliquot me adierunt, ex te auditum qui aibant hodie
      filiam

535   meam nubere tuo gnato. id viso tune an illi insaniant.

SIM ausculta pauca, et quid ego te velim et tu quod quaeris
      scies.

CHR ausculto. loquere quid velis.

SIM per te deos oro et nostram amicitiam, Chreme,
      quae incepta a parvis cum aetate accrevit simul,

540   perque unicam gnatam tuam et gnatum meum,
      quoius tibi potestas summa servandi datur,
      ut me adiuves in hac re atque ita uti nuptiae
      fuerant futurae, fiant.

CHR   ah! ne me obsecra.
      quasi hoc te orando a me impetrare oporteat!

545   alium esse censes nunc me atque olim quom dabam?
      si in remst utrique ut fiant, accersi iube.
      sed si ex ea re plus malist quam commodi
      utrique, id oro te in commune ut consulas,
      quasi si illa tua sit Pamphiluque ego sim pater.

550 SIM immo ita volo itaque postulo ut fiat, Chreme,
      neque postulem abs te ni ipsa res moneat.

CHR   quid est?

SIM irae sunt inter Glycerium et gnatum.

CHR   audio.

SIM ita magnae ut sperem posse avelli.

CHR   fabulae!

SIM profecto sic est.

CHR A number of people have come up to me to say that they've heard from you that my daughter is marrying your son today. I've come to see whether it is you who have taken leave of your senses or they.

SIM Just listen a moment, and I'll tell you what I want and answer your question.

CHR I'm listening. Say what you want.

SIM (*earnestly*) I beg you in the name of the gods, Chremes, and of our friendship, which began when we were young and has grown stronger with age, and in the name of your only daughter and my son, whose salvation rests entirely in your hands, to support me in this matter and allow the wedding to take place as planned.

CHR Ah! Please don't beseech me. This isn't a favour to be gained by begging. Do you think I'm a different man from before when I offered my daughter? If it is in both their interests that the wedding takes place, have her fetched.[34] But if it is going to cause them both more harm than good, I beg you to look to our common interest, as if she were your daughter and Pamphilus my son.

SIM You misunderstand me, Chremes. Those are my wishes; that's what I'm asking to happen. And I wouldn't ask it of you if the circumstances weren't favourable.

CHR How do you mean?

SIM (*significantly*) Glycerium and my son have fallen out.

CHR (*unimpressed*) I'm listening.

SIM So seriously that I am confident they can be parted.

CHR (*still unimpressed*) Nonsense!

SIM It's true, I assure you.

---

[34] *Accersere* (fetch) is the technical term for the summoning of the bride to the bridegroom's house as part of the marriage ceremony.

CHR   sic hercle ut dicam tibi,
555   amantium irae amoris integratiost.

SIM   em, id te oro ut ante eamus. dum tempus datur
        dumque eius lubido occlusast contumeliis,
        prius quam harum scelera et lacrumae confictae dolis
        redducunt animum aegrotum ad misericordiam,
560   uxorem demus. spero consuetudine et
        coniugio liberali devinctum, Chreme,
        dein facile ex illis sese emersurum malis.

CHR   tibi ita hoc videtur. at ego non posse arbitror
        neque illum hanc perpetuo habere neque me perpeti.
565 SIM   qui scis ergo istuc, nisi periclum feceris?

CHR   at istuc periclum in filia fieri gravest.

SIM   nempe incommoditas denique huc omnis redit
        si eveniat, quod di prohibeant, discessio.
        at si corrigitur, quot commoditates vide.
570   principio amico filium restitueris,
        tibi generum firmum et filiae invenies virum.

CHR   quid istic? si ita istuc animum induxti esse utile,
        nolo tibi ullum commodum in me claudier.

SIM   merito te semper maxumi feci, Chreme.

575 CHR   sed quid ais?

SIM   quid?

CHR   qui scis eos nunc discordare inter se?

SIM   ipsus mihi Davos, qui intumust eorum consiliis, dixit.
        et is mihi suadet nuptias quantum queam ut maturem.
        num censes faceret, filium nisi sciret eadem haec velle?
        tute adeo iam eius verba audies. heus! evocate huc
        Davom.

THE WOMAN OF ANDROS

CHR (*with a hint of impatience*) I'll tell you what's true, by god:
     lovers' quarrels are love's renewal.

SIM Well then, I beg you, let's prevent that happening. While
     the opportunity offers, while his desires are disrupted
     by their quarrels, before those women's wicked ways
     and cunningly contrived tears can work on his lovesick
     mind and reduce him to pity, let's give him a wife. I ex-
     pect that, once he is tied down by a respectable marriage,
     Chremes, he will easily extricate himself from the other
     situation.

CHR That's what you think. I don't believe he can. But he can't
     keep that woman for ever, nor can I put up with it.

SIM So how do you know, if you don't take the risk?

CHR It's a serious business to risk your daughter.

SIM After all, the worst thing that it could come to in the end
     is a separation, which heaven forbid! But if he mends his
     ways, consider all the advantages. In the first place, you'll
     have given a friend back his son, and you'll gain a steady
     son-in-law for yourself and husband for your daughter.

CHR (*reluctantly*) All right, then. If you are convinced that this
     is in everybody's interests, I don't want to stand in your
     way.

SIM You deserve the high regard which I have always had for
     you, Chremes.

CHR But tell me this.

SIM What?

CHR How do you know they're quarrelling?

SIM Davus told me himself; he's in on all their plans. And he's
     urging me to hasten the wedding with all speed. Do you
     suppose he would do that, if he didn't know that my son
     was keen on it? You can hear it from his own mouth.
     (*shouting to slaves inside the house*) Hey there! Send

113

580 atque eccum video ipsum foras exire.

III. iv: DAVOS . SIMO. CHREMES.

DAV   ad te ibam.
SIM   quidnamst?
DAV quor uxor non accersitur? iam advesperascit.
SIM   audin?
ego dudum non nil veritus sum, Dave, abs te ne faceres idem
quod volgus servorum solet, dolis ut me deluderes
propterea quod amat filius.
DAV   egon istuc facerem?
SIM   credidi,
585 idque adeo metuens vos celavi quod nunc dicam.
DAV   quid?
SIM   scies.
nam propemodum habeo iam fidem.
DAV   tandem cognosti qui siem?
SIM non fuerant nuptiae futurae.
DAV   quid? non?
SIM   sed ea gratia
simulavi vos ut pertemptarem.
DAV   quid ais?
SIM   sic res est.
DAV   vide!
numquam istuc quivi ego intellegere. vah! consilium callidum!
590 SIM hoc audi: ut hinc te introire iussi, opportune hic fit mi obviam.
DAV   hem!
numnam perimus?
SIM   narro huic quae tu dudum narrasti mihi.

Davus out here. Look, the very man. He's coming out.

Enter DAVUS *from Simo's house.*

DAV   (*to Simo*) I was coming for you.

SIM   What's the matter?

DAV   Why isn't the bride being fetched? It's already evening.[35]

SIM   Listen to me. I was quite worried before, Davus, that you
       would behave like the common run of slaves and play
       some trick on me because of my son's love affair.

DAV   (*with feigned innocence*) I do that?

SIM   I believed you would, and being afraid of that I concealed
       from you what I will now tell you.

DAV   What's that?

SIM   You shall hear, since I now just about trust you.

DAV   You've at last recognised my true character?

SIM   There wasn't going to be a wedding.

DAV   (*with feigned surprise*) What? There wasn't?

SIM   But I pretended there was, in order to test you.

DAV   You don't say!

SIM   That's the truth.

DAV   Look at that! I'd never have realised. Huh! What a clever
       scheme!

SIM   Now listen. After I told you to go indoors, by a stroke of
       luck *he* appeared (*indicating Chremes*).

DAV   (*aside*) What! Is this the end of us?

SIM   I told him what you just told me.

---

[35] The evening was the traditional time for weddings, both in
Greece and in Rome (see, for example, Catullus 62).

DAV   quidnam audio?

SIM   gnatam ut det oro vixque id exoro.

DAV   occidi!

SIM   hem!
quid dixti?

DAV   optume inquam factum.

SIM   nunc per hunc nullast mora.

CHR domum modo ibo, ut apparetur dicam, atque huc renuntio.

595 SIM nunc te oro, Dave, quoniam solus mi effecisti has nuptias—

DAV   ego vero solus.

SIM   —mihi corrigere gnatum porro enitere.

DAV   faciam hercle sedulo.

SIM   potes nunc, dum animus irritatus est.

DAV   quiescas.

SIM   age igitur, ubi nunc est ipsus?

DAV   mirum ni domist.

SIM   ibo ad eum atque eadem haec quae tibi dixi dicam itidem illi.

DAV   nullus sum!

600   quid causaest quin hinc in pistrinum recta proficiscar via?

nil est preci loci relictum. iam perturbavi omnia:
erum fefelli, in nuptias conieci erilem filium,
feci hodie ut fierent insperante hoc atque invito Pamphilo.
em astutias! quod si quiessem, nil evenisset mali.

605   sed eccum ipsum video. occidi!

DAV   (*aside*) What am I hearing?

SIM   I asked him to give his daughter in marriage, and with some difficulty I persuaded him.

DAV   (*aside*) Damnation!

SIM   What! What did you say?

DAV   (*hastily covering himself*) I said, congratulations.

SIM   Now there's no delay on his side.

CHR   (*coming forward*) I'll go home now and tell them to get things ready. I'll report back. (*he exits right in the direction of his house*)

SIM   Now I beg you, Davus, since you have brought about this wedding for me singlehanded—

DAV   (*aside*) Singlehanded indeed!

SIM   —endeavour to reform my son for the future.

DAV   God knows I'll do my best.

SIM   You can now, while he's in this angry mood.

DAV   Rest assured.

SIM   Come on then, where is he now?

DAV   At home, I expect.

SIM   I'll go to him and tell him what I've just told you. (*he goes into his house, leaving Davus alone on stage*)

DAV   (*to himself*) I'm done for! Is there any reason why I shouldn't go straight to the mill?[36] There's no room left for mercy. I've now confounded everything—deceived the master, propelled the master's son into a wedding, and fixed the ceremony for today, which is more than the old man dared to hope and not at all what Pamphilus wanted. There's real cleverness for you! If I hadn't interfered, everything would have been all right. (*seeing Pamphilus emerging*) But here's the man himself. Dam-

---

36 See note 17.

utinam mi esset aliquid hic quo nunc me praecipitem
darem!

III. V: PAMPHILUS. DAVOS.

PAM   ubi ille est scelus qui perdidit me?

DAV   perii!

PAM   atque hoc confiteor iure
mi obtigisse, quandoquidem tam iners tam nulli consili
sum.

servon fortunas meas me commisisse futtili!

610   ego pretium ob stultitiam fero. sed inultum numquam id
auferet.

DAV   posthac incolumem sat scio fore me, nunc si devito hoc
malum.

PAM   nam quid ego nunc dicam patri? negabon velle me, modo
qui sum pollicitus ducere? qua audacia id facere au-
deam?

nec quid nunc me faciam scio.

DAV   nec mequidem, atque id ago sedulo.

615   dicam aliquid me inventurum, ut huic malo aliquam pro-
ducam moram.

PAM   oh!

DAV   visus sum.

PAM   ehodum, bone vir, quid ais? viden me consiliis tuis
miserum impeditum esse?

DAV   at iam expediam.

PAM   expedies?

DAV   certe, Pamphile.

PAM   nempe ut modo.

DAV   immo melius spero.

PAM   oh! tibi ego ut credam, furcifer?

nation! If only there was a pit to throw myself into head first!

Enter PAMPHILUS *from Simo's house in an angry mood.*

PAM Where's that villain who's destroyed me?

DAV (*aside*) This is the end of me!

PAM I admit I've deserved this, for being so feeble and so helpless. Fancy entrusting my fortunes to a blabbering slave! I'm paying the price for my stupidity. But he'll never get away with it.

DAV (*aside*) If I escape a thrashing now, I'm quite sure I'll be safe in the future.

PAM What am I going to say to my father now? Say I refuse to marry her, when I've just promised to? How would I dare to be so bold? Now I don't know what to do with myself.

DAV (*aside*) Nor do I, and I'm doing my best. I'll tell him I'll work something out; that should postpone my punishment a little.

PAM (*catching sight of Davus*) Ah!

DAV (*aside*) He's seen me.

PAM Here you, my good man, answer me this. Do you realise that your schemes have entangled me in a web of misery?

DAV I'll soon disentangle you.

PAM Disentangle me?

DAV Yes, for sure, Pamphilus.

PAM You mean, in the same way as before?

DAV No, better, I hope.

PAM Oh! Do you expect me to believe you, you rascal? You

---

613 audacia *gloss. edd.*, fiducia Σ *Don.*

tu rem impeditam et perditam restituas? em quo fretus
    sim,

620   qui me hodie ex tranquillissuma re coniecisti in nuptias!

an non dixi esse hoc futurum?

DAV   dixti.

PAM   quid meritu's?

DAV   crucem.

sed sine paullulum ad me redeam. iam aliquid dispiciam.

PAM   ei mihi,

quom non habeo spatium ut de te sumam supplicium ut
    volo!

namque hoc tempus praecavere mihi me, haud te ulcisci
    sinit.

ACTUS IV

IV. i: CHARINUS. PAMPHILUS. DAVOS.

625 CHA hocine credibile aut memorabile,

tanta vecordia innata quoiquam ut siet

ut malis gaudeant atque ex incommodis

alterius sua ut comparent commoda? ah!

idnest verum? immo id est genus hominum pessumum,
    in

630   denegando modo quis pudor paullum adest.

post ubi tempus promissa iam perfici,

tum coacti necessario se aperiunt,

---

[37] Crucifixion is the most extreme of the punishments anticipated
by slaves in comedy; it is mentioned several times in Plautus but only in
this one play of Terence's, where it occurs twice (also in line 786), and
never in Menander. It is attested historically in slave revolts in Roman

undo this disastrous entanglement? Here he is, the man I
relied on, who, when there wasn't a cloud on the horizon,
has propelled me into a marriage today. Didn't I say this
would happen?

DAV You did.

PAM What do you deserve?

DAV Crucifixion.[37] But give me a moment to recover my wits.
I'll soon see a way through.

PAM I don't have time to punish you as I'd like, confound it! In
this situation I need to look out for myself first rather
than take my revenge on you.

ACT FOUR

*Enter CHARINUS right from the direction of the forum in a state
of great agitation.*

CHA (*to himself, singing*)[38] It's unbelievable, unimaginable!
That a man can be so morally deranged
As to delight in another man's misfortunes
And seek his own gain from another's loss!
Oh! Can it be true? It's the worst kind of men
Who for a while feel shame to go back on their word
But, when the time comes to make good their promises,
Reveal their true selves as needs they must,

times, but was presumably not a real-life punishment for domestic
slaves.

[38] This is the second of the lyric passages in the play (cf. line 481).
The lyric is here intended to heighten the emotional effect. It may be
part of the characterisation of Charinus that the ideas expressed are
both trite and muddled.

et timent et tamen res premit denegare.
ibi tum eorum impudentissuma oratiost:
635 "quis tu es? quis mihi's? quor meam tibi?
heus! proxumus sum egomet mihi."
at tamen "ubi fides?" si roges, nil pudet
hic ubi opus; illi ubi nil opust, ibi verentur.

sed quid agam? adeamne ad eum et cum eo iniuriam
hanc expostulem?
640 ingeram mala multa? atque aliquis dicat "nil promove-
ris."
multum. molestus certe ei fuero atque animo morem
gessero.
PAM Charine, et me et te imprudens, nisi quid di respiciunt,
perdidi.
CHA itane "imprudens"? tandem inventast causa: solvisti
fidem.
PAM quid "tandem"?
CHA   etiamnunc me ducere istis dictis postulas?
645 PAM quid istuc est?
CHA   postquam me amare dixi, complacitast tibi.
heu me miserum, qui tuom animum ex animo spectavi
meo!
PAM falsus es.
CHA   non tibi sat esse hoc solidum visumst gaudium,
nisi me lactasses amantem et falsa spe produceres?
habeas.
PAM   habeam? ah! nescis quantis in malis vorser miser,

650 quantasque hic suis consiliis mihi conflavit sollicitudines
meus carnufex.

Afraid to prove false but they have no option.
Then their impudence knows no bounds:
"Who are you? What are you to me?
Why give you my girl? I come first with me."
Yet, if you ask "What about your word?"
They've no shame then, when shame is wanted.
It's when you don't want it, they have their scruples.

(*more calmly*) But what shall I do? Go up to him and complain about this outrage? Heap abuse on him? People may say "You won't achieve anything." But I'll achieve a lot. At least I'll have annoyed him and given vent to my anger.

PAM (*coming forward*) Charinus, I didn't mean to, but I've destroyed us both, unless the gods take pity on us.

CHA (*angrily*) Didn't mean to? You've finally found an excuse and broken your promise.

PAM How do you mean "finally"?

CHA Do you still think you can lead me on by that sort of talk?

PAM What's this about?

CHA It was only after I said I loved her that you fell for her. What a fool I was to judge your character by my own!

PAM You're mistaken.

CHA Did you think your joy was not complete unless you'd enticed me to love her and led me on with false hope? You can have her.

PAM Have her? Ah! You don't realise the torments of misery that I'm suffering and the agonies that this despicable slave of mine has contrived for me by his schemes.

---

650 conflavit *Don. in comm.*, confecit Σ

CHA   quid istuc tam mirumst de te si exemplum capit?

PAM haud istuc dicas, si cognoris vel me vel amorem meum.

CHA scio. cum patre altercasti dudum et is nunc propterea tibi
suscenset nec te quivit hodie cogere illam ut duceres.

655 PAM immo etiam, quo tu minus scis aerumnas meas,
hae nuptiae non apparabantur mihi
nec postulabat nunc quisquam uxorem dare.

CHA scio. tu coactus tua voluntate es.

PAM   mane.
nondum scis.

CHA   scio equidem illam ducturum esse te.

660 PAM quor me enicas? hoc audi. numquam destitit
instare ut dicerem me ducturum patri,
suadere, orare usque adeo donec perpulit.

CHA quis homo istuc?

PAM   Davos.

CHA   Davos?

PAM   interturbat.

CHA   quam ob rem?

PAM   nescio,
nisi mihi deos satis scio fuisse iratos qui auscultaverim.

665 CHA factum hoc est, Dave?

DAV   factum.

CHA   hem! quid ais, scelus?
at tibi di dignum factis exitium duint!
eho, dic mi, si omnes hunc coniectum in nuptias
inimici vellent, quod nisi hoc consilium darent?

DAV deceptus sum, at non defetigatus.

CHA   scio.

CHA   What's so surprising if he follows your example?

PAM   You wouldn't say that if you knew the truth about me and my love.

CHA   (*with bitter irony*) I see. You've been having an argument with your father all this time, and he's now furious with you, having failed to compel you to marry her today.

PAM   On the contrary. You have no idea about my problems. This marriage was not taking place; nobody was asking me to take a wife.

CHA   (*scornfully*) I see. You were compelled of your own free will.

PAM   Hold on. You still don't know the facts.

CHA   I know one fact: you are about to marry her.

PAM   Why do you try my patience? Listen. He never stopped pressing me to tell my father I would marry her. He urged me, begged me, until in the end he persuaded me.

CHA   Who did?

PAM   Davus.

CHA   Davus?

PAM   He's the cause of all this trouble.

CHA   Why?

PAM   I've no idea, though the gods must have been angry with me to make me listen.

CHA   (*to Davus*) Is this true, Davus?

DAV   (*reluctantly*) Yes.

CHA   What! What do you have to say for yourself, you villain? May the gods destroy you as your deeds deserve! Hey, tell me, if all his enemies wanted him propelled into a marriage, could they have conceived a better scheme?

DAV   I made a mistake but I haven't given up.

CHA   I see.

670 DAV   hac non successit, alia aggrediemur via;
        nisi si id putas, quia primo processit parum,
        non posse iam ad salutem convorti hoc malum.

PAM   immo etiam. nam satis credo, si advigilaveris,
        ex unis geminas mihi conficies nuptias.

675 DAV   ego, Pamphile, hoc tibi pro servitio debeo,
        conari manibus pedibus noctesque et dies,
        capitis periclum adire, dum prosim tibi.
        tuomst, si quid praeter spem evenit, mi ignoscere.
        parum succedit quod ago; at facio sedulo.

680   vel melius tute reperi, me missum face.

PAM   cupio. restitue in quem me accepisti locum.

DAV   faciam.

PAM   at iam hoc opust.

DAV   em. sed mane. concrepuit a Glycerio ostium.

PAM   nil ad te.

DAV   quaero—

PAM   hem! nuncin demum?

DAV   at iam hoc tibi inventum dabo.

    IV. ii: MYSIS. PAMPHILUS. CHARINUS. DAVOS.

MYS   iam ubiubi erit inventum tibi curabo et mecum adduc-
        tum
        tuom Pamphilum. modo tu, anime mi, noli te macerare.

685 PAM   Mysis!

MYS   quis est? ehem, Pamphile! optume mihi te offers.

PAM   quid id est?

---

[39] See note 14.

[40] The emergence of a character from a stage house in comedy is regularly preceded by a reference to the noise made by the door opening, caused presumably by the rattling of bolts or creaking of hinges.

DAV (*to Pamphilus*) We didn't succeed this way, but we'll try another one. Unless you think that, because it didn't work out at first, we can never find a happy ending to the situation.

PAM (*with heavy irony*) Of course not. I'm quite sure that, if you keep your wits about you, you can arrange me two marriages, not just one.

DAV (*with dignity*) It is my duty, Pamphilus, as your slave, to strive with might and main,[39] night and day, and risk my neck in order to serve your interests. In return, if anything goes wrong, it is for you to forgive me. If my plan doesn't work out, at least I'm doing my best. Otherwise devise something better for yourself, and forget about me.

PAM I wish I could. Just put me back where you found me.

DAV I will.

PAM I mean now.

DAV Very well. But wait. I heard Glycerium's door.[40]

PAM It's nothing to do with you.

DAV I'm racking my brains—

PAM Really! After all this time?

DAV I'll soon have it all worked out for you.

Enter MYSIS from Glycerium's house.

MYS (*speaking back inside to Glycerium*) Wherever he is, I'll make sure I find your Pamphilus for you and bring him back with me. Just don't torment yourself, my darling.

PAM (*coming forward*) Mysis!

MYS Who's that? Oh hello, Pamphilus! Excellent!

PAM What is it?

127

MYS	orare iussit, si se ames, era iam ut ad sese venias.
	videre ait te cupere.
PAM	vah! perii! hoc malum integrascit.
	sicin me atque illam opera tua nunc miseros sollicitari!
690	nam idcirco accersor nuptias quod mi apparari sensit.
CHA	quibus quidem quam facile potuerat quiesci, si hic quiesset!
DAV	age, si hic non insanit satis sua sponte, instiga.
MYS	atque edepol
	ea res est, proptereaque nunc misera in maerorest.
PAM	Mysis,
	per omnis tibi adiuro deos numquam eam me deserturum,
695	non si capiundos mihi sciam esse inimicos omnis homines.
	hanc mi expetivi, contigit, conveniunt mores. valeant
	qui inter nos discidium volunt. hanc nisi mors mi adimet nemo.
MYS	resipisco.
PAM	non Apollinis magis verum atque hoc responsumst.
	si poterit fieri ut ne pater per me stetisse credat
700	quo minus hae fierent nuptiae, volo. sed si id non poterit,
	id faciam, in proclivi quod est, per me stetisse ut credat.
	quis videor?
CHA	miser, aeque atque ego.
DAV	consilium quaero.
PAM	forti's.
	scio quid conere.
DAV	hoc ego tibi profecto effectum reddam.
PAM	iam hoc opus est.

MYS My mistress told me to beg you to come and see her straightaway, if you love her. She says she's longing to see you.

PAM (*aside*) Oh, damn it! Here we go again! (*to Davus*) To think that she and I are tortured with worries because of your meddling! She's sending for me because she's heard about the wedding preparations.

CHA How easily things could have been kept quiet, (*pointing to Davus*) if *he* had kept quiet!

DAV (*to Charinus*) Go on, goad him on, as if he isn't out of his mind on his own account.

MYS (*to Pamphilus*) That's just it, for god's sake, and that's why the poor girl's pining away.

PAM (*solemnly*) Mysis, I swear to you by all the gods that I will never abandon her, not if it means I must have all the world as my enemies. I courted her, I won her, we suit each other. Good riddance to those who want to separate us! Nothing but death will take her from me.

MYS (*aside*) I breathe again.

PAM Apollo's oracle does not speak more truly. If it's possible to convince my father that it's not my fault that the wedding's called off, that's what I wish. But if it's not possible, I'll do the easy thing, and let him believe that it *is* my fault. (*to Charinus*) How am I doing?

CHA Miserably, the same as me.

DAV (*to Pamphilus*) I'm searching for a plan.

PAM (*sarcastically*) Well done! I know your efforts.

DAV I'll carry this one through, I promise you.

PAM I need it now.

---

698 resipisco *Mysi dant edd. pl., Charino* Σ
702 forti's *Pamphilo dant edd. nonn., Charino* Σ

	DAV	quin iam habeo.
	CHA	quid est?
	DAV	huic non tibi habeo, ne erres.
705	CHA	sat habeo.
	PAM	quid facies? cedo.
	DAV	dies hic mi ut satis sit vereor

ad agendum, ne vacuom esse me nunc ad narrandum
   credas.

proinde hinc vos amolimini; nam mi impedimento estis.

	PAM	ego hanc visam.
	DAV	quid tu? quo hinc te agis?
	CHA	verum vis dicam?
	DAV	immo etiam.

narrationis incipit mi initium.

| | CHA | quid me fiet? |
| 710 | DAV | eho tu, impudens, non satis habes quod tibi dieculam addo, |

quantum huic promoveo nuptias?

	CHA	Dave, at tamen—
	DAV	quid ergo?
	CHA	ut ducam.
	DAV	ridiculum!
	CHA	huc face ad me ut venias, si quid poteris.
	DAV	quid veniam? nil habeo.
	CHA	at tamen si quid.
	DAV	age, veniam.
	CHA	si quid,

domi ero.

	DAV	tu, Mysis, dum exeo, parumper me opperire hic.
715	MYS	quapropter?
	DAV	ita factost opus.
	MYS	matura.

DAV   I've got it now.

CHA   (*to Davus*) What is it?

DAV   (*to Charinus*) It's for him, not for you. Don't get it wrong.

CHA   All right.

PAM   (*to Davus*) What are you going to do? Tell me.

DAV   I'm afraid it'll take me all day to carry it out, so you needn't think I've the time to explain it. You two clear out of here. You're getting in my way.

PAM   I'll go and see her. (*he exits into Glycerium's house*)

DAV   (*to Charinus*) What about you? Where are *you* going?

CHA   Do you want me to tell you the truth?

DAV   Yes indeed. (*aside*) Here begins a tale.

CHA   What will become of me?

DAV   Hey, you've got a nerve! Isn't it enough for you that I've won you a little time by postponing the wedding?

CHA   Yes, Davus, but—

DAV   What?

CHA   Help me to marry her.

DAV   Don't be ridiculous!

CHA   (*moving away*) Be sure you come and tell me, if you can do anything.

DAV   Why should I? I've no plans for you.

CHA   But even so, if you can—

DAV   All right, I'll come.

CHA   If you can, I'll be at home. (*he exits left in the direction of his house*)

DAV   Mysis, you wait here a moment until I come out.

MYS   What for?

DAV   I need you.

MYS   Hurry then.

DAV	iam, inquam, hic adero.

IV. iii: MYSIS. DAVOS.

MYS	nilne esse proprium quoiquam! di vostram fidem!

     summum bonum esse erae putabam hunc Pamphilum,
amicum, amatorem, virum in quovis loco
paratum. verum ex eo nunc misera quem capit
720   laborem! facile hic plus malist quam illic boni.
sed Davos exit. mi homo, quid istuc, obsecro, est?
quo portas puerum?

DAV   Mysis, nunc opus est tua
    mihi ad hanc rem expromta memoria atque astutia.

MYS   quidnam incepturu's?

DAV   accipe a me hunc ocius
725   atque ante nostram ianuam appone.

MYS   obsecro,
    humine?

DAV   ex ara hinc sume verbenas tibi
    atque eas substerne.

MYS   quam ob rem id tute non facis?

DAV   quia, si forte opus sit ad erum iurandum mihi
    non apposisse, ut liquido possim.

MYS   intellego.
730   nova nunc religio in te istaec incessit. cedo.

DAV   move ocius te, ut quid agam porro intellegas.
    pro Iuppiter!

MYS   quid est?

---

41 The Roman stage regularly had an altar, usually of Apollo, in front
of one of the stage houses, which would be decked with boughs or

DAV   I'll be straight back, I say. (*he exits into Glycerium's house*)

MYS   (*to herself*) Nobody can count on anything! Heaven help us! I used to think Pamphilus was the perfect answer for my mistress, a friend, a lover, a husband ready for all occasions. But now look what distress he's causing the poor girl! With him, the bad easily outweighs the good. But here comes Davus. (*Davus reappears from the house, carrying a baby*) My dear man, what are you doing, for heaven's sake? Where are you taking that baby?

DAV   Mysis, for this job I need your presence of mind and your cunning.

MYS   What are you plannng to do?

DAV   Take this from me quickly and put it on our doorstep. (*he gives her the baby*)

MYS   On the ground? For heaven's sake!

DAV   Take some branches from this altar[41] and put them underneath.

MYS   Why don't you do it yourself?

DAV   Because, if it so happens that I need to swear to my master that I didn't put it here, I want to do so with a clear conscience.

MYS   I see. You didn't use to be so scrupulous. Give it here. (*she takes the baby and turns to put it on the doorstep*)

DAV   Get a move on, and I'll tell you what I'm going to do next. (*looking down the street*) Great Jupiter!

MYS   What's the matter?

---

twigs. According to the fourth-century commentator Servius (on Virgil, *Aeneid* 12.120), Menander specifically mentioned myrtle boughs at this point.

DAV		sponsae pater intervenit.
	repudio quod consilium primum intenderam.	
MYS	nescio quid narres.	
DAV		ego quoque hinc ab dextera
735	venire me assimulabo. tu ut subservias	
	orationi, ut quomque opus sit, verbis vide.	
MYS	ego quid agas nil intellego. sed si quid est	
	quod mea opera opus sit vobis, ut tu plus vides,	
	manebo, ne quod vostrum remorer commmodum.	

IV. iv: CHREMES. MYSIS. DAVOS.

740	CHR	revortor, postquam quae opus fuere ad nuptias
		gnatae paravi, ut iubeam accersi. sed quid hoc?
		puer herclest. mulier, tun posisti hunc?
	MYS	ubi illic est?
	CHR	non mihi respondes?
	MYS	nusquamst. vae miserae mihi!
		reliquit me homo atque abiit.
	DAV	di vostram fidem!
745		quid turbaest apud forum! quid illi hominum litigant!
		tum annona carast. quid dicam aliud nescio.

---

738 ut *edd.,* aut Σ *Don. Eugr.*

---

42 There are several problems in reconstructing the staging of this passage. Chremes enters from the audience's right, his house being located in the direction of the forum (line 361). Davus also reenters from the audience's right, pretending to have come from the forum (line 745). When Davus tells Mysis that he too will enter "from the right" (line 734), he must therefore mean the audience's right, which is possible only if he has his back to the audience at the time (he is facing Mysis, who is laying the baby on the doorstep), so that actors' right and audi-

DAV   The bride's father's coming. I'm abandoning my original plan.

MYS   I don't know what you're talking about.

DAV   I'll pretend that I too am arriving here from the right. Make sure you back up my story when the need arises. (*he exits to the left*)

MYS   I haven't a clue what you're up to. But, if there's anything in which you people need my help, since you know best, I'll stay. I don't want to impede your progress.

Enter CHREMES *right from the direction of his house.*[42]

CHR   (*to himself*) I've made the necessary preparations for my daughter's wedding, and I'm returning to tell them to fetch her. (*seeing the baby*) But what's this? Good heavens, it's a baby! (*seeing Mysis*) Woman, did you put it here?

MYS   (*aside*) Where's Davus got to?

CHR   Aren't you going to answer me?

MYS   (*still aside*) He's nowhere to be seen. Oh damn and blast! He's gone off and left me.

DAV   (*reappearing from the right, and pretending not to see Mysis or Chremes*) Heaven help us! What a crowd in the forum! People arguing everywhere! And the high prices! (*aside*) I don't know what else to say.

ence's right coincide. However, Davus must exit to the audience's left, to avoid meeting Chremes on the latter's approach, so we have to assume that he runs round behind the stage building in order to return from the audience's right. In line 751 Davus draws Mysis aside "to the right," which could now be actors' right, depending on where we assume Chremes to be now standing.

MYS quor tu, obsecro, hic me solam—?

DAV   hem! quae haec est fabula?
    eho, Mysis, puer hic undest? quisve huc attulit?

MYS satin sanu's qui me id rogites?

DAV   quem ego igitur rogem

750   qui hic neminem alium videam?

CHR   miror unde sit.

DAV dictura's quod rogo?

MYS   au!

DAV   concede ad dexteram.

MYS deliras. non tute ipse—?

DAV   verbum si mihi
    unum praeterquam quod te rogo faxis, cave!
    male dicis? undest? dic clare.

MYS   a nobis.

DAV   hahae!

755   mirum vero impudenter mulier si facit
    meretrix.

CHR   ab Andriast haec, quantum intellego.

DAV adeon videmur vobis esse idonei
    in quibus sic illudatis?

CHR   veni in tempore.

DAV propera adeo puerum tollere hinc ab ianua.

760   mane. cave quoquam ex istoc excessis loco.

MYS di te eradicent! ita me miseram territas.

DAV tibi ego dico an non?

MYS   quid vis?

MYS (*to Davus*) Why did you leave me here alone, for heaven's sake?

DAV (*ignoring her*) Hey! What's this nonsense? (*to Mysis*) Here you, Mysis, where does this baby come from? Who brought it here? (*he winks at her*)

MYS (*uncomprehending*) Are you in your right mind? Asking me that?

DAV Who am I supposed to ask? There's no one else here.

CHR (*aside*) I wonder where it does come from.

DAV (*to Mysis, threateningly*) Are you going to answer my question?

MYS (*as Davus grabs her arm*) Ow!

DAV Come over here to the right. (*drawing her further away from Chremes*)

MYS You're crazy. Didn't you yourself—?

DAV (*whispering*) Just answer my questions. If you utter a single word more, look out! (*aloud*) Abusing me, are you? Where does it come from? Tell me straight.

MYS It's from our house.

DAV Ha! Just the shameless behaviour you'd expect from that class of woman!

CHR (*aside*) This is the Andrian woman's maid, unless I'm mistaken.

DAV Do you think we're the sort of people you can make fools of?

CHR (*aside*) I arrived in the nick of time.

DAV Hurry up and remove the baby from the doorstep. (*whispering*) Wait! Don't move an inch from where you are.

MYS May the gods blast you! You're frightening a poor woman out of her wits.

DAV (*aloud*) Are you listening to me or not?

MYS What do you want?

DAV   at etiam rogas?
        cedo, quoium puerum hic apposisti? dic mihi.

MYS   tu nescis?

DAV   mitte id quod scio. dic quod rogo.

765 MYS   vostri.

DAV   quoius nostri?

MYS   Pamphili.

DAV   hem! quid? Pamphili?

MYS   eho, an non est?

CHR   recte ego has semper fugi nuptias.

DAV   o facinus animadvortendum!

MYS   quid clamitas?

DAV   quemne ego heri vidi ad vos afferri vesperi?

MYS   o hominem audacem!

DAV   verum. vidi Cantharam

770   suffarcinatam.

MYS   dis pol habeo gratiam
        quom in pariundo aliquot adfuerunt liberae.

DAV   ne illa illum haud novit quoius causa haec incipit:
        "Chremes si positum puerum ante aedis viderit,
        suam gnatam non dabit." tanto hercle magis dabit.

775 CHR   non hercle faciet.

DAV   nunc adeo, ut tu sis sciens,
        nisi puerum tollis, iam ego hunc in mediam viam
        provolvam teque ibidem pervolvam in luto.

MYS   tu pol homo non es sobrius.

---

[43] Free women are presumed to be more trustworthy than slaves

DAV You're not still asking? Come on, whose baby have you put here? Tell me.

MYS (*still puzzled*) Don't you know?

DAV (*whispering*) Never mind what I know. Tell me what I ask.

MYS Your master's.

DAV Which master?

MYS Pamphilus.

DAV What, really? Pamphilus' baby?

MYS Oh! Isn't it?

CHR (*aside*) I was right to be against this wedding all along.

DAV (*shouting*) It's wicked! It's criminal!

MYS What are you shouting for?

DAV Isn't this the baby I saw being brought in to you yesterday evening?

MYS (*aside*) The impudence of the man!

DAV It's true. I saw Canthara with something under her cloak.

MYS I thank the gods that there were several free women present at the birth.[43]

DAV (*aside, for Chremes to hear*) She doesn't realise what sort of man she's scheming against. (*imitating Glycerium's voice*) "Chremes won't give his daughter in marriage if he sees a baby lying on the doorstep." He'll do so all the more, for god's sake.

CHR (*aside*) He won't, for god's sake.

DAV Now, you be warned, if you don't remove this baby at once, I'll roll it down the middle of the street and roll you there in the mud with it.

MYS Good heavens! You must be drunk.

(whose evidence was admissible in a court of law only when obtained under torture).

DAV		fallacia

alia aliam trudit. iam susurrari audio
780   civem Atticam esse hanc.

CHR   hem!

DAV   coactus legibus

eam uxorem ducet.

MYS   eho, obsecro, an non civis est?

CHR   iocularium in malum insciens paene incidi.

DAV   quis hic loquitur? o Chreme, per tempus advenis.

ausculta.

CHR   audivi iam omnia.

DAV   anne haec tu omnia?

785 CHR   audivi, inquam, a principio.

DAV   audistin, obsecro? em

scelera! hanc iam oportet in cruciatum hinc abripi.
hic est ille. non te credas Davom ludere.

MYS   me miseram! nil pol falsi dixi, mi senex.

CHR   novi omnem rem. est Simo intus?

DAV   est.

MYS   ne me attigas,

790   sceleste. si pol Glycerio non omnia haec—

DAV   eho, inepta, nescis quid sit actum?

MYS   qui sciam?

DAV   hic socer est. alio pacto haud poterat fieri
ut sciret haec quae voluimus.

MYS   praediceres.

DAV   paullum interesse censes, ex animo omnia,
795   ut fert natura, facias an de industria?

787 non . . . credas *codd. pl. Don.*, non . . . credes *PDL*, ne . . . credas
Prisc.

140

DAV One fabrication leads to another. I now hear it whispered that she's an Athenian citizen.

CHR (*aside*) What!

DAV So he'll have to marry her under the law.

MYS Oh, for goodness' sake, is she not a citizen?

CHR (*aside*) It's laughable. I nearly fell into the trap without seeing it.

DAV Who's that speaking? (*turning round to Chremes*) Oh, Chremes! You're just in time. Listen.

CHR I've already heard everything.

DAV You have? Everything?

CHR I tell you, I heard it from the beginning.

DAV You heard it, really? It's criminal! The woman ought to be dragged off and crucified. (*to Mysis*) See who this is. Don't suppose it's Davus you're fooling.

MYS Poor me! (*to Chremes*) Heaven knows I haven't told a lie, sir.

CHR I know the whole situation. (*to Davus*) Is Simo at home?

DAV Yes. (*Chremes exits into Simo's house*)

MYS (*as Davus tries to embrace her*) Don't touch me, you villain. By heaven, if I don't tell Glycerium all about this—

DAV Oh, you silly creature! Don't you know what we've been doing?

MYS How should I know?

DAV That was the father-in-law. It was the only way we could make him believe what we wanted.

MYS You could have warned me.

DAV Do you suppose it doesn't make any difference whether you are behaving sincerely and naturally or are acting a part?

IV. V: CRITO. MYSIS. DAVOS.

CRI	in hac habitasse platea dictumst Chrysidem,
	quae sese inhoneste optavit parere hic ditias
	potius quam in patria honeste pauper viveret.
	eius morte ea ad me lege redierunt bona.
800	sed quos perconter video. salvete.
MYS	obsecro,
	quem video? estne hic Crito, sobrinus Chrysidis?
	is est.
CRI	o Mysis, salve.
MYS	salvos sis, Crito.
CRI	itan Chrysis—? hem!
MYS	nos quidem pol miseras perdidit.
CRI	quid vos? quo pacto hic? satine recte?
MYS	nosne? sic
805	ut quimus, aiunt, quando ut volumus non licet.
CRI	quid Glycerium? iam hic suos parentis repperit?
MYS	utinam!
CRI	an nondum etiam? haud auspicato huc me appuli.
	nam pol si id scissem numquam huc tetulissem pedem.
	semper eius dictast esse haec atque habitast soror.
810	quae illius fuere possidet. nunc me hospitem
	litis sequi quam hic mihi sit facile atque utile
	aliorum exempla commonent. simul arbitror
	iam aliquem esse amicum et defensorem ei. nam fere
	grandicula iam profectast illinc. clamitent

---

[44] In Athenian law the property of those who died without heirs reverted to their nearest relatives.

[45] The word *sobrinus* denotes a second cousin.

[46] These words are ironic; the implication is that it was difficult for a foreigner to obtain justice at Athens.

Enter CRITO *left from the direction of the harbour in travelling clothes.*

CRI   (*to himself*) This is the street where I'm told Chrysis lived, having chosen to get rich here dishonourably rather than live a poor but honourable life in her homeland. Now that she's dead, by law her possessions revert to me.[44] (*seeing Davus and Mysis*) But here are some people I can ask. Good day.

MYS   (*aside*) For heaven's sake, who's this? Is it Chrysis' cousin Crito?[45] It is.

CRI   (*recognising her*) Oh Mysis, good day.

MYS   And good day to you, Crito.

CRI   Has Chrysis really—? (*as Mysis wipes away a tear*) I'm sorry.

MYS   Yes, and, heaven knows, it's been the end of us, poor things.

CRI   What about you? How are you doing here? All right?

MYS   Us? So so. We live how we can, as the saying goes, since we can't live how we will.

CRI   What about Glycerium? Has she found her parents here yet?

MYS   If only she had!

CRI   Still not? So this was an inauspicious voyage. If I'd known, by heaven, I wouldn't have made the journey. It was said she was Chrysis' sister and she was always so regarded. She's now in possession of Chrysis' property. (*with a wry smile*) I know from other people's experience how easy and advantageous[46] it would be for me as a foreigner here to take her to court. Besides, I'm sure she has a friend and protector now; she was almost grown up when she left home. The cry would go up that I'm a

143

815   me sycophantam, hereditatem persequi
              mendicum. tum ipsam despoliare non lubet.
MYS o optume hospes! pol, Crito, antiquom obtines.
CRI   duc me ad eam quando huc veni ut videam.
MYS   maxume.
DAV sequar hos. nolo me in tempore hoc videat senex.

ACTUS V

V. i: CHREMES. SIMO.

820 CHR satis iam satis, Simo, spectata erga te amicitiast mea.
              satis pericli incepi adire. orandi iam finem face.
              dum studeo obsequi tibi, paene illusi vitam filiae.
SIM immo enim nunc quom maxume abs te postulo atque
                  oro, Chreme,
              ut beneficium verbis initum dudum nunc re comprobes.
825 CHR vide quam iniquos sis prae studio. dum id efficias quod
                  cupis,
              neque modum benignitatis neque quid me ores cogitas.
              nam si cogites remittas iam me onerare iniuriis.
SIM quibus?
CHR   at rogitas? perpulisti me ut homini adulescentulo
              in alio occupato amore, abhorrenti ab re uxoria,
830   filiam ut darem in seditionem atque in incertas nuptias,
              eius labore atque eius dolore gnato ut medicarer tuo.

---

823 quom *Don. edd.*, quam Σ

poverty-stricken trickster looking for a legacy. Besides, for her own sake, I don't like to leave her penniless.

MYS What a splendid man! By heaven, you're the same old Crito.

CRI Well, take me in, since I've come to see her.

MYS Certainly. (*they exit into Glycerium's house*)

DAV I'll follow them. I don't want the old master to see me just at the moment. (*he follows them in, leaving the stage empty*)

ACT FIVE

Enter CHREMES and SIMO from Simo's house.

CHR I've already given enough proof of my friendship for you, Simo. I've taken enough risks. Now stop your entreaties. I almost gambled away my daughter's life in my eagerness to fall in with your wishes.

SIM On the contrary, now more than ever, I beg and beseech you to make good in practice the favour you promised a while ago.

CHR Look how unreasonable your eagerness for this marriage makes you. So long as you get what you want, you don't realise that there is a limit to my generosity or see what you are asking me to do. If you did, you would now stop troubling me with these unjust demands.

SIM What unjust demands?

CHR A fine question! You persuaded me to promise my daughter to a young lad involved in another love affair who had no intention of taking a wife, condemning her to squabbling and an unstable marriage, all so that your son could be cured through *her* pain and *her* suffering. You got

145

       impetrasti. incepi, dum res tetulit. nunc non fert: feras.
       illam hinc civem esse aiunt, puer est natus: nos missos
          face.

SIM   per ego te deos oro, ut ne illis animum inducas credere,
835   quibus id maxume utilest illum esse quam deterrumum.
       nuptiarum gratia haec sunt ficta atque incepta omnia.
       ubi ea causa quam ob rem haec faciunt erit adempta his,
          desinent.

CHR erras. cum Davo egomet vidi iurgantem ancillam.
SIM   scio.
CHR   at
       vero voltu, quom ibi me adesse neuter tum praesenserat.
840 SIM credo, et id facturas Davos dudum praedixit mihi. et
       nescio qui id tibi sum oblitus hodie ac volui dicere.

         V. ii: DAVOS. CHREMES. SIMO. DROMO.

DAV animo nunciam otioso esse impero—
CHR   em Davom tibi!
SIM   unde egreditur?
DAV   —meo praesidio atque hospitis.
SIM   quid illud malist?
DAV ego commodiorem hominem adventum tempus non vidi.
SIM   scelus,
845   quemnam hic laudat?
DAV   omnis rcs iam est in vado.
SIM   cesso alloqui?

your way. I agreed, so long as the circumstances permitted. Now they don't. So accept the situation. They claim she's an Athenian citizen, and they have a baby. You can forget about us.

SIM I beg you in the name of the gods not to let yourself believe these women. It suits their best interests to put my son in the worst possible light. These are all schemes and inventions designed to prevent the wedding. Take away their reason for doing this, and they'll stop.

CHR You're mistaken. I saw the maid arguing with Davus myself.

SIM (*ironically*) Quite so.

CHR They weren't pretending. Neither of them had realised that I was present.

SIM (*ironically*) Of course. Davus warned me some time ago that they'd do this. I meant to tell you today but somehow I forgot.

Enter DAVUS *from Glycerium's house.*

DAV (*speaking back inside to Glycerium*) Just take things easy now. That's an order.

CHR (*to Simo*) There you are, there's Davus.

SIM (*to Chremes*) Coming from that house?

DAV (*to Glycerium*) You're in good hands, mine and our visitor's.

SIM (*to Chremes*) What the hell's going on?

DAV (*to Glycerium*) I've never known a better person to arrive at a better time.

SIM (*to Chremes*) The villain! Who's he praising?

DAV (*to Glycerium*) Our boat's now in shallow water.

SIM Why don't I talk to him? (*he goes up to Davus*)

147

DAV   erus est. quid agam?
SIM   o salve, bone vir.
DAV   ehem, Simo! o noster Chremes!
     omnia apparata iam sunt intus.
SIM   curasti probe.
DAV   ubi voles accerse.
SIM   bene sane. id enimvero hinc nunc abest.
     etiam tu hoc responde: quid istic tibi negotist?
DAV   mihin?
SIM   ita.
850 DAV   mihin?
SIM   tibi ergo.
DAV   modo introii—
SIM   quasi ego quam dudum rogem.
DAV   —cum tuo gnato una.
SIM   anne est intus Pamphilus? crucior miser.
     eho, non tu dixti esse inter eos inimicitias, carnufex?
DAV   sunt.
SIM   quor igitur hic est?
CHR   quid illum censes? cum illa litigat.
DAV   immo vero indignum, Chreme, iam facinus faxo ex me
     audies.
855   nescioquis senex modo venit—ellum—confidens catus.
     quom faciem videas videtur esse quantivis preti.
     tristis severitas inest in voltu atque in verbis fides.
SIM   quidnam apportas?
DAV   nil equidem nisi quod illum audivi dicere.
SIM   quid ait tandem?
DAV   Glycerium se scire civem esse Atticam.

    857 severitas *codd. pl.*, veritas $P^1C^1p^1$

148

DAV   (*aside*) It's the master. What shall I do?

SIM   Good day, my fine fellow.

DAV   Oh hello, Simo! And our friend Chremes! (*remembering his instructions*)[47] Everything's now ready at home.

SIM   (*with heavy irony*) You've managed things well.

DAV   You can fetch the bride when you wish.

SIM   (*still ironically*) Why yes, of course. That's the one thing that's missing now. (*changing his tone*) Now answer me this. What were you doing in there?

DAV   (*evasively*) Me?

SIM   Yes, you.

DAV   I went in just now—

SIM   As if I asked you how long ago!

DAV   —together with your son.

SIM   Is Pamphilus in there? It's heartbreaking! (*a thought strikes him*) Hey, didn't you say that there was a quarrel between them, you scoundrel?

DAV   There is.

SIM   Then why is he in there?

CHR   (*sarcastically*) Why do you think? He's arguing with her.

DAV   Not at all. It's a shocking business, Chremes, and I'll put you in the picture. An old man arrived just now—he's in there (*pointing to Glycerium's house*)—a crafty confident type. To look at, he seems a very worthy man, with a severe expression on his face and truth upon his lips.

SIM   What are you trying to tell us?

DAV   Nothing, except what I overheard him say.

SIM   Well, what did he say?

DAV   That he knows Glycerium to be an Athenian citizen.

[47] See line 523.

SIM	hem!
860	Dromo, Dromo!
DAV	quid est?
SIM	Dromo!
DAV	audi.
SIM	verbum si addideris—Dromo!

DAV	audi, obsecro.
DRO	quid vis?
SIM	sublimem intro rape hunc quantum potest.
DRO	quem?
SIM	Davum.
DAV	quam ob rem?
SIM	quia lubet. rape, inquam.
DAV	quid feci?
SIM	rape.
DAV	si quicquam invenies me mentitum occidito.
SIM	nil audio.
	ego iam te commotum reddam.
DAV	tamen etsi hoc verumst?
SIM	tamen.
865	cura asservandum vinctum atque (audin?) quadrupedem
	constringito.

	age nunciam. ego pol hodie, si vivo, tibi
	ostendam erum quid sit pericli fallere,
	et illi patrem.
CHR	ah! ne saevi tanto opere.
SIM	o Chreme,
	pietatem gnati! nonne te miseret mei?

SIM   (*furious*) What! (*calling inside his house*) Dromo!
        Dromo!

DAV   What's the matter?

SIM   (*calling*) Dromo!

DAV   Listen to me.

SIM   (*to Davus*) If you utter another word—(*calling*) Dromo!

DAV   Listen, I beseech you.

DRO   (*appearing from Simo's house, a thuggish looking slave
        carrying a whip*) What do you want?

SIM   Pick him up and take him inside, and quickly.

DRO   Who?

SIM   Davus.

DAV   Why?

SIM   Because I want it. (*to Dromo*) Take him off, I say.

DAV   What have I done?

SIM   (*ignoring him*) Take him.

DAV   If you discover I've told a lie, put me to death.

SIM   I'm not listening. I'll give you a real stirring up.

DAV   Even if all this is true?

SIM   Even so. (*to Dromo*) Make sure he's tied up and guarded,
        and (do you hear me?) bind him hands to feet. Go on
        then. (*to Davus, as Dromo carries him into Simo's house*)
        As sure as I live, by heaven, I'll show you how risky it is for
        you to deceive your master, and him his father.

CHR   (*to Simo*) Oh! Don't be so harsh.

SIM   Oh, Chremes! How's that for filial duty? Aren't you sorry

---

863 nil audio *Simoni vel Dromoni varie dant* Σ *edd.*
864 ego . . . reddam *Simoni dant codd. pl., Dromoni* G¹L

151

870   tantum laborem capere ob talem filium!
        age, Pamphile. exi, Pamphile. ecquid te pudet?

           V. iii: PAMPHILUS. SIMO. CHREMES.

PAM   quis me volt? perii! pater est.

SIM   quid ais, omnium—?

CHR   ah!
        rem potius ipsam dic ac mitte male loqui.

SIM   quasi quicquam in hunc iam gravius dici possiet.

875   ain tandem, civis Glyceriumst?

PAM   ita praedicant.

SIM   "ita praedicant"? o ingentem confidentiam!
        num cogitat quid dicat? num facti piget?
        vide num eius color pudoris signum usquam indicat.
        adeo impotenti esse animo ut praeter civium

880   morem atque legem et sui voluntatem patris
        tamen hanc habere studeat cum summo probro!

PAM   me miserum!

SIM   hem! modone id demum sensti, Pamphile?
        olim istuc, olim quom ita animum induxti tuom,
        quod cuperes aliquo pacto efficiundum tibi,

885   eodem die istuc verbum vere in te accidit.
        sed quid ego? quor me excrucio? quor me macero?
        quor meam senectutem huius sollicito amentia?
        an ut pro huius peccatis ego supplicium sufferam?
        immo habeat, valeat, vivat cum illa.

PAM   mi pater!

for me? Suffering so much trouble for such a son! (*going to Glycerium's door and shouting inside*) Come on, Pamphilus! Come out here, Pamphilus! Aren't you ashamed of yourself?

Enter PAMPHILUS from Glycerium's house.

PAM   Who wants me? (*seeing Simo*) Damn it! It's my father.

SIM   (*angrily*) What have you to say for yourself, you worst of all—?

CHR   Oh! Keep to the facts and never mind the abuse.

SIM   As if it were possible to speak too harshly to him! (*to Pamphilus*) Well, are you saying Glycerium is a citizen?

PAM   So they claim.

SIM   "So they claim?" What monstrous insolence! Does he think what he's saying? Does he regret what he's done? See if there's a blush on his face which might indicate shame. How can he be so headstrong as to defy social custom and the law and the wishes of his own father? He's determined to have this woman whatever the disgrace.

PAM   I'm a miserable wretch!

SIM   What! Have you only now realised that, Pamphilus? Long long ago, when you decided that you must get what you wanted by whatever means you could, that was the day when you really earned that description. But why do I bother? Why torture myself? Why torment myself? Why worry my old age with his folly? Just so that I can suffer the punishment for his misdeeds? No, let him have her, let him live with her, and good riddance!

PAM   Father!

153

890	SIM	quid "mi pater"? quasi tu huius indigeas patris.
		domus, uxor, liberi inventi invito patre.
		adducti qui illam hinc civem dicant. viceris.
	PAM	pater, liceatne pauca?
	SIM	quid dices mihi?
	CHR	at
		tamen, Simo, audi.
	SIM	ego audiam? quid audiam,
895		Chreme?
	CHR	at tandem dicat.
	SIM	age dicat. sino.

PAM ego me amare hanc fateor. si id peccarest, fateor id
      quoque.
   tibi, pater, me dedo. quidvis oneris impone. impera.
   vis me uxorem ducere? hanc vis mittere? ut potero
      feram.
   hoc modo te obsecro ut ne credas a me allegatum hunc
      senem.
900   sine me expurgem atque illum huc coram adducam.
SIM   adducas?
PAM   sine, pater.
CHR aequom postulat. da veniam.
PAM   sine te hoc exorem.
SIM   sino.
   quidvis cupio dum ne ab hoc me falli comperiar,
      Chreme.
CHR pro peccato magno paullum supplici satis est patri.

V. iv: CRITO. CHREMES. SIMO. PAMPHILUS.

CRI mitte orare. una harum quaevis causa me ut faciam
      monet,

SIM   How do you mean "Father"? You don't need me for a father. You've found your own home, wife, and children against your father's wishes. You've brought in people to declare that she's an Athenian citizen. Enjoy your victory.

PAM   Father, may I speak briefly?

SIM   There's nothing you can say.

CHR   Even so, listen, Simo.

SIM   Listen? Listen to what, Chremes?

CHR   But let him speak.

SIM   All right, let him speak. I give my permission.

PAM   I confess that I love her. If that is a sin, I confess that too. I put myself in your hands, father. Impose whatever burden you wish. Give me my orders. Do you wish me to take a wife? Do you wish me to send *her* away? I will bear it as best I can. But I make this one entreaty: don't believe that I brought in this old gentleman. Let me clear myself; let me bring him here to meet you.

SIM   Bring him here?

PAM   Let me, father.

CHR   It's a fair request. Grant it.

PAM   Let me persuade you.

SIM   I give my permission. (*to Chremes, as Pamphilus goes into Glycerium's house to get Crito*) I'd give anything rather than find out that he's deceiving me, Chremes.

CHR   However great the misdeed, a father should be content with a small punishment.

Enter PAMPHILUS and CRITO from Glycerium's house.

CRI   You don't have to beg me. I'll do it for any one of three

155

905	vel tu vel quod verumst vel quod ipsi cupio Glycerio.
CHR	Andrium ego Critonem video? certe is est.
CRI	salvos sis, Chreme.
CHR	quid tu Athenas insolens?
CRI	evenit. sed hicinest Simo?
CHR	hic.
CRI	Simo, men quaeris?
SIM	eho tu, Glycerium hinc civem esse ais?
CRI	tu negas?
SIM	itane huc paratus advenis?
CRI	qua re?
SIM	rogas?
910	tune impune haec facias? tune hic homines adulescentu- los
	imperitos rerum, eductos libere, in fraudem illicis?
	sollicitando et pollicitando eorum animos lactas?
CRI	sanun es?
SIM	ac meretricios amores nuptiis conglutinas?
PAM	perii! metuo ut substet hospes.
CHR	si, Simo, hunc noris satis,
915	non ita arbitrere. bonus est hic vir.
SIM	hic vir sit bonus?
	itane attemperate evenit, hodie in ipsis nuptiis
	ut veniret, antehac numquam? est vero huic credundum,
	Chreme.

---

[908] men quaeris *Simoni dant codd. pl., Critoni C¹p¹*

reasons, for you or because it's true or because I want to for Glycerium's sake.

CHR (*looking closely at Crito*) Is that Crito from Andros? I'm sure it is.

CRI (*recognising him*) Good day to you, Chremes.

CHR Why this rare visit to Athens?

CRI (*vaguely*) Things turned out that way. But is this Simo?

CHR Yes.

CRI Simo, are you looking for me?

SIM (*gruffly*) Here you, are you saying that Glycerium is an Athenian citizen?

CRI Are you saying she isn't?

SIM So you've come here all primed, have you?

CRI What do you mean?

SIM Well may you ask! Do you think you'll get away with this? Coming here and luring young men into wrongdoing, young lads ignorant of the ways of the world and brought up as gentlemen? Leading them astray with temptations and promises?

CRI Are you in your right mind?

SIM Cementing love affairs[48] with the glue of marriage?

PAM (*aside*) Damn it! I'm afraid our visitor won't be able to stand this.

CHR If you knew him well, Simo, you wouldn't judge him like this. He's a good man.

SIM Him a good man? Did it just happen that he arrived today in time for the wedding when he'd never been here before? (*sarcastically*) We really should believe him, Chremes.

---

[48] Literally "affairs with courtesans."

PAM ni metuam patrem, habeo pro illa re illum quod moneam
 probe.
SIM sycophanta!
CRI hem!
CHR sic, Crito, est hic. mitte.
CRI videat qui siet.
920 si mihi perget quae volt dicere, ea quae non volt audiet.
 ego istaec moveo aut curo? non tu tuom malum aequo
 animo feras?
 nam ego quae dico vera an falsa audierim iam sciri po-
 test.
 Atticus quidam olim navi fracta ad Andrum eiectus est
 et istaec una parva virgo. tum ille egens forte applicat
925 primum ad Chrysidis patrem se.
SIM fabulam inceptat.
CHR sine.
CRI itane vero obturbat?
CHR perge.
CRI tum is mihi cognatus fuit
 qui eum recepit. ibi ego audivi ex illo sese esse Atticum.
 is ibi mortuost.
CHR eius nomen?
CRI nomen tam cito? Phania? hem!

 perii! verum hercle opinor fuisse Phaniam. hoc certo
 scio,
930 Rhamnusium se aiebat esse.
CHR o Iuppiter!

928 Phania *Critoni dant* A¹Π*b*Σ, *Pamphilo* A². hem *Chremeti dant*
Σ, *Critoni* A¹, *Simoni* A²
 929 perii *Chremeti dant codd. pl.*, *Simoni* P¹C², *Pamphilo* A²

PAM   (*aside*) If I wasn't afraid of my father, I could give him some good advice on this matter.

SIM   (*to Crito*) You trickster!

CRI   What!

CHR   He's like this, Crito. Ignore it.

CRI   He'd better look to his behaviour. If he insists on saying what he likes, he'll hear what he doesn't like. (*to Simo*) Did I cause this situation? Is it any concern to me? It's your problem: can't you handle it without losing your temper? As for my story, you can soon check whether what I've heard is true or false. Some time ago an Athenian was shipwrecked on the coast of Andros. He had a small girl with him. He'd lost everything, and quite by chance the first person he turned to was Chrysis' father.

SIM   Here begins the fairy tale.

CHR   Let him continue.

CRI   Is he really going to interrupt like this?

CHR   Go on.

CRI   The man who took him in was a relative of mine. I was there and I heard him say that he was an Athenian citizen. He died on Andros.

CHR   His name?

CRI   His name? Just a moment. Was it Phania? (*trying to remember*) Oh damn it! (*after a pause*) Yes, by god, I think it was Phania. One thing I'm quite sure about: he said he came from Rhamnus.[49]

CHR   (*aside*) Jupiter!

[49] Athenians were identified by their father's name and their deme of origin. Rhamnus was a deme on the east coast of Attica.

CRI	eadem haec, Chreme, multi alii in Andro audivere.
CHR	utinam id sit quod spero! eho, dic mihi, quid eam tum? suamne esse aibat?
CRI	non.
CHR	quoiam igitur?
CRI	fratris filiam.
CHR	certe meast.
CRI	quid ais?
SIM	quid tu ais?
PAM	arrige auris, Pamphile.
SIM	qui credis?
CHR	Phania illic frater meus fuit.
SIM	noram et scio.

935 CHR is bellum hinc fugiens meque in Asiam persequens
proficiscitur.
tum illam relinquere hic est veritus. postilla hoc primum
audio
quid illo sit factum.

PAM vix sum apud me. ita animus commotust metu,
spe, gaudio, mirando tanto hoc tam repentino bono.

SIM ne istam multimodis tuam inveniri gaudeo.

PAM credo, pater.

940 CHR at mi unus scrupulus etiam restat qui me male habet.

PAM dignus es
cum tua religione, odium. nodum in scirpo quaeris.

---

936 hoc *Kauer*, hunc A¹, nunc *cett.*

---

50 Andros was on the sea route to Asia Minor for anyone fleeing
from Athens. There were a number of civil wars in Athens in

CRI   There were lots of people on Andros who heard him say it, Chremes.

CHR   (*aside*) May my hopes come true! (*to Crito*) Hey, tell me, what about the girl? Did he say that she was his daughter?

CRI   No.

CHR   Whose, then?

CRI   His brother's.

CHR   She must be mine.

CRI   What did you say?

SIM   What did you say?

PAM   (*aside*) Prick up your ears, Pamphilus.

SIM   (*to Chremes*) What makes you believe that?

CHR   This Phania was my brother.

SIM   I knew him. It's true.

CHR   He left Athens to avoid the war and follow me to Asia.[50] He was afraid to leave the girl here. This is the first time since then that I've heard what became of him.

PAM   (*aside*) I'm beside myself. I'm a jumble of emotions, fear, hope, joy, at this wonderful unexpected good news.

SIM   (*to Chremes*) I'm absolutely delighted that she turns out to be your daughter.

PAM   (*aside*) I'm sure you are, father.

CHR   But there's one little thing[51] which still worries me.

PAM   (*aside*) Serve you right, you and your scruples, you tiresome man! You're looking for a knot in a bullrush.[52]

Menander's lifetime between the Macedonian rulers and the democratic movement.   [51] In the Latin idiom the reference is to a stone (*scrupulus*) in the shoe.

[52] A proverbial expression for finding difficulties where there are none, a bullrush being smooth.

161

CRI   quid istud est?

CHR   nomen non convenit.

CRI   fuit hercle huic aliud parvae.

CHR   quod, Crito?
   numquid meministi?

CRI   id quaero.

PAM   egon huius memoriam patiar meae
   voluptati obstare, quom ego possim in hac re medicari
     mihi?

945   non patiar. heus, Chreme, quod quaeris Pasibulast.

CHR   ipsast.

CRI   east.

PAM   ex ipsa miliens audivi.

SIM   omnis nos gaudere hoc, Chreme,
   te credo credere.

CHR   ita me di ament, credo.

PAM   quod restat, pater,—

SIM   iamdudum res redduxit me ipsa in gratiam.

PAM   o lepidum patrem!
   de uxore, ita ut possedi, nil mutat Chremes?

CHR   causa optumast,

950   nisi quid pater ait aliud.

PAM   nempe id.

SIM   scilicet.

CHR   dos, Pamphile, est
   decem talenta.

PAM   accipio.

---

941 istud *Dziatzko metro consulens,* istuc Σ

---

53 The language in this and the following lines has a legal ring.

CRI   (*to Chremes*) What is it?

CHR   The name isn't right.

CRI   She had another one when she was small, for god's sake.

CHR   What was it, Crito? Can you remember?

CRI   I'm thinking.

PAM   (*aside*) Shall I allow my happiness to be spoiled by his forgetfulness, when the remedy is in my own hands? No. I shan't. (*aloud*) Listen, Chremes, the name you want is Pasibula.

CHR   That's her.

CRI   It is.

PAM   I've heard it from her a thousand times.

SIM   All of us are delighted at the news, Chremes, as I'm sure you are.

CHR   Heaven help me, I certainly am.

PAM   It only remains, father—

SIM   I'm on your side now we know the facts.

PAM   Father, you're splendid. As for my wife, given I'm in possession, I presume Chremes has no objection?[53]

CHR   You have an excellent claim, unless your father says otherwise.

PAM   He agrees.

SIM   Of course.

CHR   Her dowry, Pamphilus, is ten talents.[54]

PAM   I accept the offer.

---

[54] This implies that Chremes is a rich man and is being very generous with the dowry. His namesake in *The Self-Tormentor* (line 838) offers two talents, and it seems that one talent was a perfectly acceptable amount in real-life Athens among the wealthy classes.

163

CHR   propero ad filiam. eho, mecum, Crito!
nam illam me credo haud nosse.
SIM   quor non illam huc transferri iubes?
PAM   recte admones. Davo ego istuc dedam iam negoti.
SIM   non potest.
PAM   qui?
SIM   quia habet aliud magis ex sese et maius.
PAM   quidnam?
SIM   vinctus est.
955 PAM   pater, non recte vinctust.
SIM   haud ita iussi.
PAM   iube solvi, obsecro.
SIM   age, fiat.
PAM   at matura.
SIM   eo intro.
PAM   o faustum et felicem diem!

V. V: CHARINUS. PAMPHILUS.

CHA   proviso quid agat Pamphilus. atque eccum.
PAM   aliquis me forsitan
putet non putare hoc verum. at mihi nunc sic esse hoc
verum lubet.

ego deorum vitam propterea sempiternam esse arbitror
960   quod voluptates eorum propriae sunt. nam mi immorta-
litas
partast, si nulla aegritudo huic gaudio intercesserit.
sed quem ego mihi potissumum exoptem quoi nunc haec
narrem dari?
CHA   quid illud gaudist?

958 putet *ad fin.* 957 AΣ, *ad init.* 958 Π*b*

CHR I can't wait to see my daughter. Hey, Crito, come with
me. I don't think she'll recognise me. (*Chremes and
Crito exit into Glycerium's house*)

SIM (*to Pamphilus*) Why don't you have her brought over
here? (*indicating his own house*)

PAM That's good advice. I'll put Davus in charge of things.

SIM He can't.

PAM Why not?

SIM It's personal. He's something more important on his
hands.

PAM What is it?

SIM He's tied up.

PAM Father, that's not proper.

SIM (*with a laugh*) I told them to tie him properly.

PAM Have him released, for heaven's sake.

SIM All right. It shall be done.

PAM But hurry up.

SIM I'm just going in. (*Simo exits into his house*)

PAM Oh blessed happy day!

Enter CHARINUS *left from the direction of his house. He pauses
on the side of the stage.*

CHA (*to himself*) I'm coming to see what Pamphilus is up to.
(*seeing him*) There he is.

PAM (*to himself*) Some people may perhaps think that I don't
believe this is true. But I choose to think it is. In my opin-
ion what gives the gods eternal life is the fact that their
pleasures are theirs to keep. *I'm* immortal, if no sorrow
comes to spoil my joy. But who would I most want to
appear and hear my news?

CHA (*aside*) What's he so joyful about?

165

PAM   Davom video. nemost quem mallem omnium.
nam hunc scio mea solide solum gavisurum gaudia.

V. vi: CHARINUS. PAMPHILUS. DAVOS.

965 DAV   Pamphilus ubinam hic est?
PAM   Dave!
DAV   quis homost?
PAM   ego sum.
DAV   o Pamphile!
PAM   nescis quid mi obtigerit.
DAV   certe. sed quid mi obtigerit scio.
PAM   et quidem ego.
DAV   more hominum evenit ut quod sim nanctus mali
prius rescisceres tu quam ego illud quod tibi evenit boni.
PAM   Glycerium mea suos parentis repperit.
DAV   factum bene!
CHA   hem!
970 PAM   pater amicus summus nobis.
DAV   quis?
PAM   Chremes.
DAV   narras probe.
PAM   nec mora ullast quin eam uxorem ducam.
CHA   num ille somniat
ea quae vigilans voluit?
PAM   tum de puero, Dave—
DAV   ah! desine.
solus est quem diligant di.
CHA   salvos sum si haec vera sunt.
colloquar.
PAM   quis homost? Charine, in tempore ipso mi advenis.
975 CHA   bene factum!

PAM (*as Simo's door opens*) Here's Davus. There's nobody in the world that I'd rather see. He's the only person I know will share my joy with his whole heart.

Enter DAVUS from Simo's house.

DAV Where's Pamphilus?
PAM Davus!
DAV Who's that?
PAM It's me.
DAV Oh, Pamphilus!
PAM You don't know what's happened to me.
DAV True. But I do know what's happened to *me*.
PAM So do I.
DAV That's the way of the world. You know the bad that's come to me before I know the good that's befallen you.
PAM My Glycerium has found her parents.
DAV Congratulations!
CHA (*aside*) What!
PAM Her father's a good friend of ours.
DAV Who?
PAM Chremes.
DAV Good news!
PAM And I can marry her immediately.
CHA (*aside*) Is he dreaming that his wishes have come true?
PAM Then about the baby, Davus . . .
DAV Enough! He must be the darling of the gods.
CHA (*aside*) If this is true, I'm saved. I'll speak to him. (*he goes up to Pamphilus*)
PAM Who's that? Charinus, you've arrived at the right moment.
CHA Congratulations!

PAM   audisti?

CHA   omnia. age, me in tuis secundis respice.
tuos est nunc Chremes. facturum quae voles scio esse
     omnia.

PAM   memini. atque adeo longumst illum me exspectare dum
     exeat.

sequere hac me. intus apud Glycerium nunc est. tu,
     Dave, abi domum,

propera, accerse hinc qui auferant eam. quid stas? quid
     cessas?

DAV   eo.

980   ne exspectetis dum exeant huc. intus despondebitur.
intus transigetur si quid est quod restet.

Ω   plaudite.

PAM You've heard?

CHA Everything. But come on, have regard for me in your good fortune. You now have Chremes where you want him. I'm sure he'll do everything you ask.

PAM I haven't forgotten you. But I haven't time to wait for him to come out. Follow me this way. He's inside with Glycerium. (*to Davus*) You go home quickly, Davus, and bring some people to form the procession. Don't stand there. What are you waiting for?

DAV I'm going. (*to the audience*) Don't wait for them to come out here. The betrothal will take place inside, together with any other remaining business.

ALL[55] (*to the audience*) Give us your applause.[56]

---

[55] All Terence's plays end with a request for applause, which in a curtainless theatre signifies to the audience the end of the play. In the MSS this request is preceded by the Greek letter omega, of which the significance is not at all clear. It is implied by Horace *Ars Poetica* 155 (*donec cantor 'vos plaudite' dicat*) that the final *plaudite* was spoken by the *cantor* (perhaps the musician who accompanied the play), but there is no other evidence to corroborate this. It is more likely that it was spoken either by all the actors onstage, as in several plays of Plautus', signified in the MSS by *grex* or *caterva*, or by one of the characters (here presumably Davus), as in the rest of Plautus' plays.

[56] A number of the later MSS preserve an alternative ending to the play in which Pamphilus persuades Chremes to betroth Philumena to Charinus. This ending was recognised by Donatus and Eugraphius as not being by Terence: its obvious intention was to create a more satisfactory outcome for the second pair of lovers.

THE SELF-TORMENTOR

INTRODUCTORY NOTE

The Self-Tormentor, which was based on Menander's play of the same name, has a double plot involving two fathers, two sons, two love affairs, and two slaves (though one of the slaves has only a very minor part). Line 6 of the prologue ("a play which has been made double out of a single plot") appears to imply that Terence himself created the double plot by adding a second set of characters to the Greek original, but this can scarcely be the case. In contrast to *The Woman of Andros,* the two sides of the plot are both well developed; they are moreover intimately linked, and it would be very difficult to reconstruct a convincing plot for Menander's play with only one set of characters centred upon the self-tormentor of the title. It is likely, therefore, that Terence's play follows the basic shape of Menander's; he may have made additions or alterations, but in the absence of any external evidence these can only be a matter of speculation.

Before the play opens, Menedemus (the self-tormentor) has driven his son Clinia overseas by his harshness over an affair with a poor Corinthian girl Antiphila. Now, full of remorse, he is punishing himself by slaving away on a farm he has recently bought. His neighbour, the busybody Chremes, rebukes him for this and reads him a lecture on proper father-son relationships; but the shallowness of Chremes' position is revealed when it transpires that his own son Clitipho, unknown to his father, is having an affair with a greedy courtesan Bacchis. Clinia returns from overseas and enjoys a brief romantic reunion with Antiphila (this is the only onstage appearance of a *virgo* in Terence). Antiphila presently turns out to be a long-lost daughter of Chremes', and the way is clear for Clinia to marry her. Meanwhile, Clitipho needs to find money to satisfy Bacchis' expensive tastes while keeping his affair secret from his father, and the family slave Syrus takes over the plot to this end with a series of complicated schemes which must have been quite difficult to follow on stage. One of these is to represent Antiphila as a maid of Bacchis', given to her by her Corinthian mother as a security for a debt, which Chremes, as her newly revealed father, is honour-bound to repay. Another is to represent Clinia as the real lover of Bacchis in order to allay any suspicions that Chremes might have of his son's involvement with her: Clinia, it is claimed, is only *pretending* to love Antiphila in order to fool Menedemus into providing money for a wedding. Eventually the truth comes out, and Chremes, despite his self-proclaimed expertise in dealing with sons, is furious; he threatens to disinherit Clitipho but is finally persuaded to relent on condition that Clitipho abandons Bacchis and takes a wife.

A major focus of the play is on the fathers and their respective attitudes towards their sons. Comedy tends to divide fathers into two types, harsh and lenient, as in Terence's later *The Brothers,* but the characterisation here is more subtle: Menedemus is the formerly harsh father who is now determined to err on the side of leniency, whereas Chremes counsels leniency, but, when put to the test, goes to extremes of harshness. The two sons present a more straightforward and typical contrast, Clinia as the romantic well-intentioned lover of a poor but in the end marriageable girl, and Clitipho as hopelessly in love with a demanding courtesan of whose vices he is only too well aware. Clinia's problem is easily solved by Menedemus' change of heart and the discovery of Antiphila's true parentage, which means that the climax of the play is the resolution of the conflict between Clitipho and Chremes, with the father finally asserting his authority. An extra dimension is provided by the appearance of Chremes' wife Sostrata, the first of several sympathetically drawn *matronae* in Terence, who skilfully manages her confession to having disobeyed Chremes' instructions to expose their baby daughter and who staunchly champions her son's cause at the end.

As the the summary of the plot makes clear, much of the play is taken up with the machinations of Syrus, who is Terence's closest approximation to the tricky slave character. Like his Plautine counterparts, he devises a series of schemes, not all of which are divulged to the audience, and changes them ingeniously to meet changing circumstances. A new twist is that Syrus is actually encouraged and abetted in his schemes by Chremes, who is anxious that Menedemus should be tricked out of his money rather than simply bestowing it on Clinia in an excess of generosity. The irony is that it is in fact Chremes himself who is being tricked, and in the end it is Menedemus who, in a reversal of the opening scene of the play, is shown to be the wiser of the two fathers. The trickery thus serves the wider interests of the play, and the danger that it becomes itself the focus of the audience's interest is thereby avoided.

SELECT BIBLIOGRAPHY

Editions and Commentaries

Brothers, A. J. (Warminster 1988).

Criticism

Brothers, A. J. "The Construction of Terence's *Heautontimorumenos.*" *Classical Quarterly* 30 (1980): 94–119.

Fantham, E. "*Heautontimorumenos* and *Adelphoe:* A Study of Fatherhood in Terence and Menander." *Latomus* 30 (1971): 970–998.

Goldberg, S. M. "The *duplex comoedia,*" in *Understanding Terence.* Princeton, 1986: 135–148.

Jocelyn, H. D. "Homo sum: humani nil a me alienum puto (Terence, *Heauton timorumenos* 77)." *Antichthon* 7 (1973): 14–46.

Konstan, D. "*Self-Tormentor,*" in *Greek Comedy and Ideology.* Oxford, 1995: 120–130.

Lefèvre, E. *Terenz' und Menanders Heautontimorumenos* (*Zetemata* Heft 91). Munich, 1994.

Lowe, J. C. B. "The Intrigue of Terence's *Heauton Timorumenos.*" *Rheinisches Museum* 141 (1998): 163–171.

Steidle, W. "Menander bei Terenz II." *Rheinisches Museum* 117 (1974): 247–276.

DIDASCALIA

**INCIPIT HEAUTON TIMORUMENOS TERENTI
ACTA LVDIS MEGALENSIBVS
L. CORNELIO LENTVLO L. VALERIO FLACCO
AEDILIBVS CVRVLIBVS
EGERE L. AMBIVIVS TVRPIO L. ATILIVS
PRAENESTINVS
MODOS FECIT FLACCVS CLAVDI
ACTA PRIMVM TIBIIS IMPARIBVS DEINDE DVABVS
DEXTRIS
GRAECA MENANDRV
FACTA III M'. IVVENTIO TI. SEMPRONIO COS.**

C. SULPICI APOLLINARIS PERIOCHA

in militiam proficisci gnatum Cliniam
amantem Antiphilam compulit durus pater
animique sese angebat facti paenitens.
mox ut reversust clam patrem devortitur
ad Clitiphonem. is amabat scortum Bacchidem.
cum accerseret cupitam Antiphilam Clinia,
ut eius Bacchis venit amica ac servolae
habitum gerens Antiphila. factum id quo patrem
suum celaret Clitipho. hic technis Syri
decem minas meretriculae aufert a sene.
Antiphila Clitiphonis reperitur soror.
hanc Clinia, aliam Clitipho uxorem accipit.

---

[1] L. Atilius is omitted by the Bembine MS (A), which names
Ambivius Turpio as the sole producer.

PRODUCTION NOTICE

Here begins the Self-Tormentor of Terence, acted at the Ludi Megalenses in the curule aedileship of L. Cornelius Lentulus and L. Valerius Flaccus. Produced by L. Ambivius Turpio and L. Atilius of Praeneste.[1] Music composed by Flaccus, slave of Claudius, first for unequal pipes, then for two right-hand pipes.[2] Greek original by Menander. The author's third play,[3] performed in the consulship of M. Iuventius and Ti. Sempronius.[4]

SYNOPSIS BY C. SULPICIUS APOLLINARIS

Clinia, the lover of Antiphila, was compelled by his strict father to go overseas as a soldier. The father regretted what he had done and suffered torments of agony. Presently, the son returns and, unknown to his father, goes to stay with Clitipho, who is in love with the courtesan Bacchis. When Clinia sends for his beloved Antiphila, Bacchis arrives, pretending to be Clinia's mistress, with Antiphila dressed as her servant; this was so that Clitipho could conceal his affair from his own father. Thanks to the schemes of Syrus, Clitipho extracts ten minas from the old man to pay the courtesan. Antiphila is discovered to be Clitipho's sister; Clinia marries her, and Clitipho takes another woman as his wife.

[2] This is the only play of Terence's where there is an apparent change of pipes during the course of the play.

[3] The second was *The Mother-in-Law*, whose first performance had to be abandoned.

[4] That is, in 163 B.C.

PERSONAE

CHREMES senex
MENEDEMUS senex
CLITIPHO adulescens
CLINIA adulescens
SYRUS servus
DROMO servus
BACCHIS meretrix
ANTIPHILA virgo
SOSTRATA matrona
NUTRIX
PHRYGIA ancilla

Scaena: Athenis

CHARACTERS

CHREMES, an old man, father of Clitipho and (as it turns out) of Antiphila

MENEDEMUS, an old man, neighbour of Chremes, father of Clinia

CLITIPHO, a young man, son of Chremes, lover of Bacchis

CLINIA, a young man, son of Menedemus, lover of Antiphila

SYRUS, slave of Chremes

DROMO, slave of Menedemus

BACCHIS, a courtesan

ANTIPHILA, a young woman, supposed daughter of a woman of Corinth, in fact daughter of Chremes and Sostrata

SOSTRATA, a matron, wife of Chremes

NURSE in Chremes' household

PHRYGIA, a maid of Bacchis

Staging

The stage represents a street in a country town in Attica, on which stand the houses of Chremes, Menedemus, and Phania. The exit on the audience's right leads to Athens, that on their left leads further into the country.[5]

[5] The play is unusual in that (like Menander's *The Bad-Tempered Man* and Plautus' *The Rope*), it is set in the country rather than in the city. In the Greek original it was specifically set in the village of Halae (see note 18).

179

HEAUTON TIMORUMENOS

ne quoi sit vostrum mirum quor partis seni
poeta dederit quae sunt adulescentium,
id primum dicam, deinde quod veni eloquar.
ex integra Graeca integram comoediam
5   hodie sum acturus Heauton Timorumenon,
duplex quae ex argumento factast simplici.
novam esse ostendi et quae esset. nunc qui scripserit
et quoia Graeca sit, ni partem maxumam
existumarem scire vostrum, id dicerem.
10   nunc quam ob rem has partis didicerim paucis dabo.
oratorem esse voluit me, non prologum.
vostrum iudicium fecit, me actorem dedit,
si hic actor tantum poterit a facundia
quantum ille potuit cogitare commode
15   qui orationem hanc scripsit quam dicturus sum.
nam quod rumores distulerunt malevoli
multas contaminasse Graecas dum facit
paucas Latinas, factum id esse hic non negat

---

[13] si *Bentley,* sed *codd.*

[6] This prologue was evidently spoken by Ambivius Turpio, as was
that of the third performance of *The Mother-in-Law* (see Introduction).

THE SELF-TORMENTOR

Some of you may be wondering why the playwright has given to an old man[6] a role usually reserved for the young. I will explain that first, and then deliver the speech I have come to deliver. Today I am about to perform a fresh comedy from a fresh Greek play, "The Self-Tormentor," a double play based on a single plot.[7] I have revealed that it is a new play and given you its name; I would tell you who wrote it and the author of the Greek original, but I judge that most of you know this already.[8]

Now I will explain briefly why I have taken on this role. The playwright wanted me as an advocate, not as a prologue speaker. He has turned this into a court, with me to act on his behalf. I only hope that the eloquence of the actor can do justice to the aptness of the arguments which the writer of this speech has contrived to put together.

Malicious people have spread rumours to the effect that the playwright has contaminated[9] many Greek plays while creating few Latin ones. He does not deny that this is so; he does not re-

[7] On the problem caused by this line see Introductory Note.

[8] The implication is that these details were posted on notices by the aediles who were in charge of the games.

[9] On "contamination" see Introduction.

181

neque se pigere et deinde facturum autumat.
20   habet bonorum exemplum, quo exemplo sibi
licere facere quod illi fecerunt putat.
tum quod malevolus vetus poeta dictitat
repente ad studium hunc se applicasse musicum,
amicum ingenio fretum, haud natura sua,
25   arbitrium vostrum, vostra existumatio
valebit. quare omnis vos oratos volo
ne plus iniquom possit quam aequom oratio.
facite aequi sitis, date crescendi copiam
novarum qui spectandi faciunt copiam
30   sine vitiis. ne ille pro se dictum existumet
qui nuper fecit servo currenti in via
decesse populum. quor insano serviat?
de illius peccatis plura dicet quom dabit
alias novas, nisi finem maledictis facit.
35   adeste aequo animo, date potestatem mihi
statariam agere ut liceat per silentium,
ne semper servos currens, iratus senex
edax parasitus, sycophanta autem impudens,
avarus leno assidue agendi sint seni
40   clamore summo, cum labore maxumo.
mea causa causam hanc iustam esse animum inducite,
ut aliqua pars laboris minuatur mihi.
nam nunc novas qui scribunt nil parcunt seni.
si quae laboriosa est, ad me curritur;

³⁹ seni Σ, mihi A

---

¹⁰ In the prologue of *The Woman of Andros* (18–20) Terence names
Naevius, Plautus, and Ennius as his models.
¹¹ That is, Luscius of Lanuvium (see Introduction).

gret it and he declares that he will do the same again. He has good writers[10] as a precedent, and he reckons that with them as a precedent he is permitted to do what they did. The malicious old playwright[11] further asserts that our author has taken up the dramatic art rather suddenly, relying on the talent of his friends[12] and not on his natural ability. This is a matter for your judgement; you shall decide the issue.

I should like you all to be persuaded not to let biassed arguments have more weight than unbiassed ones. Make sure that you are fair, and give those writers a chance to flourish who give you the chance to see new plays not marred by faults. The playwright[13] who recently portrayed a crowd making way for a running slave in the street[14] should not imagine that I am including him in this: why should anyone defend a madman? Our author will have more to say about *his* failings when he writes other new plays, if he doesn't put an end to his slanders.

Listen with open minds, and give me the opportunity to perform a quiet[15] play without interruption. I do not wish in my old age to be continually playing running slaves, angry old men, hungry parasites, brazen tricksters, and greedy pimps, all at the top of my voice and with a great effort. For my sake, be convinced that my cause is just, so that I may enjoy some diminution of my labours. Those who write new plays nowadays have no concern for my old age. If it's a play full of action, they come

[12] The reference is to members of the so-called "Scipionic circle" (see Introduction).

[13] This is Luscius again.

[14] The "running slave" scene is a standard scene of Roman comedy, which Terence himself uses four times in six plays.

[15] That is, one which depends on talk (Latin *stataria*) rather than on action (Latin *motoria*).

45 si lenis est, ad alium defertur gregem.
in hac est pura oratio. experimini
in utramque partem ingenium quid possit meum.
[si numquam avare pretium statui arti meae
et eum esse quaestum in animum induxi maxumum
50 quam maxume servire vostris commodis,]
exemplum statuite in me, ut adulescentuli
vobis placere studeant potius quam sibi.

ACTUS I

I. i: CHREMES. MENEDEMUS.

CHR quamquam haec inter nos nuper notitia admodumst
(inde adeo quod agrum in proxumo hic mercatus es)
55 nec rei fere sane amplius quicquam fuit,
tamen vel virtus tua me vel vicinitas,
quod ego in propinqua parte amicitiae puto,
facit ut te audacter moneam et familiariter,
quod mihi videre praeter aetatem tuam
60 facere et praeterquam res te adhortatur tua.
nam, pro deum atque hominum fidem, quid vis tibi aut
quid quaeris? annos sexaginta natus es
aut plus eo, ut conicio. agrum in his regionibus
meliorem neque preti maioris nemo habet.
65 servos compluris; proinde quasi nemo siet,

48–50 = *Hec.* 49–51 *om. edd.*, 48–9 *om.* A

---

16 These lines recur at *The Mother-in-Law* 49–51 and are therefore suspect, especially as the first two are omitted here by the Bembine MS (A).

17 The jerkin is the suggestion of Varro, *On Agriculture* 2.11.11.

to me; if it's a sedate one, they go to another company. This play depends purely on its language. Try what my talent can achieve in either type of play. [If I have never been greedy in setting a price on my art, and am resolved that my greatest reward is to serve your interests as best I can][16] set me up as a precedent, so that young writers may be eager to please you rather than themselves.

ACT ONE

Enter CHREMES *from the left with* MENEDEMUS, *who is wearing a leather jerkin*[17] *and carrying several large hoes.*

CHR (*pompously*) Although our acquaintance is quite recent (in fact it dates from the time you bought the farm next door) and we have scarcely had any further dealings with each other, nonetheless your good character and the fact that we are neighbours (which I think is the nearest thing to being friends) persuade me to offer you a bold piece of advice, person to person, to the effect that you seem to me to be behaving inappropriately for your years and for the requirements of your circumstances. In the name of gods and men, what are you up to? What are you trying to achieve? You're sixty years of age, or more, at a guess. Nobody in this area has better or more valuable land.[18] You have quite a lot of slaves, but you perform their tasks

[18] We possess the corresponding passage of Menander (fr. 77 Kassel-Austin), which reads: "In the name of Athena, you're insane, when you're so old; you must be about sixty. Of the people of Halae you've acquired the finest piece of land among the three, and, best of all, it's unmortgaged." There were two villages called Halae in Attica. The reference of "among the three" is not clear.

ita attente tute illorum officia fungere.
numquam tam mane egredior neque tam vesperi
domum revertor quin te in fundo conspicer
fodere aut arare aut aliquid ferre. denique
70 nullum remittis tempus neque te respicis.
haec non voluptati tibi esse satis certo scio. "at
enim" dices "quantum hic operis fiat paenitet."
quod in opere faciundo operae consumis tuae,
si sumas in illis exercendis, plus agas.
75 MEN Chreme, tantumne ab re tuast oti tibi
aliena ut cures ea quae nil ad te attinent?
  CHR homo sum; humani nil a me alienum puto.
vel me monere hoc vel percontari puta.
rectumst, ego ut faciam; non est, te ut deterream.
80 MEN mihi sic est usus; tibi ut opus facto est face.
  CHR an quoiquam est usus homini se ut cruciet?
  MEN   mihi.
  CHR si quid laborist, nollem. sed quid istuc malist?
quaeso, quid de te tantum meruisti?
  MEN   eheu!
  CHR ne lacruma atque istuc quidquid est fac me ut sciam.
85 ne retice, ne verere; crede, inquam, mihi.
aut consolando aut consilio aut re iuvero.
  MEN scire hoc vis?
  CHR   hac quidem causa qua dixi tibi.
  MEN dicetur.
  CHR   at istos rastros interea tamen
appone, ne labora.
  MEN   minume.

yourself as assiduously as if you had none. I never go out so early in the morning or return home so late in the evening that I don't see you on your farm digging or ploughing or carrying something. In short you never slacken off or take any thought for yourself. I'm pretty sure you're not enjoying this way of life. "Well," you may say, "I'm not satisfied with the amount of work that's getting done here." But if you spent the effort which you spend on doing the work on putting *them* to work, you'd be better off.

MEN Chremes, do you have so much free time from your own business that you concern yourself with other people's affairs when they have nothing to do with you?

CHR I'm human, and I regard no human business as other people's. Take it as advice or, if you like, as a question. If your behaviour's right, I'll follow your example; if not, I'll try to dissuade you.

MEN I need to behave this way; you do what you want to do.

CHR Does anyone need to torment himself?

MEN Yes, I do.

CHR If you've a problem, I'm sorry. But what's wrong? Tell me, how do you deserve such treatment?

MEN (*sobbing*) Oh dear, oh dear!

CHR Don't weep. Whatever your trouble is, tell me all about it; don't keep it to yourself. Don't be afraid; trust me, I say. I'll help you whether you need consolation or counsel or money.

MEN Do you really want to know?

CHR Yes, and I've explained why.

MEN I'll tell you.

CHR But first put down those hoes. Don't burden yourself.

MEN Certainly not.

	CHR	quam rem agis?
90	MEN	sine me vocivom tempus ne quod dem mihi
		laboris.
	CHR	non sinam, inquam.
	MEN	ah! non aequom facis.
	CHR	hui! tam gravis hos, quaeso?
	MEN	sic meritumst meum.
	CHR	nunc loquere.
	MEN	filium unicum adulescentulum

habeo. at quid dixi habere me? immo habui, Chreme.
95   nunc habeam necne incertumst.

	CHR	quid ita istuc?
	MEN	scies.

est e Corintho hic advena anus paupercula.
eius filiam ille amare coepit perdite,
prope iam ut pro uxore haberet. haec clam me omnia.
ubi rem rescivi, coepi non humanitus
100   neque ut animum decuit aegrotum adulescentuli
tractare sed vi et via pervolgata patrum.
cotidie accusabam: "hem! tibine haec diutius
licere speras facere me vivo patre,
amicam ut habeas prope iam in uxoris loco?
105   erras, si id credis, et me ignoras, Clinia.
ego te meum esse dici tantisper volo
dum quod te dignumst facies. sed si id non facis,
ego quod me in te sit facere dignum invenero.
nulla adeo ex re istuc fit nisi ex nimio otio.
110   ego istuc aetatis non amori operam dabam
sed in Asiam hinc abii propter pauperiem atque ibi
simul rem et gloriam armis belli repperi."
postremo adeo res rediit. adulescentulus
saepe eadem et graviter audiendo victus est.

CHR What are you trying to achieve?

MEN Allow me to deny myself time off from work.

CHR I won't allow you, I say. (*he relieves Menedemus of the hoes*)

MEN Oh! That's not fair.

CHR (*weighing the hoes*) Wow! Are they really so heavy?

MEN It's what I deserve.

CHR (*putting them down*) Now tell me your story.

MEN I have a one and only son, a young lad. But why did I say, have? Had, rather, Chremes; it's not clear whether I have one now or not.

CHR How do you mean?

MEN I'll tell you. There's a penniless old woman here, an immigrant from Corinth. My son fell desperately in love with her daughter, and practically treated her as his wife. All this unknown to me. When I found out, I didn't handle him humanely and with due regard to the feelings of a lovesick lad, but harshly, as is the common way of fathers. Day after day I would find fault with him: "What! Do you expect to be allowed to carry on like this any longer while your father's alive? Treating a mistress practically as a wife? If you believe that, you're making a mistake. You don't know me, Clinia. I am willing for you to be called my son only as long as your behaviour is worthy of you. If it isn't, I will devise some action against you which is worthy of me. In fact, this is only happening because you have time on your hands. When I was your age, I didn't spend my time on love affairs. I had no money, so I went off to Asia and gained both wealth and glory on the battlefield." Finally matters came to a head. The poor lad was worn down by hearing the same things emphasised

115	putavit me et aetate et benevolentia
	plus scire et providere quam se ipsum sibi.
	in Asiam ad regem militatum abiit, Chreme.
CHR	quid ais?
MEN	clam me profectus mensis tris abest.
CHR	ambo accusandi, etsi illud inceptum tamen
120	animist pudentis signum et non instrenui.
MEN	ubi comperi ex iis qui ei fuere conscii,
	domum revortor maestus atque animo fere
	perturbato atque incerto prae aegritudine.
	assido: accurrunt servi, soccos detrahunt.
125	video alios festinare, lectos sternere,
	cenam apparare. pro se quisque sedulo
	faciebant quo illam mihi lenirent miseriam.
	ubi video, haec coepi cogitare: "hem! tot mea
	solius solliciti sunt causa ut me unum expleant?
130	ancillae tot me vestiant? sumptus domi
	tantos ego solus faciam? sed gnatum unicum,
	quem pariter uti his decuit aut etiam amplius,
	quod illa aetas magis ad haec utenda idoneast,
	eum ego hinc eieci miserum iniustitia mea.
135	malo quidem me dignum quovis deputem,
	si id faciam. nam usque dum ille vitam illam colet
	inopem carens patria ob meas iniurias,
	interea usque illi de me supplicium dabo,
	laborans, parcens, quaerens, illi serviens."
140	ita facio prorsus. nil relinquo in aedibus
	nec vas nec vestimentum; corrasi omnia.

---

[19] The reference is to mercenary service in the army of one of the
Hellenistic kings who came into power after the death of Alexander in
323 B.C.

over and over again. He reckoned that with my age and concern for him I was wiser than he was and had a better understanding of what was good for him. He went off to Asia to serve under the king, Chremes.[19]

CHR What are you saying?

MEN He left without telling me, and he's been away three months.

CHR You're both at fault, though his action does suggest a sense of shame and a certain amount of enterprise.

MEN When I found out from those who were in his confidence, I returned home, sad, pretty upset, and uncertain what to do in my distress. I sat down, and slaves ran up and took off my shoes. I saw others bustling about, setting the table,[20] preparing the dinner, every one of them doing his very best to soothe my grief. When I saw them, I began to think: "What! So many people taking all this trouble just for my sake, to satisfy one man's needs? Should I have so many maids to dress me? Should I be so extravagant when I'm living at home alone? And my only son, who should be enjoying these things as much—or indeed more, since he's at a more suitable age to enjoy them—I've driven him out of here, poor boy, by my unjust treatment. I should regard myself as deserving any misfortune you care to name, if I carried on like this. So long as he lives a life of poverty and exile through my injustice, I shall punish myself on his behalf, toiling, scraping, earning my living, slaving away for him." I'm doing exactly that. I've left nothing in the house, no silver plate, no fine clothing; I collected it all up. All my maids

---

[20] Literally, "spreading the couches"; the couches at which diners reclined while eating were spread with coverlets.

ancillas, servos, nisi eos qui opere rustico
faciundo facile sumptum exsercirent suom,
omnis produxi ac vendidi. inscripsi ilico

145   aedis mercede. quasi talenta ad quindecim
coegi. agrum hunc mercatus sum. hic me exerceo.
decrevi tantisper me minus iniuriae,
Chreme, meo gnato facere dum fiam miser,
nec fas esse ulla me voluptate hic frui,

150   nisi ubi ille huc salvos redierit meus particeps.

CHR   ingenio te esse in liberos leni puto,
et illum obsequentem si quis recte aut commode
tractaret. verum nec tu illum satis noveras
nec te ille. hoc qui fit? ubi non vere vivitur.

155   tu illum numquam ostendisti quanti penderes
nec tibi illest credere ausus quaest aequom patri.
quod si esset factum, haec numquam evenissent tibi.

MEN   ita res est, fateor. peccatum a me maxumest.

CHR   Menedeme, at porro recte spero et illum tibi

160   salvom adfuturum esse hic confido propediem.

MEN   utinam ita di faxint!

CHR   facient. nunc, si commodumst,
Dionysia hic sunt hodie; apud me sis volo.

MEN   non possum.

CHR   quor non? quaeso, tandem aliquantulum
tibi parce. idem absens facere te volt filius.

---

[143] exsercirent *Paumier*, resarcirent *schol. Bemb.*, exercerent *codd*.
[154] qui *codd. pl.*, ibi *Pp*

and slaves, except those who could readily earn their
keep by working on the farm, I put on the market and
sold. I advertised my house for sale on the spot, and
raised about fifteen talents.[21] I bought this piece of land,
and here I keep myself busy. I've decided, Chremes, that
I'll be doing my son less injustice so long as I make myself
miserable; it is not right for me to enjoy any pleasure
here, until he comes safe home to share it with me.

CHR I judge you to be a liberal-minded father and him a duti-
ful son, if he were treated rightly and considerately. But
you didn't know him well enough, nor he you. And how
does this arise? When there's a lack of truthfulness in the
way people live. You never showed him how much you
thought of him, and he didn't dare confide to you what a
son should to a father. If he had, this situation would
never have arisen.

MEN It's true, I admit. I was very much in the wrong.

CHR But I expect it'll turn out all right in the end, Mene-
demus, and I am sure you'll have him back here safe and
sound before too long.

MEN If only the gods would grant that!

CHR They will. Now, it's the Dionysia today,[22] and if it's con-
venient, I'd like you to join me at home.

MEN I can't.

CHR Why not? Please spare yourself just a little. Your absent
son would want that too.

---

[21] A considerable sum; for comparison the value of Knemon's estate
in Menander's *The Bad Tempered Man* is two talents.

[22] The reference is to the Rural Dionysia, a festival in honour of
Dionysus held on various days in December in the country towns of
Attica.

165 MEN non convenit, qui illum ad laborem impepulerim,
nunc me ipsum fugere.

CHR   sicin est sententia?

MEN sic.

CHR   bene vale.

MEN   et tu.

CHR   lacrumas excussit mihi
miseretque me eius. sed, ut diei tempus est,
tempust monere me hunc vicinum Phaniam
170 ad cenam ut veniat. ibo, visam si domist.
nil opus fuit monitore. iamdudum domi
praesto apud me esse aiunt. egomet convivas moror.
ibo adeo hinc intro. sed quid crepuerunt fores
hinc a me? quisnam egreditur? huc concessero.

I. ii: CLITIPHO. CHREMES.

175 CLIT nil adhuc est quod vereare, Clinia. haudquaquam etiam
cessant
et illam simul cum nuntio tibi hic adfuturam hodie scio.
proin tu sollicitudinem istam falsam quae te excruciat
mittas.

CHR quicum loquitur filius?

CLIT pater adest quem volui. adibo. pater, opportune advenis.

180 CHR quid id est?

CLIT   hunc Menedemum nostin nostrum vicinum?

---

165 impepulerim *Kauer-Lindsay,* hinc pepulerim *Bentley,* impule-
rim *codd.*   169 tempust *add. Bentley*

---

23 This momentary vacating of the stage is awkward and unusual. It
is likely that in the Greek original there was a divine prologue (omitted
by Terence) between Chremes' disappearance and reappearance. It is
also likely that Phania's house was conceived of as situated somewhere

MEN It's not proper, when I've imposed hardship on him, for me to avoid it myself.

CHR Is your mind made up?

MEN Yes.

CHR Goodbye.

MEN Goodbye. (*he picks up his hoes and goes into his house*)

CHR (*to himself*) He made me shed a tear, and I'm sorry for him. But, seeing what time of day it is, it's time to remind my neighbour Phania here to come over for dinner. I'll go and see if he's at home. (*he disappears into Phania's house and reappears almost immediately*).[23] He didn't need reminding. They say he's been over at my place for some time. I'm the one who's keeping the guests waiting. I'll go straight in. But that's my door.[24] Who's coming out? I'll stand aside here. (*he does so*)

Enter CLITIPHO *from Chremes' house.*

CLIT (*speaking back inside the house*) There's nothing to be afraid of, Clinia. They're not at all late, and I'm sure she'll be here for you today when the messenger returns. So put aside that worry which is tormenting you: it isn't warranted.

CHR (*aside*) Who's my son talking to?

CLIT (*aside*) It's my father, just who I wanted. I'll approach him. (*to Chremes*) Father, your return is well timed.

CHR What's this about?

CLIT You know our neighbour Menedemus here?

offstage in the Greek version; this passage is the only reason for placing it onstage in Terence.

[24] See *The Woman of Andros* note 40.

195

CHR   probe.

CLIT huic filium scis esse?
CHR   audivi esse in Asia.
CLIT   non est, pater;
    apud nos est.
CHR   quid ais?
CLIT   advenientem, e navi egredientem ilico
    abduxi ad cenam. nam mihi cum eo iam inde usque a
       pueritia
    fuit semper familiaritas.
CHR   voluptatem magnam nuntias.
185   quam vellem Menedemum invitatum ut nobiscum esset
       amplius
    ut hanc laetitiam necopinanti primus obicerem ei domi!
    atque etiam nunc tempus est.
CLIT   cave faxis. non opus est, pater.
CHR quapropter?
CLIT   quia enim incertumst etiam quid se faciat. modo venit,
    timet omnia, patris iram et animum amicae erga se ut sit
       suae.
190   eam misere amat. propter eam haec turba atque abitio
    evenit.
CHR   scio.
CLIT nunc servolum ad eam in urbem misit et ego nostrum
    una Syrum.
CHR quid narrat?
CLIT   quid ille? miserum se esse.
CHR   miserum? quem minus crederest?
    quid relicuist quin habeat quae quidem in homine dicun-
      tur bona?

CHR   Well.

CLIT   You know he has a son?

CHR   I've heard he's in Asia.

CLIT   He's not, father; he's at our house.

CHR   What are you saying?

CLIT   When he arrived, as soon as he disembarked from the ship, I brought him here to dinner. We've always been good friends right from boyhood.

CHR   This is splendid news. If only I'd pressed my invitation to Menedemus to join us a bit harder! I could have been the first to present him with this unexpected joyful news in my own home. And there's still time.

CLIT   Don't do it, father. It's not a good idea.

CHR   How so?

CLIT   Because it's still unclear what he's going to do with himself. He's only just arrived, he's apprehensive about everything—his father's anger and how his girl friend feels towards him. He's desperately in love with her. It was because of her that this trouble arose and he left home.

CHR   I know.

CLIT   Now he's sent his slave into town[25] to fetch her, and I've sent our Syrus along with him.

CHR   What does he have to say himself?

CLIT   Him? That he's miserable.

CHR   Miserable? Can you imagine anyone less miserable? What does he lack of the so-called blessings of human

[25] Namely, Athens.

parentis, patriam incolumem, amicos, genus, cognatos,
ditias.
195 atque haec perinde sunt ut illius animus qui ea possidet:
qui uti scit, ei bona, illi qui non utitur recte, mala.

CLIT immo ill' fuit senex importunus semper, et nunc nil magis
vereor quam ne quid in illum iratus plus satis faxit, pater.

CHR illicine? sed reprimam me; nam in metu esse hunc illist
utile.

200 CLIT quid tute tecum?

CHR dicam. utut erat, mansum tamen oportuit.
fortasse aliquanto iniquior erat praeter eius lubidinem:
pateretur. nam quem ferret si parentem non ferret
suom?
huncin erat aequom ex illius more an illum ex huius
vivere?
et quod illum insimulat durum, id non est. nam paren-
tum iniuriae
205 unius modi sunt ferme, paullo quist homo tolerabilis.
scortari crebro nolunt, nolunt crebro convivarier,
praebent exigue sumptum; atque haec sunt tamen ad vir-
tutem omnia.
verum ubi animus semel se cupiditate devinxit mala,
necessest, Clitipho, consilia consequi consimilia. hoc
210 scitumst, periclum ex aliis facere tibi quod ex usu siet.

CLIT ita credo.

CHR ego ibo hinc intro, ut videam nobis quid cenae siet.
tu, ut tempus est diei, vide sis ne quo hinc abeas longius.

---

199 illicine *Fleckeisen metro consulens,* illene *codd. Eugr.*

life—parents, a secure fatherland, friends, family, relatives, wealth? And yet what these things are depends on the attitude of the man who possesses them; they're good for those who know how to enjoy them, bad for those who don't enjoy them properly.

CLIT There's more to it than that. The old man was always bullying him, and what I most fear now is that he'll lose his temper and overreact, father.

CHR Him? (*aside*) But I must restrain myself. It's in his interest for his son to be afraid of him.

CLIT What are you saying to yourself?

CHR I'll tell you. Whatever the situation, the boy should have stayed at home. Perhaps his father was a bit too harsh for his liking. He should have put up with it. Who was he going to bear with if he couldn't bear with his own father? Should we expect the son to live by the father's rules or the father by the son's? He accuses his father of being strict, but it's not so. The restrictions parents impose are nearly all of the same kind, if they're at all reasonable people. They don't like continuous chasing after girls, they don't like continuous drinking parties, and they keep their sons short of money. But, after all, the intention of all this is to preserve their morals; once a character's in the grip of base desires, Clitipho, it's inevitable that it will continue down the same path. The smart thing is to test on others what is going to be good for yourself.

CLIT (*totally unconvinced*) I suppose so.

CHR I'll go inside and see what's for dinner. As for you, seeing what time of day it is, please make sure you don't go too far away. (*he goes into his house, leaving Clitipho onstage alone*)

ACTUS II

II. i: CLITIPHO.

CLIT quam iniqui sunt patres in omnis adulescentis iudices!
qui aequom esse censent nos a pueris ilico nasci senes,
215   neque illarum affinis esse rerum quas fert adulescentia.
ex sua lubidine moderantur nunc quaest, non quae olim
    fuit.
mihi si umquam filius erit, ne ille facili me utetur patre.
nam et cognoscendi et ignoscendi dabitur peccati locus.
non ut meus, qui mihi per alium ostendit suam senten-
    tiam.
220   perii! is mi, ubi adbibit plus paullo, sua quae narrat faci-
    nora!
nunc ait "periclum ex aliis facito tibi quod ex usu siet,"
astutus! ne ille haud scit quam mihi nunc surdo narret
    fabulam.
magis nunc me amicae dicta stimulant, "da mihi" atque
    "affer mihi."
quoi quod respondeam nil habeo, neque me quisquamst
    miserior.
225   nam hic Clinia, etsi is quoque suarum rerum satagit, at
    tamen
habet bene et pudice eductam, ignaram artis mere-
    triciae.
meast potens, procax, magnifica, sumptuosa, nobilis.
tum quod dem "recte" est. nam nil esse mihi religiost
    dicere.
hoc ego mali non pridem inveni neque etiamdum scit
    pater.

ACT TWO

CLIT (*to himself*) How unfair all fathers are in their judgment of the young! They expect us to be born into old age right from boyhood and to have no liking for what youth offers. They control us on the basis of their own desires, their present ones, not those they once had. If I ever have a son, he'll find me an easygoing father, believe me. There'll be times when misdeeds are looked into and times when they're overlooked. I won't be like my own father, who reveals what he thinks through the example of somebody else. Damn it all! The escapades of his own he recounts to me when he's had a bit too much to drink! But now he says, "Test in others what is going to be good for yourself," the cunning old blighter! He doesn't realise that with me he's telling tales to the deaf,[26] believe me. At the moment I'm more troubled by what my mistress says: "give me this" and "bring me that." I've no way of responding, and no one's more miserable than me. Clinia here, although he too has his hands full with his affair, at least has a girl brought up in purity and innocence, ignorant of the wiles of courtesans. Mine is a strong-willed, demanding, arrogant, expensive, high and mighty creature. As for giving her gifts, it's a case of "yes, of course"; I haven't the nerve to to tell her that I haven't a thing. I've only got myself into this situation recently, and my father still doesn't know about it.

---

[26] The phrase is proverbial.

II. ii: CLINIA. CLITIPHO.

230 CLIN   si mihi secundae res de amore meo essent, iamdudum
      scio

      venissent. sed vereor ne mulier me absente hic corrupta
      sit.

      concurrunt multae opiniones quae mihi animum exau-
      geant,

      occasio, locus, aetas, mater quoius sub imperiost mala,
      quoi nil iam praeter pretium dulcest.

CLIT   Clinia!

CLIN   ei misero mihi!

235 CLIT   etiam caves ne videat forte hic te a patre aliquis exiens?

CLIN   faciam. sed nescioquid profecto mi animus praesagit
      mihi.

CLIT   pergin istuc prius diiudicare quam scis quid veri siet?

CLIN   si nil mali esset, iam hic adessent.

CLIT   iam aderunt.

CLIN   quando istuc erit?

CLIT   non cogitas hinc longule esse? et nosti mores mulierum.

240   dum moliuntur, dum conantur, annus est.

CLIN   o Clitipho,
      timeo.

CLIT   respira. eccum Dromonem cum Syro una. adsunt tibi.

II. iii: SYRVS. DROMO. CLINIA. CLITIPHO.

SYR   ain tu?

DRO   sic est.

SYR   verum interea, dum sermones caedimus,
      illae sunt relictae.

CLIT   mulier tibi adest. audin, Clinia?

Enter CLINIA *from Chremes' house in an agitated mood.*

CLIN (*to himself*) If fortune looked kindly on my love affair, the
women would have been here long ago, I know. But I'm
afraid that she has been corrupted here in my absence.
There are lots of factors which combine to increase my
anxiety: the opportunity, the situation, her age, and that
wicked mother who has her under her thumb, who cares
for nothing but money.

CLIT Clinia!

CLIN Oh dear! I'm so miserable!

CLIT Be careful. Somebody may come out of my father's house
and see you here.

CLIN I will. But I foresee trouble ahead, I promise you.

CLIT Do you insist on prejudging the situation before you
know the truth?

CLIN If nothing was wrong, they'd be here by now.

CLIT They'll be here soon.

CLIN And when will that be?

CLIT Don't you realise that it's some distance from here? And
you know how women are. While they're making their
preparations and getting themselves going, a year goes
by.

CLIN Oh Clitipho! I'm afraid.

CLIT (*looking down the street*) You can breathe again. Look,
there's Dromo, and Syrus with him. They're here.

Enter SYRUS *and* DROMO *from the right.*

SYR Do you say so?

DRO It's true.

SYR In the meantime, while we've been chatting away, the
women have been left behind.

CLIT (*to Clinia*) Your girl's here. Do you hear, Clinia?

	CLIN	ego vero audio nunc demum et video et valeo, Clitipho.
245	SYR	minume mirum: adeo impeditae sunt. ancillarum gre- gem
		ducunt secum.
	CLIN	perii! unde illi sunt ancillae?
	CLIT	men rogas?
	SYR	non oportuit relictas. portant quid rerum!
	CLIN	ei mihi!
	SYR	aurum, vestem! et vesperascit et non noverunt viam.
		factum a nobis stultest. abi dum tu, Dromo, illis obviam.
250		propera. quid stas?
	CLIN	vae misero mi! quanta de spe decidi!
	CLIT	quid istuc? quae res te sollicitant autem?
	CLIN	rogitas quid siet?
		viden tu? ancillas, aurum, vestem, quam ego cum una ancillula
		hic reliqui, unde esse censes?
	CLIT	vah! nunc demum intellego.
	SYR	di boni! quid turbaest? aedes nostrae vix capient, scio.
255		quid comedent! quid ebibent! quid sene erit nostro mise- rius?
		sed video eccos quos volebam.
	CLIN	o Iuppiter, ubinamst fides?
		dum ego propter te errans patria careo demens, tu interea loci
		conlocupletasti te, Antiphila, et me in his deseruisti malis,
		propter quam in summa infamia sum et meo patri minus obsequens.
260		quoius nunc pudet me et miseret, qui harum mores can- tabat mihi,

204

CLIN (*to Clitipho*) I do indeed hear at last, and I see them, and I'm restored to health, Clitipho.

SYR (*to Dromo*) It's not at all surprising: they've so much baggage. They're bringing a flock of maids with them.

CLIN Damn it! Where did *she* get maids from?

CLIT Are you asking me?

SYR (*to Dromo*) We shouldn't have left them behind. They're carrying an awful lot.

CLIN Oh dear!

SYR (*to Dromo*) All that gold and fine clothing! Evening's coming on and they don't know the way. We've acted stupidly. You go and meet them, Dromo. Hurry up. What are you waiting for? (*Dromo exits right*)

CLIN Oh damn and blast! Such high hopes dashed!

CLIT What's the matter? What's upsetting you?

CLIN Need you ask? Can't you see? Maids, gold, fine clothing—where do you suppose she got these from, when I left her here with one little maid?

CLIT Huh! Now I understand at last.

SYR (*aside*) Good gods! What a crowd! Our house will barely hold them, I'm sure. How much they'll eat! How much they'll drink! Who will be more miserable than our old man? (*seeing Clinia and Clitipho*) But there are the people I'm looking for.

CLIN (*to himself*) By Jupiter, where has loyalty gone? While I was wandering in exile out of my mind on your account, Antiphila, you used the time to enrich yourself; you abandoned me in my troubles, when for your sake I'm in utter disgrace and have disobeyed my father. I now feel shame and regret towards him because, when he harangued me

---

245–6 minume . . . secum *Syro dant codd. pl., Dromoni* P[2]

monuisse frustra neque eum potuisse umquam ab hac
    me expellere.
quod tamen nunc faciam; tum quom gratum mi esse po-
    tuit nolui.
nemost miserior me.

SYR   hic de nostris verbis errat videlicet
quae hic sumus locuti. Clinia, aliter tuom amorem at-
    quest accipis.

265   nam et vitast eadem et animus te erga idem ac fuit,
quantum ex ipsa re coniecturam fecimus.

CLIN quid est, obsecro? nam mihi nunc nil rerum omniumst
quod malim quam me hoc falso suspicarier.

SYR   hoc primum, ut ne quid huius rerum ignores: anus
270   quaest dicta mater esse ei antehac, non fuit.
ea obiit mortem. hoc ipsa in itinere alterae
dum narrat forte audivi.

CLIT   quaenamst altera?

SYR   mane. hoc quod coepi primum enarrem, Clitipho;
post istuc veniam.

CLIT   propera.

SYR   iam primum omnium
275   ubi ventum ad aedis est, Dromo pultat fores.
anus quaedam prodit. haec ubi aperuit ostium,
continuo hic se coniecit intro. ego consequor.
anus foribus obdit pessulum, ad lanam redit.
hic sciri potuit aut nusquam alibi, Clinia,
280   quo studio vitam suam te absente exegerit,
ubi de improvisost interventum mulieri.
nam ea res dedit tum existumandi copiam
cotidianae vitae consuetudinem,
quae quoiusque ingenium ut sit declarat maxume.

on the character of such women, his warnings fell on deaf ears, and he was never able to make me give her up. I'll do it now, but I refused to when I could have earned his favour. Nobody is more miserable than me.

SYR   (*aside*) He's evidently misunderstood what we were saying just now. (*to Clinia*) Clinia, you're mistaken about your girl. Her way of life and her feelings for you are the same as they were, to judge from the facts of the situation.

CLIN   What facts, for heaven's sake? There's nothing in the world that I'd like better now than to find my suspicions unfounded.

SYR   The first point is this, to give you the whole picture. The old woman who was previously said to be her mother wasn't. And she's now dead. I happened to hear your girl telling this to the other woman on the way.

CLIT   Who's this other woman?

SYR   Wait a minute. Let me finish my story first, Clitipho. Then I'll come to that.

CLIT   Hurry up, then.

SYR   First of all, when we came to the house, Dromo knocked on the door. An old woman came out. When she opened the door, he immediately rushed in, and I followed. The old woman bolted the door and went back to her spinning. If ever there was a way to find out how she spent her life in your absence, Clinia, this was it, when we burst in unexpectedly. That gave us the means to judge how she lived her everyday life, which is what gives the clearest picture of a person's character. We found her busily

285 texentem telam studiose ipsam offendimus,
mediocriter vestitam veste lugubri,
(eius anuis causa opinor quae erat mortua)
sine auro, tum ornatam ita uti quae ornantur sibi,
nulla arte malas expolitam muliebri;

290 capillus passus, prolixus, circum caput
reiectus neglegenter. pax!

CLIN   Syre mi, obsecro
ne me in laetitiam frustra conicias.

SYR   anus
subtemen nebat. praeterea una ancillula
erat. ea texebat una, pannis obsita,

295 neglecta, immunda illuvie.

CLIT   si haec sunt, Clinia,
vera, ita uti credo, quis test fortunatior?
scin hanc quam dicit sordidatam et sordidam?
magnum hoc quoque signumst dominam esse extra
   noxiam,
quom eius tam negleguntur internuntii.

300 nam disciplinast isdem munerarier
ancillas primum, ad dominas qui affectant viam.

CLIN perge, obsecro te, et cave ne falsam gratiam
studeas inire. quid ait ubi me nominas?

SYR ubi dicimus redisse te et rogare uti

305 veniret ad te, mulier telam desinit
continuo et lacrumis opplet os totum sibi,
facile ut scires desiderio id fieri tuo.

CLIN prae gaudio, ita me di ament, ubi sim nescio.
ita timui.

---

289 nulla arte malas *Fleckeisen*, nulla mala (malam Σ) re esse *codd.*
edd. dubitanter vel desperantes

weaving at her loom, clothed modestly in mourning clothes (I presume for the sake of the old lady who had died), with no jewellery, dressed in fact like those who dress to please themselves, her cheeks untouched by women's arts, her hair loose and flowing and tossed back carelessly behind her head. Enough said!

CLIN My dear Syrus, I beg you, don't raise my hopes in vain.

SYR The old woman was spinning the yarn. Apart from her there was one young maid. She was weaving alongside, dressed in rags, unkempt, filthy.

CLIT If this is true, Clinia, as I believe it is, who is luckier than you? You heard the maid described as shabby and dirty? It is a sure sign that the mistress is beyond reproach when her go-betweens are so neglected. It's standard practice for those who seek access to the mistress to give presents to the maid first.

CLIN (to Syrus) Go on, I beg you, and mind you don't try to earn my gratitude by falsifying the truth. What did she say when you mentioned my name?

SYR When we said that you had returned and were asking her to come to you, she stopped her weaving at once and covered her whole face with tears; anyone could see that she had been longing for you.

CLIN Heaven help me, I don't know where I am for joy. I was so afraid.

---

290 passus Σ, pexus A Don ad Ph. 106

305 desinit A, deserit Σ Eugr.

307 facile ut . . . tuo *scripsi metro consulens*, ut facile . . . tuo *codd.*, ut facile (tuo *secluso*) edd.

CLIT   at ego nil esse scibam, Clinia.

310   agedum vicissim, Syre, dic quae illast altera.

SYR   adducimus tuam Bacchidem.

CLIT   hem! quid? Bacchidem?

        eho, sceleste, quo illam ducis?

SYR   quo ego illam? ad nos scilicet.

CLIT   ad patrem?

SYR   ad eum ipsum.

CLIT   o hominis impudentem audaciam!

SYR   heus,

        non fit sine periclo facinus magnum nec memorabile.

315 CLIT hoc vide: in mea vita tu tibi laudem is quaesitum, scelus?

        ubi si paullulum modo quid te fugerit, ego perierim.

        quid illo facias?

SYR   at enim—

CLIT   quid "enim"?

SYR   si sinas, dicam.

CLIN   sine.

CLIT sino.

SYR   ita res est haec nunc quasi quom—

CLIT   quas, malum, ambages mihi

        narrare occipit?

CLIN   Syre, verum hic dicit. mitte, ad rem redi.

320 SYR enimvero reticere nequeo. multimodis iniurius,

        Clitipho, es neque ferri potis es.

CLIN   audiendum herclest: tace.

SYR vis amare, vis potiri, vis quod des illi effici:

        tuom esse in potiundo periclum non vis. haud stulte sapis,

        siquidem id saperest velle te id quod non potest contingere.

CLIT Well, I knew it was nothing, Clinia. But, to change the subject, Syrus, tell me who the other woman is.

SYR We're bringing your Bacchis.

CLIT What! Really? Bacchis? Hey, you villain, where are you bringing her?

SYR Where? To our house, of course.

CLIT To my father's?

SYR Exactly.

CLIT Oh, the brazen impudence of the fellow!

SYR Listen, no great or memorable deed is ever achieved without a risk.

CLIT Look here: are you trying to win glory for yourself at the risk of my life, you villain? If you make the slightest slip, I'm the one who'll be ruined. (*to Clinia*) What would you do with him?

SYR Well—

CLIT How do you mean "Well"?

SYR If you'd let me, I'd tell you.

CLIN Let him.

CLIT All right.

SYR The present situation is rather like when—

CLIT (*impatiently*) What the hell's this rigmarole he's embarking on?

CLIN He's right, Syrus. Forget that, and come to the point.

SYR (*angrily*) Very well, I'm going to speak out. You ill-treat me in many ways, Clitipho, and I won't stand for it.

CLIN (*to Clitipho, who is visibly exasperated by this remark*) You need to listen to him, heaven knows. Say nothing.

SYR You want to love your girl, you want to possess her, you want the means to give her presents; but you don't want the risks of possessing her. This is no foolish wisdom, if it *is* wisdom to want what you can't possibly have. You have

211

325   aut haec cum illis sunt habenda aut illa cum his mittenda
           sunt.
       harum duarum condicionum nunc utram malis vide;
       etsi consilium quod cepi rectum esse et tutum scio.
       nam apud patrem tua amica tecum sine metu ut sit co-
           piast.
       tum quod illi argentum es pollicitus, eadem hac inveniam
           via,
330   quod ut efficerem orando surdas iam auris reddideras
           mihi.
       quid aliud tibi vis?

CLIT   siquidem hoc fit.
SYR   siquidem? experiundo scies.
CLIT age age, cedo istuc tuom consilium. quid id est?
SYR   assimulabimus
       tuam amicam huius esse.
CLIT   pulchre. cedo, quid hic faciet sua?
       an ea quoque dicetur huius, si una haec dedecorist pa-
           rum?
335 SYR immo ad tuam matrem abducetur.
CLIT   quid eo?
SYR   longumst, Clitipho,
       si tibi narrem quam ob rem id faciam. vera causast.
CLIT   fabulae!
       nil satis firmi video quam ob rem accipere hunc mi expe-
           diat metum.
SYR mane, habeo aliud, si istuc metuis, quod ambo confitea-
           mini
       sine periclo esse.
CLIT   huius modi, obsecro, aliquid reperi.

333 esse *edd.*, esse amicam *codd.*

212

either to take the good with the bad or do without both. So choose which of the two alternatives you prefer. I'm sure though that the plan I've conceived is the right one—and it's safe. It gives you the means to enjoy your mistress's company in your father's house without any worry. And I'll find the money you promised her in this same way—something you've deafened me with your pleas to achieve. What else do you want?

CLIT That's if it works.

SYR If? Try it and see.

CLIT Come on then, tell me this scheme of yours. What is it?

SYR We will pretend that your mistress is *his* mistress (*pointing to Clinia*).

CLIT (*sarcastically*) Brilliant! What will he do with his own? Will she be called his as well, as if one isn't disgrace enough?

SYR No, we'll take her to your mother.[27]

CLIT Why there?

SYR It would take too long, Clitipho, to explain why I'm doing this. There's a good reason.

CLIT Nonsense! I can see no convincing reason why it should be worth my while to take on the worry this would cause.

SYR Hold on, then. If you're worried about this plan, I've another one which you will both admit is risk-free.

CLIT (*eagerly*) Yes, please, find me one like that.

[27] That is, to the women's quarters, which in a Greek house were separate, where her presence would not be noticed.

---

336 vera causast *Syro continuat*Σ, *Cliniae dat* A
339 maxume *Syro dant*Σ, *Cliniae* A

SYR   maxume.

340   ibo obviam, hinc dicam ut revortantur domum.

CLIT   hem!
quid dixti?

SYR   ademptum tibi iam faxo omnem metum,
in aurem utramvis otiose ut dormias.

CLIT   quid ago nunc?

CLIN   tune? quod boni—

CLIT   Syre, dic modo
verum.

SYR   age modo. hodie sero ac nequiquam voles.

345 CLIN —datur, fruare dum licet. nam nescias—

CLIT   Syre, inquam.

SYR   perge porro, tamen istuc ago.

CLIN —eius sit potestas posthac an numquam tibi.

CLIT   verum hercle istuc est. Syre, Syre, inquam! heus, heus,
Syre!

SYR   concaluit. quid vis?

CLIT   redi, redi.

SYR   adsum. dic quid est.

350   iam hoc quoque negabis tibi placere.

CLIT   immo, Syre,
et me et meum amorem et famam permitto tibi.
tu's iudex; ne quid accusandus sis vide.

SYR   ridiculumst istuc me admonere, Clitipho,
quasi istic minor mea res agatur quam tua.

355   hic si quid nobis forte advorsi evenerit,
tibi erunt parata verba, huic homini verbera.
quapropter haec res ne utiquam neglectust mihi.

---

[28] The phrase is proverbial; compare Plautus, *Pseudolus* 123–124.

SYR   Certainly. I'll go to meet the women, and tell them to go back home.

CLIT   What! What did you say?

SYR   I'll soon have all your worry removed, so that you can sleep soundly on either ear.[28]

CLIT   (*helplessly, to Clinia*) What do I do now?

CLIN   You? When something good—

CLIT   (*to Syrus, ignoring Clinia*) Syrus, just be frank with me.

SYR   Come on now. You'll wish I'd done it later, and it'll be too late. (*he turns to go*)

CLIN   (*continuing regardless*)—is on offer, enjoy it while you can. You never know—

CLIT   (*still ignoring Clinia*) Syrus, I say!

SYR   You carry on. I'm going to do it anyway. (*he moves away*)

CLIN   (*still continuing*)—whether you will ever have the opportunity again.

CLIT   (*at last paying attention to Clinia*) That's true, for heaven's sake. (*to Syrus*) Syrus! Syrus, I say! Hey there, Syrus!

SYR   (*aside*) That's raised his temperature. (*to Clitipho*) What do you want?

CLIT   Come back, come back!

SYR   (*returning*) Here I am. Tell me what's the matter. You'll soon be saying you don't like this plan either.

CLIT   On the contrary, Syrus, I entrust myself, my love affair, and my reputation to you. You're the judge; make sure you don't become the defendant.

SYR   It's ridiculous for you to give me that sort of warning, Clitipho, as if my interests were any less at stake than yours. If anything happens to go wrong here, you face a talking-to but I face a thrashing. So I can't afford to be at all careless in this. But persuade him (*indicating Clinia*)

215

	sed istunc exora ut suam esse assimulet.
CLIN	scilicet
	facturum me esse. in eum iam res rediit locum
360	ut sit necessus.
CLIT	merito te amo, Clinia.
CLIN	verum illa ne quid titubet.
SYR	perdoctast probe.
CLIT	at hoc demiror qui tam facile potueris
	persuadere illi, quae solet quos spernere.
SYR	in tempore ad eam veni, quod rerum omniumst
365	primum. nam quendam misere offendi ibi militem
	eius noctem orantem. haec arte tractabat virum,
	ut illius animum cupidum inopia incenderet
	eademque ut esset apud te hoc quam gratissumum.
	sed heus tu, vide sis ne quid imprudens ruas.
370	patrem novisti ad has res quam sit perspicax.
	ego te autem novi quam esse soleas impotens.
	inversa verba, eversas cervices tuas,
	gemitus, screatus, tussis, risus abstine.
CLIT	laudabis.
SYR	vide sis.
CLIT	tutemet mirabere.
375 SYR	sed quam cito sunt consecutae mulieres!
CLIT	ubi sunt? quor retines?
SYR	iam nunc haec non est tua.
CLIT	scio, apud patrem. at nunc interim—
SYR	nihilo magis.
CLIT	sine.
SYR	non sinam, inquam.
CLIT	quaeso, paullisper.
SYR	veto.

to pretend that the girl's his.

CLIN   You can be sure I will. Things have reached the point where there's no choice.

CLIT   You're a true friend, Clinia.

CLIN   But make sure *she* doesn't give the game away.

SYR   She's been well schooled.

CLIT   I can't imagine how you were able to persuade her so easily, when you consider what lovers she scorns.

SYR   I caught her at just the right time, which is the most important thing. I found a soldier with her begging her desperately for a night. She was treating him with all her skill, inflaming his desires by denying them and at the same time looking to maximise your gratitude. But listen, please make sure you don't spoil everything by being careless. You know how keen-scented your father is for this sort of thing; and I know how headstrong you can be. None of your double meanings, side glances, sighs, throat clearing, coughs, laughs.

CLIT   You'll congratulate me.

SYR   Please make sure.

CLIT   Even you will be amazed.

SYR   (*looking down the street*) But how quickly the women have caught up!

CLIT   (*making to go to meet them*) Where are they? (*as Syrus restrains him*) Why are you holding me back?

SYR   She's not your girl any more.

CLIT   I know, in my father's house. But now, in the meantime—

SYR   It makes no difference.

CLIT   Let me.

SYR   I won't, I say.

CLIT   Just for a little, please.

SYR   I forbid you.

CLIT saltem salutem—

SYR   abeas si sapias.

CLIT   eo.

380   quid istic?

SYR   manebit.

CLIT   hominem felicem!

SYR   ambula.

II. iv: BACCHIS. ANTIPHILA. CLINIA. SYRUS.

BAC edepol te, mea Antiphila, laudo et fortunatam iudico,
id quom studuisti isti formae ut mores consimiles forent;
minumeque, ita me di ament, miror si te sibi quisque
     expetit.
nam mihi quale ingenium haberes fuit indicio oratio;

385 et quom egomet nunc mecum in animo vitam tuam
     considero
omniumque adeo vostrarum volgus quae ab se segre-
     gant,
et vos esse istius modi et nos non esse haud mirabilest.
nam expedit bonas esse vobis; nos, quibuscumst res, non
     sinunt.
quippe forma impulsi nostra nos amatores colunt:

390 haec ubi imminutast, illi suom animum alio conferunt.
nisi si prospectum interea aliquid est, desertae vivimus.
vobis cum uno semel ubi aetatem agere decretumst viro,
quoius mos maxume consimilis vostrum, hi se ad vos
     applicant.
hoc beneficio utrique ab utrisque vero devincimini,

395 ut numquam ulla amori vostro incidere possit calamitas.

ANT nescio alias; mequidem semper scio fecisse sedulo
ut ex illius commodo meum compararem commodum.

CLIT Just a greeting.

SYR You'll make yourself scarce, if you've any sense.

CLIT All right. What about him (*indicating Clinia*)?

SYR He can stay.

CLIT Lucky man!

SYR Off you go. (*Clitipho exits into Chremes' house*)

Enter BACCHIS *and* ANTIPHILA *from the left, accompanied by maids and baggage.*

BAC In heaven's name, my dear Antiphila, I congratulate you and I judge you fortunate, in that you have made it your concern to see that your character matches your beauty. And, as heaven is my witness, I'm not at all surprised, if everyone wants you for himself. For me your conversation has been an indication of your true nature. And now, when I ponder your life and the lives of all of you who shun common lovers, I don't wonder you're the way you are and we aren't. It's in your interest to be good, but our clients don't allow us to. Lovers cultivate us because they are attracted by our beauty; once that's faded, they take their affections elsewhere; and, unless we have meanwhile made some provision for the future, we're left to live on our own. With you, on the other hand, once you have decided to live your life with the one man whose character is most compatible with yours, they devote themselves to you. In this happy relationship each is truly bound to the other, so that no disaster can ever befall your love.

ANT I don't know about other women, but for my part I know that I've always done my best to base my own interests on his.

219

CLIN   ah!

        ergo, mea Antiphila, tu nunc sola reducem me in patriam
           facis.

        nam dum abs te absum, omnes mihi labores fuere quos
           cepi leves

400   praeterquam tui carendum quod erat.

SYR   credo.

CLIN   Syre, vix suffero.

        hocin me miserum non licere meo modo ingenium frui!

SYR   immo ut patrem tuom vidi esse habitum, diu etiam duras
           dabit.

BAC   quisnam hic adulescens est qui intuitur nos?

ANT   ah, retine me, obsecro.

BAC   amabo, quid tibist?

ANT   disperii, perii misera!

BAC   quid stupes,

405   Antiphila?

ANT   videon Cliniam an non?

BAC   quem vides?

CLIN salve, anime mi.

ANT   o mi Clinia, salve.

CLIN   ut vales?

ANT   salvom venisse gaudeo.

CLIN   teneone te,
        Antiphila, maxume animo exoptatam meo?

SYR   ite intro. nam vos iamdudum exspectat senex.

CLIN (*to himself*) Ah! My dear Antiphila, it was you and you alone who brought me back to my homeland. While I was away from you, all the hardships I endured were light compared with the fact that I had to do without you.

SYR (*aside*) I'm sure they were.

CLIN (*to Syrus*) Syrus, I can hardly bear it. Poor me, to think that I'm not permitted to enjoy her lovely nature in my own way!

SYR No. And, as I understand your father's attitude, he'll be giving you a hard part to play for some time.

BAC (*seeing Clinia*) Who's that young man who's staring at us?

ANT (*fainting*) Ah! Hold me up, I beg you.

BAC My darling, what's the matter?

ANT Oh dear, I'm overcome, quite overcome.

BAC What's come over you, Antiphila?

ANT Do I see Clinia or not?

BAC See who?

CLIN (*approaching cautiously*) Good day, my darling.

ANT Oh my Clinia! Good day.

CLIN How are you?

ANT I'm glad to see you safely back.

CLIN (*stepping forward and embracing her*) Am I really holding you, Antiphila? I've longed for you with all my heart.

SYR Come on inside. The old man has been expecting you for some time. (*they all exit into Chremes' house, leaving the stage empty*)

221

ACTUS III

III. i: CHREMES. MENEDEMUS.

410 CHR lucescit hoc iam. cesso pultare ostium
vicini, primum ex me ut sciat sibi filium
redisse? etsi adulescentem hoc nolle intellego.
verum quom videam miserum hunc tam excruciarier
eius abitu, celem tam insperatum gaudium,
415 quom illi nihil pericli ex indicio siet?
haud faciam. nam quod potero adiutabo senem.
item ut filium meum amico atque aequali suo
video inservire et socium esse in negotiis,
nos quoque senes est aequom senibus obsequi.
420 MEN aut ego profecto ingenio egregio ad miserias
natus sum aut illud falsumst quod volgo audio
dici, diem adimere aegritudinem hominibus.
nam mihi quidem cotidie augescit magis
de filio aegritudo, et quanto diutius
425 abest, magis cupio tanto et magis desidero.
CHR sed ipsum foras egressum video. ibo adloquar.
Menedeme, salve. nuntium apporto tibi
quoius maxume te fieri participem cupis.
MEN numquidnam de gnato meo audisti, Chreme?
430 CHR valet atque vivit.
MEN   ubinamst, quaeso?
CHR   apud me, domi.

---

29 This is very rare in comedy, where the convention is that the action of the play takes place within a single day. The only other possible example in Greek or Roman comedy is in Menander's *The Arbitration*, and even there the time frame is disputable.

THE SELF-TORMENTOR

ACT THREE

Night has passed.[29] CHREMES *appears at his door.*

CHR It's getting light. Why don't I knock at my neighbour's door, so as to be the first to tell him that his son has returned? I realise that this is not what the young man wants. But when I see the poor father so tortured by his son's absence, how can I keep from him this unexpected joy, when there is no danger to the son from the disclosure? I can't do it. I'll help the old man as best I can. I see my son standing by a friend and comrade and helping him in his affairs; it's only right that we old men too should stick together.

MENEDEMUS appears at his door.

MEN Either I've been born with a special predisposition to misery or it's not true what is commonly said, that time heals men's sorrows. In my case my sorrow for my son increases day by day, and the longer he's away, the more I long for him and want him back.

CHR (*seeing Menedemus*) But there he is outside his house. I'll go and speak to him. (*going up to him*) Good day, Menedemus. I'm bringing you the news which you most long to hear.

MEN You haven't heard something about my son, Chremes?

CHR He's alive and well.

MEN Where is he? Please tell me.

CHR At home, at my house.

MEN meus gnatus?
CHR   sic est.
MEN   venit.
CHR   certe.
MEN   Clinia
     meus venit?
CHR   dixi.
MEN   eamus. duc me ad eum, obsecro.
CHR non volt te scire se redisse etiam et tuom
     conspectum fugitat. propter peccatum hoc timet,
435   ne tua duritia antiqua illa etiam adaucta sit.
MEN non tu illi dixisti ut essem?
CHR   non.
MEN   quam ob rem, Chreme?
CHR quia pessume istuc in te atque in illum consulis,
     si te tam leni et victo esse animo ostenderis.
MEN non possum. satis iam satis pater durus fui.
CHR   ah!
440   vehemens in utramque partem, Menedeme, es nimis,
     aut largitate nimia aut parsimonia.
     in eandem fraudem ex hac re atque ex illa incides.
     primum olim potius quam paterere filium
     commetare ad mulierculam, quae paullulo
445   tum erat contenta quoique erant grata omnia,
     proterruisti hinc. ea coacta ingratiis
     postilla coepit victum volgo quaerere.
     nunc quom sine magno intertrimento non potest
     haberi, quidvis dare cupis. nam ut tu scias
450   quam ea nunc instructa pulchre ad perniciem siet,
     primum iam ancillas secum adduxit plus decem

MEN My son?

CHR Yes.

MEN He's come back?

CHR For sure.

MEN My son Clinia has come back?

CHR That's what I said.

MEN Let's go. Take me to him, I beseech you.

CHR He doesn't want you to know yet that he's back. He's keeping out of your sight. He's afraid that your old severity towards him because of his misbehaviour may now have increased.

MEN Didn't you tell him how I feel?

CHR No.

MEN Why not, Chremes?

CHR Because you are acting very much against your own interests and his, if you let him see that you've given in and are taking a lenient view.

MEN I can't do it. I've had enough of being a severe father, quite enough.

CHR Ah! You go to extremes in one direction or the other, Menedemus, either too much generosity or too much meanness. You'll fall into the same pitfall one way or the other. Previously, instead of allowing your son to visit a girl who was then content with very little and took everything as a favour, you frightened him away from home. After that she was compelled against her will to make a living on the streets. Now, when she can't be had without a great deal of expense, you're willing to give him whatever he wants. If you want to know quite how well equipped she is to ruin you, she's brought more than ten

oneratas veste atque auro. satrapes si siet
amator, numquam sufferre eius sumptus queat,
nedum tu possis.

MEN   estne ea intus?

CHR   sit rogas?

455   sensi. nam unam ei cenam atque eius comitibus
dedi. quod si iterum mihi sit danda, actum siet.
nam, ut alia omittam, pytissando modo mihi
quid vini absumpsit "sic hoc" dicens; "asperum,
pater, hoc est. aliud lenius sodes vide."
460   relevi dolia omnia, omnis serias.
omnis sollicitos habui—atque haec una nox.
quid te futurum censes quem assidue exedent?
sic me di amabunt ut me tuarum miseritumst,
Menedeme, fortunarum.

MEN   faciat quidlubet,
465   sumat, consumat, perdat. decretumst pati
dum illum modo habeam mecum.

CHR   si certumst tibi
sic facere, illud permagni referre arbitror
ut ne scientem sentiat te id sibi dare.

MEN quid faciam?

CHR   quidvis potius quam quod cogitas.
470   per alium quemvis ut des, falli te sinas
techinis per servolum; etsi subsensi id quoque,
illos ibi esse, id agere inter se clanculum.
Syrus cum illo vostro consusurrant, conferunt
consilia ad adulescentes; et tibi perdere
475   talentum hoc pacto satius est quam illo minam.

---

[30] Chremes is under the impression that it is Bacchis who is Clinia's
girl.

maids with her, all loaded with fine clothing and jewels.[30]
If she had a satrap[31] for a lover, he'd never be able to sustain her extravagance, let alone you.

MEN (*unimpressed by this lecture*) Is she inside?

CHR Inside? I'll say she is! I've provided one dinner for her and her retinue; if I had to do it again, I'd be bankrupt. To say nothing of the rest, how much wine she wasted just by spitting it out! "This is so-so, this is rough, father," she says. "See if you've a smoother one, if you don't mind." I opened all my casks and jars;[32] I had all my slaves running around. And this was just one night! What do you think will become of you when they're eating you out of house and home on a regular basis? As heaven is my witness, Menedemus, I pity your plight.

MEN Let him do what he likes, let him spend, squander, waste. I'm determined to put up with it so long as I have him with me.

CHR If that's what you've decided to do, I consider it of the utmost importance that he shouldn't realise that you're giving him the money knowingly.

MEN What shall I do?

CHR Anything rather than what you are proposing. Contrive to give it through somebody else; let yourself be deceived by your slave's wiles. I've an inkling, though, that they're already at it, that they're plotting secretly among themselves. Syrus is whispering with that slave of yours, and they're reporting their plans to the young men. It's better for you to lose a talent this way than a mina the other.[33]

---

[31] Satraps were provincial governors in the Persian empire; their wealth was proverbial.   [32] Both the Latin terms refer to earthenware vessels.   [33] There were 60 minas to the talent.

non nunc pecunia agitur sed illud quo modo
minumo periclo id demus adulescentulo.
nam si semel tuom animum ille intellexerit,
prius proditurum te tuam vitam et prius
480   pecuniam omnem quam abs te amittas filium, hui,
quantam fenestram ad nequitiem patefeceris,
tibi autem porro ut non sit suave vivere!
nam deteriores omnes sumus licentia.
quod quoique quomque inciderit in mentem volet,
485   neque id putabit pravom an rectum sit; petet.
tu rem perire et ipsum non poteris pati.
dare denegaris, ibit ad illud ilico
qui maxume apud te se valere sentiet:
abiturum se abs te esse ilico minitabitur.
490 MEN videre vera atque ita uti res est dicere.
      CHR somnum hercle ego hac nocte oculis non vidi meis,
dum id quaero tibi qui filium restituerem.
      MEN cedo dextram. porro te idem oro ut facias, Chreme.
      CHR paratus sum.
      MEN   scin quid nunc facere te volo?
495 CHR dic.
      MEN   quod sensisti illos me incipere fallere,
id uti maturent facere. cupio illi dare
quod volt, cupio ipsum iam videre.
      CHR   operam dabo.
paullum negoti mi obstat. Simus et Crito
vicini nostri hic ambigunt de finibus;
500   me cepere arbitrum. ibo ac dicam, ut dixeram
operam daturum me, hodie non posse eis dare.
continuo hic adero.

---

[34] It was normal practice in Athenian law for disputes between citi-

It's not now a matter of the money, but of how we're going to give it to the lad at the least risk. If once he realises your feelings—that you would rather sacrifice your life and all your money than lose your son—wow, what a window you'll have opened up for debauchery, and you won't get much pleasure from life in the future! We're all worse when there are no restraints. Everyone wants whatever comes into his head; he doesn't weigh whether it is good or bad, he goes after it. You won't be able to endure the loss of your money *and* your son. But if you refuse to give him it, he'll immediately go where he knows he has you at his mercy: he'll threaten to leave home on the spot.

MEN I suppose you're right; that's the way it is.

CHR God knows I didn't sleep a wink last night, wondering how I could restore your son to you.

MEN Give me your hand. I beg you to continue that way, Chremes.

CHR I'm ready and willing.

MEN Do you know what I'd like you to do now?

CHR Tell me.

MEN You observed that they were planning to deceive me: see that they hurry up and do it. I'm eager to give him what he wants, I'm eager to set eyes on him.

CHR I'll see to it. I've a little business to do first. Our neighbours Simus and Crito here are in dispute over their boundaries, and they've named me as their arbitrator.[34] I'll go and tell them that I can't attend to their affairs today as I promised. I'll be back straightaway.

zens to be settled by an arbitrator. Any private citzen could fulfil this role: the only necessary qualification was that he was acceptable to both parties.

MEN		ita quaeso. di vostram fidem!

MEN   ita quaeso. di vostram fidem!
ita comparatam esse hominum naturam omnium
aliena ut melius videant et diiudicent
505   quam sua! an eo fit quia in re nostra aut gaudio
sumus praepediti nimio aut aegrititudine?
hic mihi nunc quanto plus sapit quam egomet mihi!
CHR   dissolvi me otiosus operam ut tibi darem.
Syrus est prendendus atque adhortandus mihi.
510   a me nescioquis exit. concede hinc domum,
ne nos inter nos congruere sentiant.

III. ii: SYRUS. CHREMES.

SYR   hac illac circumcursa. inveniendumst tamen
argentum, intendenda in senem fallacia.
CHR   num me fefellit hosce id struere? videlicet
515   ill' Cliniai servos tardiusculust.
idcirco huic nostro traditast provincia.
SYR   quis hic loquitur? perii! numnam haec audivit?
CHR   Syre.
SYR   hem!
CHR   quid tu istic?
SYR   recte equidem. sed te miror, Chreme,
tam mane, qui heri tantum biberis.
CHR   nil nimis.

509–11 *post 487 habent codd., transtulit Bentley*

---

[35] This is the money for Clitipho to give to Bacchis. See lines 329–330.

[36] Syrus means Chremes, though Chremes will imagine that he is referring to Menedemus.

MEN Please do. (*Chremes exits left*) Heaven help us, to think
that human nature is so constituted that we can see the
solutions to other people's problems better than we can
our own! Is it because in our own affairs our judgment is
clouded by excesses of joy or sorrow? How much wiser
this man is on my behalf than I am on my own! (*Chremes
returns left*)

CHR I've excused myself, and now I'm free to attend to your
affairs. I must get hold of Syrus and urge him on. (*there is
a noise at his door*) Somebody's coming out of my house.
You go back home; they mustn't notice that we are put-
ting our heads together. (*Menedemus exits into his house*)

Enter SYRUS *from Chremes' house.*

SYR (*to himself*) Run here, run there. Still, we've got to find
the money.[35] We need to set a trap for the old man.[36]

CHR (*aside*) Didn't I say that they were devising a plan? Evi-
dently this slave of Clinia's is a bit slow. That's why the job
has been handed over to ours.

SYR Who's that speaking? (*seeing Chremes*) Damn it! Did he
hear what I said?

CHR Syrus!

SYR What!

CHR What are you up to?

SYR I'm all right. But I'm surprised to see you up so early,
Chremes, when you drank so much last night.

CHR Nothing in excess.[37]

[37] The old Greek proverb inscribed over the portal of Apollo's
temple at Delphi.

520	SYR	"nil" narras? visa verost, quod dici solet,
		aquilae senectus.
	CHR	heia!
	SYR	mulier commoda et
		faceta haec meretrix.
	CHR	sane.
	SYR	idem visast tibi?
		et quidem hercle forma luculenta.
	CHR	sic satis.
	SYR	ita non ut olim, sed uti nunc, sane bona,
525		minumeque miror Clinia hanc si deperit.
		sed habet patrem quendam avidum, miserum atque ari-
		dum
		vicinum hunc (nostin?). at quasi is non ditiis
		abundet, gnatus eius profugit inopia.
		scis esse factum ut dico?
	CHR	quid ego ni sciam?
530		hominem pistrino dignum!
	SYR	quem?
	CHR	istum servolum
		dico adulescentis—
	SYR	Syre, tibi timui male!
	CHR	—qui passus est id fieri.
	SYR	quid faceret?
	CHR	rogas?
		aliquid reperiret, fingeret fallacias
		unde esset adulescenti amicae quod daret,
535		atque hunc difficilem invitum servaret senem.

522 SYR. idem visast tibi? *A*, CHR. idem visast mihi Σ *(nisi D¹G¹ tibi)*

SYR Did you say "nothing"? It was like the old age of the eagle, as the saying goes.[38]

CHR Come off it!

SYR That courtesan is an attractive and witty woman.

CHR Indeed.

SYR Did you think so too? And, by god, a lovely figure.

CHR Good enough.

SYR Not like they used to be, but by today's standards pretty good, and I'm not at all surprised if Clinia has fallen for her. But he has a miserly, miserable, tight-fisted father, our neighbour here—you know him? And, as if he wasn't rolling in wealth, his son ran away because he hadn't a penny. You know this is what happened, don't you?

CHR Of course I know. The fellow should be sent to the mill.[39]

SYR (*alarmed*) Who?

CHR I mean the young man's slave boy—

SYR (*aside, with a sigh of relief*) Syrus, that gave you a nasty fright!

CHR —who allowed this to happen.

SYR What was he supposed to do?

CHR You ask? Invent something, devise a trick to get money for the young man to give to his mistress, and to save the bad-tempered old man in spite of himself.

[38] This is a reference to the old Greek proverb "The old age of the eagle is as the youth of the lark." The nearest English equivalent is "There's life in the old dog yet."

[39] See *The Woman of Andros* note 17.

SYR garris.

CHR   haec facta ab illo oportebant, Syre.

SYR eho, quaeso, laudas qui eros fallunt?

CHR   in loco
ego vero laudo.

SYR   recte sane.

CHR   quippe qui
magnarum saepe id remedium aegritudinumst.

540   iam huic mansisset unicus gnatus domi.

SYR iocone an serio ille haec dicat nescio,
nisi mihi quidem addit animum quo lubeat magis.

CHR et nunc quid exspectat, Syre? an dum hic denuo
abeat, quom tolerare illius sumptus non queat?

545   nonne ad senem aliquam fabricam fingit?

SYR   stolidus est.

CHR at te adiutare oportet adulescentuli
causa.

SYR   facile equidem facere possum si iubes.
etenim quo pacto id fieri soleat calleo.

CHR tanto hercle melior.

SYR   non est mentiri meum.

550 CHR fac ergo.

SYR   at heus tu, facito dum eadem haec memineris,
si quid huius simile forte aliquando evenerit,
ut sunt humana, tuos ut faciat filius.

CHR non usus veniet, spero.

SYR   spero hercle ego quoque,
neque eo nunc dico quo quicquam illum senserim,

555   sed si quid, ne quid. quae sit eius aetas vides;
et ne ego te, si usus veniat, magnifice, Chreme,
tractare possim.

SYR   You're joking.

CHR   This is what he should have done, Syrus.

SYR   Hey, tell me, do you approve of slaves who deceive their masters?

CHR   In the right circumstances, yes, I do.

SYR   And rightly so.

CHR   Because this is often the remedy for serious problems. In his case (*pointing to Menedemus' house*) his only son would have stayed at home.

SYR   (*aside*) I don't know whether he's saying this seriously or in jest, but I'll take it as an invitation to enjoy myself.

CHR   And now what's he waiting for, Syrus? For the son to go away a second time because he can't support the expense? Isn't he inventing some plot to use against the old man?

SYR   He's too slow-witted.

CHR   You should help him out, for the young lad's sake.

SYR   I can do that easily if you give me the word. I'm pretty experienced and I know how these things are done.

CHR   (*ironically*) So much the better, by god.

SYR   (*feigning hurt*) I'm not used to telling lies.

CHR   Get on with it then.

SYR   But listen, make sure you remember this conversation, if by chance, human nature being what it is, it should so happen some day that your son is in a similar situation.

CHR   The need won't arise, I hope.

SYR   I hope so too, god knows, and I don't raise the matter now because I've noticed him up to anything. But if he does, don't. You see how old he is; and, believe me, Chremes, I could handle you splendidly if the need arose.

CHR   de istoc, quom usus venerit,
       videbimus quid opus sit. nunc istuc age.

SYR   numquam commodius umquam erum audivi loqui,
560   nec quom male facere crederem mi impunius
       licere. quisnam a nobis egreditur foras?

         III. iii: CHREMES. CLITIPHO. SYRUS.

CHR   quid istuc, quaeso? qui istic mos est, Clitipho? itane fieri
         oportet?

CLIT   quid ego feci?

CHR   vidin ego te modo manum in sinum huic meretrici
       inserere?

SYR   acta haec res est! perii!

CLIT   mene?

CHR   hisce oculis: ne nega.
565   facis adeo indigne iniuriam illi qui non abstineas manum.
       nam istaec quidem contumeliast,
       hominem amicum recipere ad te atque eius amicam su-
         bigitare.
       vel here in vino quam immodestus fuisti—

SYR   factum.

CHR   —quam molestus!
       ut equidem, ita me di ament, metui quid futurum de-
         nique esset!
570   novi ego amantium animum: advortant graviter quae non
         censeas.

CLIT   at mihi fides apud hunc est nil me istius facturum, pater.

CHR   esto. at certe concedas aliquo ab ore eorum aliquantis-
         per.
       multa fert lubido: ea facere prohibet tua praesentia.

CHR We'll see what to do about that when the need arises. For now, concentrate on the matter in hand. (*he exits into his house*)

SYR I've never heard the master say anything so welcome, and there's never been a time when I believed I could misbehave with less fear of punishment. (*there is a noise at the door*) Who's this coming out of our house? (*he stands aside*)

Enter CHREMES *from his house, dragging a reluctant* CLITIPHO.

CHR Tell me, what are you up to? What sort of behaviour's this, Clitipho? Is this the proper way to act?

CLIT What have I done?

CHR Didn't I see you just now putting your hand inside that woman's bosom?

SYR (*aside*) It's all over! I'm lost!

CLIT Me?

CHR With my own eyes, so don't deny it. You're doing Clinia a terrible injustice in not keeping your hands to yourself. It really is outrageous to invite a friend to your house and then fondle his mistress. For instance, yesterday when you were drunk how shameless you were—

SYR (*aside*) It's true.

CHR —and how disagreeable. Heaven knows how afraid I was of what would happen in the end! I understand how lovers feel. They get very upset at things you wouldn't imagine.

CLIT But he trusts me not to do that sort of thing, father.

CHR All right. But at least take yourself off somewhere out of their sight for a while. Lovers have their desires, but they can't indulge themselves with you around. I'm talking

237

ego de me facio coniecturam: nemost meorum amico-
     rum hodie
575   apud quem expromere omnia mea occulta, Clitipho,
     audeam.
apud alium prohibet dignitas, apud alium ipsius facti
     pudet,
ne ineptus, ne protervus videar. quod illum facere cre-
     dito.
sed nostrumst intellegere utquomque atque ubiquom-
     que opus sit obsequi.

SYR quid istic narrat?

CLIT   perii!

SYR   Clitipho, haec ego praecipio tibi?

580 hominis frugi et temperantis functu's officium?

CLIT   tace, sodes.

SYR recte sane.

CLIT   Syre, pudet me.

SYR   credo, neque id iniuria. quin
     mihi molestumst.

CLIT   perdis hercle.

SYR   verum dico quod videtur.

CLIT nonne accedam ad illos?

CHR   eho, quaeso, una accedundi viast?

SYR actumst! hic prius se indicarit quam ego argentum effe-
     cero.

585 Chreme, vin tu homini stulto mi auscultare?

CHR   quid faciam?

SYR   iube hunc
     abire hinc aliquo.

CLIT   quo ego hinc abeam?

SYR   quo lubet. da illis locum.
     abi deambulatum.

from my own experience. There's none of my friends to whom I would venture to reveal all my secrets, Clitipho. In one case it's my social standing which prevents it, in another it's shame at the deed: I don't want to seem vulgar or brash. You should realise that your friend feels the same. It's up to us to perceive when and where we should leave him alone.

SYR (*coming up to Clitipho*) What's he talking about?

CLIT (*realising that Syrus has overheard the conversation*) Damn it!

SYR Clitipho, were these my instructions? Is this how a respectable well-behaved person should act?

CLIT Stop it, please!

SYR (*ironically*) A fine thing to suggest!

CLIT Syrus, I'm ashamed.

SYR I'm sure you are, and so you should be. I find it quite annoying.

CLIT For god's sake, you're destroying me.

SYR I'm saying what I take to be the truth.

CLIT Can't I go near to them?

CHR Hey, tell me, have you only one way of getting near?

SYR (*aside*) It's all over. He'll have given himself away before I get the money. (*to Chremes*) Chremes, will you take some advice from a foolish man like me?

CHR What advice?

SYR Tell him to go away somewhere.

CLIT Go where?

SYR Where you like. Give them some space to breathe. Go for a stroll.

---

581 Syre, pudet me *Clitiphoni dat* A, *Chremeti* Σ

CLIT   deambulatum? quo?

SYR   vah, quasi desit locus!
abi sane istac, istorsum, quovis.

CHR   recte dicit, censeo.

CLIT di te eradicent qui me hinc extrudis, Syre!

590 SYR tu pol tibi istas posthac comprimito manus.

censen vero? quid illum porro credas facturum, Chreme,
nisi eum, quantum tibi opis di dant, servas, castigas, mo-
     nes?

CHR ego istuc curabo.

SYR   atqui nunc, ere, tibi istic asservandus est.

CHR fiet.

SYR   si sapias. nam mihi iam minus minusque obtemperat.

595 CHR quid tu? ecquid de illo quod dudum tecum egi egisti,
     Syre, aut
repperisti tibi quod placeat an non?

SYR   de fallacia
dicis? est. inveni nuper quandam.

CHR   frugi's. cedo, quid est?

SYR dicam, verum ut aliud ex alio incidit.

CHR   quidnam, Syre?

SYR pessuma haec est meretrix.

CHR   ita videtur.

SYR   immo, si scias.

600 vah! vide quod inceptet facinus. fuit quaedam anus Co-
     rinthia
hic. huic drachumarum haec argenti mille dederat mu-
     tuom.

CHR quid tum?

CLIT Go for a stroll? Where?

SYR Huh! As if there was a shortage of places! Go this way, that way, any way.

CHR He's right. It's a good idea.

CLIT May the gods utterly destroy you, Syrus, for pushing me out of here. (*he goes off unwillingly to the left*)

SYR (*shouting after him*) You keep your hands to yourself in future, for heaven's sake. (*to Chremes*) Do you really think it's a good idea? What do you suppose will become of him, Chremes, if you don't watch him, rebuke him, admonish him with all the power the gods give you?

CHR I'll see to it.

SYR But you need to watch him now, master.

CHR It will be done.

SYR It will, if you're wise. He takes less and less notice of me these days.

CHR But what about you? Have you done anything about that business I was discussing with you just now, Syrus? Have you found one that appeals to you or not?

SYR You're talking about a trick? I do have one. I've just thought of it.

CHR Good for you! Tell me, what is it?

SYR I'll tell you, but first things first.

CHR What do you mean, Syrus?

SYR That courtesan is a wicked woman.

CHR So it seems.

SYR If only you knew! Huh! Just look what she's up to now! There was an old woman here from Corinth, to whom she'd given a thousand silver drachmas as a loan.

CHR What of it?

241

SYR   ea mortuast. reliquit filiam adulescentulam.
      ea relicta huic arrabonist pro illo argento.

CHR   intellego.

SYR   hanc secum huc adduxit, ea quaest nunc apud uxorem
      tuam.

605 CHR   quid tum?

SYR   Cliniam orat sibi uti nunc det. illam illi tamen
      post daturam. mille nummum poscit.

CHR   et poscit quidem?

SYR   hui!
      dubium id est? ego sic putavi.

CHR   quid nunc facere cogitas?

SYR   egon? ad Menedemum ibo. dicam hanc esse captam ex
      Caria
      ditem et nobilem: si redimat magnum inesse in ea lu-
      crum.

610 CHR   erras.

SYR   quid ita?

CHR   pro Menedemo nunc tibi ego respondeo:
      "non emo." quid ages?

SYR   optata loquere.

CHR   qui?

SYR   non est opus.

---

[607] ego sic putavi *Syro continuat* A, *Chremeti dat* Σ
[611] non est opus *Syro dat* A, *Chremeti* Σ

---

[40] Under the laws of Solon it was forbidden at Athens to make loans on the security of a person, but the law may not have applied to foreigners or necessarily have been observed among the lower classes.

SYR   The old woman died, leaving a young daughter. This girl was left to the courtesan as a security for the money.⁴⁰

CHR   I see.

SYR   Bacchis brought the girl here along with her. She's the one who's now staying with your wife.

CHR   What of it?

SYR   She's asking Clinia to pay the money now. She says she'll give him the girl after that. She's demanding a thousand drachmas.⁴¹

CHR   Demanding? Really?

SYR   Wow! Do you doubt it? It's the impression I got.

CHR   What are you proposing to do now?

SYR   Me? I'll go to Menedemus, and tell him that she's a rich well-born captive from Caria;⁴² if he purchases her, he'll make a good profit.

CHR   You're making a mistake.

SYR   How so?

CHR   I'll give you Menedemus' response: "I'm not buying her." What will you do?

SYR   Just what I wanted to hear.

CHR   How?

SYR   It's not necessary.

---

⁴¹ There were 100 drachmas to the mina, so that this sum is equivalent to ten minas. For comparison Thais in *The Eunuch* extracts gifts from Phaedria to the vaue of twenty minas (line 169), and a young man in Plautus' *Epidicus* pays forty minas to buy his girlfriend from a pimp (lines 51–52).

⁴² Caria is in the southwest corner of Asia Minor. The girl might be supposed to have been kidnapped from its coastline by pirates or captured in war during the campaigns that followed the death of Alexander the Great.

CHR non opus est?
SYR   non hercle vero.
CHR   qui istuc? miror.
SYR   iam scies.
CHR mane, mane. quid est quod tam a nobis graviter crepue-
     runt fores?

ACTUS IV

IV. i: SOSTRATA. CHREMES. NUTRIX. SYRUS.

SOS nisi me animus fallit, hic profectost anulus quem ego sus-
     picor,
615 is quicum expositast gnata.
CHR   quid volt sibi, Syre, haec oratio?
SOS quid est? isne tibi videtur?
NUT   dixi equidem, ubi mi ostendisti, ilico
     eum esse.
SOS   at tu satis contemplata modo sis, mea nutrix.
NUT   satis.
SOS abi nunciam intro atque illa si iam laverit mihi nuntia.
     hic ego virum interea opperibor.
SYR   te volt: videas quid velit.
620 nescioquid tristis est: non temerest. timeo quid sit.
CHR   quid siet?
     ne ista hercle magno iam conatu magnas nugas dixerit.

612 *sic A, personas invertit* Σ
613 *Chremeti dat G, Syro continuant cett.*

244

CHR Not necessary?

SYR No, for god's sake.

CHR How do you mean? I'm puzzled.

SYR You'll find out presently.[43] (*he makes to leave*)

CHR Wait, wait! What's all that noise at our door?

ACT FOUR

Enter SOSTRATA *and an old* NURSE *from Chremes' house.*

SOS Unless I'm mistaken, this is fact the ring that I think it is, the one with which my daughter was exposed.

CHR (*aside to Syrus*) What does she mean by that remark, Syrus?

SOS Well? Do you think it's the one?

NUR I said it was at once, as soon as you showed it to me.

SOS Make sure you've examined it closely enough, nurse dear.

NUR I have.

SOS Go inside then and, if she's finished her bath, come and tell me.[44] Meanwhile I'll wait here for my husband. (*the nurse goes back into the house*)

SYR (*to Chremes*) She wants you: find out why. She's rather distressed and there must be a reason. I dread to think what it is.

CHR (*to Syrus*) What it is? Believe me, after a mighty effort, god knows she'll produce some mighty nonsense.

[43] Syrus is bluffing in the manner of Plautine tricky slaves who claim to have plans up their sleeves when they haven't.

[44] The nurse never reports back; this is simply a device to remove her from the stage.

SOS   ehem, mi vir!

CHR   ehem, mea uxor!

SOS   te ipsum quaero.

CHR   loquere quid velis.

SOS   primum hoc te oro, ne quid credas me advorsum edic-
       tum tuom
  facere esse ausam.

CHR   vin me istuc tibi, etsi incredibilest, credere?

625   credo.

SYR   nescioquid peccati portat haec purgatio.

SOS   meministin me gravidam et mihi te maxumo opere edi-
       cere,
  si puellam parerem, nolle tolli?

CHR   scio quid feceris:
  sustulisti.

SYR   sic est factum: domina ego, erus damno auctus est.

SOS   minume. sed erat hic Corinthia anus haud impura. ei
       dedi

630   exponendam.

CHR   o Iuppiter, tantam esse in animo inscitiam!

SOS   perii! quid ego feci?

CHR   rogitas?

SOS   si peccavi, mi Chreme,
  insciens feci.

CHR   id equidem ego, si tu neges, certo scio,
  te inscientem atque imprudentem dicere ac facere om-
       nia.

---

45 The exposure of unwanted babies is common in New Comedy and no doubt reflects real-life practice. Female babies were particularly at risk for the economic reason that they would need to be provided

SOS (*seeing Chremes*) Oh hello, my dear husband!

CHR (*to Sostrata*) Oh hello, my dear wife!

SOS I was looking for you.

CHR Say what you want.

SOS (*defensively*) First I beg you not to believe that I have ventured to do anything against your instructions.

CHR You want me to believe that, when it's unbelievable? (*with a shrug*) I believe it.

SYR (*aside*) This self-justification means that she's been up to some mischief.

SOS Do you remember I was pregnant and you gave strict instructions that, if it was a girl, you didn't want it to be raised?

CHR I know what you did: you raised it.[45]

SYR (*aside*) That's what she's done, which means another mistress for me and another expense for the master.

SOS No, I didn't. But there was an old Corinthian woman here, a respectable woman. I gave the child to her to expose.

CHR By Jupiter, to think that anyone could be so naive!

SOS Damn it! What have I done?

CHR Need you ask?

SOS If I've done wrong, my dear Chremes, I did so unwittingly.

CHR I know perfectly well, even if you deny it, that you do and say everything unwittingly—and unthinkingly. Anyone

with a dowry when they married. If the father was unwilling to raise the child, the mother might, as here and often elsewhere in drama, give the baby to someone else to expose, in the hope that it might in fact be spared and one day be recognised through a ring or other token which was given with it.

247

635	tot peccata in hac re ostendis. nam iam primum, si meum imperium exsequi voluisses, interemptam oportuit, non simulare mortem verbis, re ipsa spem vitae dare. at id omitto. misericordia, animus maternus: sino. quam bene vero abs te prospectumst quod voluisti cogi- ta.
640	nempe anui illi prodita abs te filiast planissume, per te vel uti quaestum faceret vel uti veniret palam. credo, id cogitasti: "quidvis satis est dum vivat modo." quid cum illis agas qui neque ius neque bonum atque ae- quom sciunt? melius peius, prosit obsit, nil vident nisi quod lubet.
sos	mi Chreme, peccavi, fateor: vincor. nunc hoc te obsecro,
645	quando tuos est animus, mi vir, natura ignoscentior, ut meae stultitiae in iustitia tua sit aliquid praesidi.
CHR	scilicet equidem istuc factum ignoscam. verum, Sostrata, male docet te mea facilitas multa. sed istuc quidquid est qua hoc occeptumst causa loquere.
sos	ut stultae et misere omnes sumus
650	religiosae, quom exponendam do illi, de digito anulum detraho et eum dico ut una cum puella exponeret; si moreretur, ne expers partis esset de nostris bonis.
CHR	istuc recte. conservasti te atque illam.
sos	is hic est anulus.
CHR	unde habes?

645 *sic Fleckeisen,* quanto tuos est animus natu gravior ignoscentior *codd. Eugr. Serv. ad Aen. 9.289,* quanto tu me es annis gravior tanto es ignoscentior *Bentley,* quanto tu me es annis gravior eo sis ignoscentior *Dziatzko*

can see that you acted wrongly here on several counts. First of all, if you'd really intended to carry out my orders, the girl should have been done away with; you shouldn't have pretended she was dead while in fact giving her the hope of life. But I pass that by. It was pity, maternal feeling: I accept that. But consider how little thought you took for the consequences of your plan. The fact is, you put your daughter totally at the mercy of the old woman, so that, as far as you were concerned, she could earn her living on the streets or be sold on the open market. I suppose you thought "Anything will do, so long as she lives." What can you do with people who have no sense of justice or of what is right and proper? Better or worse, helpful or harmful, they can see nothing but what they want to see.

SOS   My dear Chremes, I've done wrong, I admit it, I submit. But now I beseech you, my dear husband, as you are inclined to be forgiving by nature, let my folly find some refuge in your sense of justice.

CHR   I suppose I'll forgive you what you have done, Sostrata, though my generosity in many ways sends you the wrong message. But, whatever it is, tell me the reason why you brought up the subject.

SOS   Foolish and desperately superstitious as we mothers all are, when I gave the woman the girl to expose, I took a ring from my finger and told her to expose it with her, so that, if she died, she would at least have some share in our possessions.

CHR   Fair enough. That was a safeguard both for yourself and for her.

SOS   (*holding up the ring*) This is the ring.

CHR   Where did you get it?

SOS   quam Bacchis secum adduxit adulescentulam—
SYR   hem!
655 CHR quid illa narrat?
SOS   ea lavatum dum it, servandum mihi dedit.
animum non advorti primum. sed postquam aspexi, ilico
cognovi, ad te exsilui.
CHR   quid nunc suspicare aut invenis
de illa?
SOS   nescio nisi ex ipsa quaeras unde hunc habuerit,
si potis est reperiri.
SYR   interii! plus spei video quam volo.
660 nostrast, si itast.
CHR   vivitne illa quoi tu dederas?
SOS   nescio.
CHR quid renuntiavit olim?
SOS   fecisse id quod iusseram.
CHR nomen mulieris cedo quid sit, ut quaeratur.
SOS   Philterae.
SYR ipsast. mirum ni illa salvast et ego perii.
CHR   Sostrata,
sequere me intro hac.
SOS   ut praeter spem evenit! quam timui male
665 ne nunc animo ita esses duro ut olim in tollendo,
Chreme!
CHR non licet hominem esse saepe ita ut volt, si res non sinit.
nunc ita tempus est mi ut cupiam filiam, olim nil minus.

---

655 quid illa narrat *Chremeti dant codd. pl., Syro continuant D²GF¹*

46 The discovery that Antiphila is Chremes' daughter will mean that Clinia can marry her; however, the pretence that Bacchis is Clinia's mis-

SOS The young lass whom Bacchis brought with her—

SYR (*aside*) What!

CHR (*aside*) What is she saying?

SOS She gave it to me to look after while she went for her bath. I didn't take any notice at first, but when I looked at it I recognised it instantly and rushed out to find you.

CHR So now what do you make of it? What have you discovered about the girl?

SOS I don't know, though you could ask her where she got it, if that can be established.

SYR (*aside*) That's me ruined! This is too hopeful for my liking.[46] She's one of the family, if this is true.

CHR Is the woman you gave her to still alive ?

SOS I don't know.

CHR What did she report to you at the time?

SOS That she'd done what I told her.

CHR Tell me the woman's name, so that we can make enquiries.

SOS Philtera.

SYR (*aside*) It's her. It looks as if the girl's saved and I'm lost.

CHR Sostrata, follow me inside.

SOS Things have turned out far better than I could have hoped. How terribly afraid I was, Chremes, that you would be as hardhearted now as you were then over bringing up the girl!

CHR Often a man can't be how he would like to be, if his circumstances don't allow it. Now my situation is such that I'm eager for a daughter; then I wanted nothing less. (*he*

tress will have to be abandoned and the truth about Clitipho's affair with Bacchis will be revealed.

IV. ii: SYRUS.

SYR nisi me animus fallit multum, haud multum a me aberit
infortunium.

ita hac re in angustum oppido nunc meae coguntur
copiae,

670 nisi aliquid video ne esse amicam hanc gnati resciscat
senex.

nam quod de argento sperem aut posse postulem me
fallere,

nil est. triumpho si licet me latere tecto abscedere.

crucior bolum tantum mi ereptum tam desubito e fauci-
bus.

quid agam? aut quid comminiscar? ratio de integro
ineundast mihi.

675 nil tam difficilest quin quaerendo investigari possiet.

quid si hoc nunc sic incipiam? nilst. quid si sic? tantun-
dem egero.

at sic opinor: non potest. immo optume. euge, habeo
optumam.

retraham hercle, opinor, ad me idem illud fugitivom
argentum tamen.

IV. iii: CLINIA. SYRUS.

CLIN nulla mihi res posthac potest iam intervenire tanta
680 quae mi aegritudinem afferat: tanta haec laetitia obor-
tast.

dedo patri me nunciam ut frugalior sim quam volt.

---

[47] Literally, "my forces are confined in a narrow space"; in this
speech Syrus is indulging in military metaphors in the manner of
Plautine slaves.

goes into his house, followed by Sostrata, leaving Syrus on stage alone)

SYR *(to himself)* Unless I'm much mistaken, disaster is not very far away. My room for maneuver[47] in this operation is now greatly restricted, unless I can see some way of preventing the old man from discovering that this is his son's mistress.[48] As for my hope about the money and my thoughts of being able to deceive him, that's come to nothing. It will be a triumph if I can effect a withdrawal with my flanks intact. It's heartbreaking to have such a tasty morsel snatched away so suddenly from my lips. What shall I do? What plan can I devise? I need to think out a scheme again from scratch. *(resolutely)* There's nothing so hard to find that it can't be tracked down if you look for it. What if I approach it this way? No good. Or this? Won't achieve any more. Well this way, perhaps. Can't be done. No, it's excellent. Hooray! I've got an excellent plan. By god, I think I'll get my hands on that elusive money after all.

Enter CLINIA from Chremes' house in a state of elation.

CLIN After this nothing can befall me so bad as to cause me any sorrow, so great is the happiness welling up inside me. I put myself in my father's hands here and now: I'll live an even more orderly life than he wants me to.

[48] In the context this must refer to Menedemus finding out that Antiphila is Clinia's girlfriend.

SYR nil me fefellit. cognitast, quantum audio huius verba.
istuc tibi ex sententia tua obtigisse laetor.

CLIN o mi Syre, audisti, obsecro?

SYR   quidni, qui usque una adfuerim?

685 CLIN quoi aeque vidisti commode quicquam evenisse?

SYR   nulli.

CLIN atque ita me di ament ut ego nunc non tam meapte causa
laetor quam illius, quam ego scio esse honore quovis
dignam.

SYR ita credo. sed nunc, Clinia, age, da te mihi vicissim.
nam amici quoque res est videnda in tuto ut collocetur,

690 ne quid de amica nunc senex.

CLIN   o Iuppiter!

SYR   quiesce.

CLIN Antiphila mea nubet mihi.

SYR   sicin me interloquere?

CLIN quid faciam? Syre mi, gaudeo: fer me.

SYR   fero hercle vero.

CLIN deorum vitam apti sumus.

SYR   frustra operam, opinor, sumo.

CLIN loquere, audio.

SYR   at iam hoc non ages.

CLIN   agam.

SYR   videndumst, inquam,

695 amici quoque res, Clinia, tui in tuto ut collocetur.
nam si nunc a nobis abis et Bacchidem hic relinquis,
senex resciscet ilico esse amicam hanc Clitiphonis.

SYR   (*aside*) I was right. From what I hear him say, her identity has been confirmed. (*to Clinia*) I'm delighted that this has turned out in accordance with your wishes.

CLIN   Oh my dear Syrus, have you heard, for heaven's sake?

SYR   Of course I have. I was present through the whole discussion.

CLIN   Have you ever known anyone for whom things have worked out so favourably?

SYR   No, nobody.

CLIN   As heaven is my witness, I am delighted not so much for my own sake as for hers. I know she's worthy of whatever honour can be bestowed on her.

SYR   I'm sure she is. But come now, Clinia, do me a favour in return. We need to make sure your friend's affairs too are put on a safe footing. The old man mustn't find out about his mistress.

CLIN   (*still thinking of his own good fortune*) Oh Jupiter!

SYR   Be quiet!

CLIN   My Antiphila is going to be my wife.

SYR   Are you going to keep interrupting me?

CLIN   What shall I do? My dear Syrus, I'm so happy. Bear with me.

SYR   I am bearing with you, for god's sake.

CLIN   We have attained the life of the gods.

SYR   I think I'm wasting my time here.

CLIN   Go on, I'm listening.

SYR   But you won't pay attention.

CLIN   Yes, I will.

SYR   As I said, we need to make sure your friend's affairs too are put on a safe footing. If you go back home now and leave Bacchis here, the old man will realise immediately that she's Clitipho's mistress. If you take her with you, the

255

si abduxeris, celabitur, itidem ut celata adhuc est.

CLIN at enim istoc nil est magis, Syre, meis nuptiis advorsum.

700   nam quo ore appellabo patrem? tenes quid dicam?

SYR   quidni?

CLIN quid dicam? quam causam afferam?

SYR   qui nolo mentiare.

aperte ita ut res sese habet narrato.

CLIN   quid ais?

SYR   iubeo:

illam te amare et velle uxorem, hanc esse Clitiphonis.

CLIN bonam atque iustam rem oppido imperas et factu faci-
       lem.

705   et scilicet iam me hoc voles patrem exorare ut celet
senem vostrum?

SYR   immo ut recta via rem narret ordine omnem.

CLIN   hem!

satis sanus es aut sobrius? tuquidem illum plane perdis.

nam qui ille poterit esse in tuto, dic mihi?

SYR   huic equidem consilio palmam do. hic me magnifice
effero,

710   qui vim tantam in me et potestatem habeam tantae as-
tutiae

vera dicendo ut eos ambos fallam; ut quom narret senex

voster nostro istam esse amicam gnati, non credat tamen.

CLIN at enim spem istoc pacto rursum nuptiarum omnem eri-
       pis.

nam dum amicam hanc meam esse credet, non commit-
       tet filiam.

715   tu fors quid me fiat parvi pendis, dum illi consulas.

secret will be kept, as it has been up to now.

CLIN But there's nothing more likely to ruin my marriage, Syrus. How am I going to face my father? Can you suggest what I should say?

SYR Of course.

CLIN What shall I say, then? What explanation shall I give?

SYR I don't want you to tell a lie. Tell him the plain facts of the situation.

CLIN What are you saying?

SYR I'm suggesting that you say that you are in love with Antiphila and want to marry her, and that the other woman belongs to Clitipho.

CLIN (*sarcastically*) That's an absolutely fine and reasonable suggestion—and easy enough to carry out. I suppose you'll also want me to persuade my father to keep this a secret from your old man.

SYR On the contrary, get him to tell the whole story straight through from beginning to end.

CLIN What! Are you mad or drunk? You'll utterly ruin Clitipho. How will this put him on a safe footing, tell me?

SYR I award my plan the first prize. I congratulate myself with great pride on possessing so much power and being capable of so much cunning that I can deceive both of them by telling the truth. When your old man tells ours that Bacchis is his son's mistress, he still won't believe it.

CLIN But that way you're again taking from me all my hope of marriage. So long as Chremes believes she's *my* mistress, he won't trust me with his daughter. Perhaps you don't care much what happens to me so long as you look after Clitipho's interests.

SYR   quid, malum, me aetatem censes velle id assimularier?
        unus est dies dum argentum eripio. pax! nil amplius.

CLIN tantum sat habes? quid tum, quaeso, si hoc pater rescive-
        rit?

SYR   quid si redeo ad illos qui aiunt "quid si nunc caelum
        ruat?"

720 CLIN metuo quid agam.

SYR   metuis? quasi non ea potestas sit tua
        quo velis in tempore ut te exsolvas, rem facias palam.

CLIN age, age, transducatur Bacchis.

SYR   optume ipsa exit foras.

IV. iv: BACCHIS. CLINIA. SYRUS. DROMO. PHRYGIA.

BAC satis pol proterve me Syri promissa huc induxerunt,
        decem minas quas mihi dare pollicitust. quod si nunc me

725   deceperit, saepe obsecrans me ut veniam frustra veniet.
        aut quom venturam dixero et constituero, quom is certe
        renuntiarit, Clitipho quom in spe pendebit animi,
        decipiam ac non veniam, Syrus mihi tergo poenas pen-
        det.

CLIN satis scite promittit tibi.

SYR   atqui tu hanc iocari credis?

730 faciet nisi caveo.

BAC   dormiunt. ego pol istos commovebo.
        mea Phrygia, audisti modo iste homo quam villam de-
        monstravit
        Charini?

PHR   audivi.

---

49 This is a proverbial expression to indicate something potentially disastrous but quite unlikely.   50 According to Suetonius (*Life of Terence* 4) this line was actually composed by Terence's friend Laelius before dinner one evening at a country villa.

SYR   Damn it all, do you suppose I intend to keep up this pretence for ever? It'll take me one day to get my hands on the money. That's it! No more!

CLIN   Do you think that's enough? Tell me, what happens if my father finds out?

SYR   There are people who say "What happens if the sky falls in?"[49] That's my response.

CLIN   I'm worried about what you're asking me to do.

SYR   Worried? As if you don't have the power any time you like to release yourself from this and reveal the truth.

CLIN   Very well then, have Bacchis brought across.

SYR   (*as Chremes' door opens*) She's coming out herself. Excellent!

Enter BACCHIS from Chremes' house with her maid PHRYGIA.

BAC   Heaven knows it was pretty brash of Syrus to entice me here with his assurances,[50] promising to give me the ten minas. But if he lets me down now, he can beg me to come as often as he likes in the future, and he'll be wasting his time. Or else I'll say I'll come and fix a time, and he's bound to report back, and Clitipho will be on tenterhooks of anticipation; and then I'll let him down and not come, Syrus will get a thrashing, and I'll get my revenge.

CLIN   (*aside to Syrus, ironically*) That's a pretty shrewd promise she's making you.

SYR   (*to Clinia*) And you suppose she's joking? She'll do it, if I'm not careful.

BAC   (*aside to Phrygia*) They're dreaming. By heaven, I'll stir them up. (*aloud*) Phrygia, my dear, you heard that man point out just now which was Charinus' house?

PHR   Yes, I did.

BAC	proxumam esse huic fundo ad dextram?
PHR	memini.
BAC	curriculo percurre. apud eum miles Dionysia agitat.
SYR	quid inceptat?
BAC	dic me hic oppido esse invitam atque asservari,

735   verum aliquo pacto verba me his daturam esse et ventu-
            ram.

SYR	perii hercle! Bacchis, mane, mane. quo mittis istanc,

        quaeso?
        iube maneat.

BAC	i.
SYR	quin est paratum argentum.
BAC	quin ego maneo.
SYR	atqui iam dabitur.
BAC	ut lubet. num ego insto?
SYR	at scin quid sodes?
BAC	quid?
SYR	transeundumst nunc tibi ad Menedemum et tua pompa

740   eo transducendast.

BAC	quem rem agis, scelus?
SYR	egon? argentum cudo

        quod tibi dem.

BAC	dignam me putas quam illudas?
SYR	non est temere.
BAC	etiamne tecum hic res mihist?
SYR	minume. tuom tibi reddo.
BAC	eatur.
SYR	sequere hac. heus, Dromo!
DRO	quis me volt?

BAC   It was the one next to this farm on the right?

PHR   Yes, as I remember it.

BAC   Run over there as fast as you can. The soldier's celebrating the Dionysia there.[51]

SYR   (*aside to Clinia*) What's she up to?

BAC   Tell him that I'm here completely against my will and being kept under guard. But I'll give them the slip somehow and come.

SYR   God damn it! (*to Bacchis*). Wait, wait! Where are you sending that girl, for heaven's sake? Tell her to stay.

BAC   (*to Phrygia*). Off you go. (*Phrygia begins to move off to the left*)

SYR   But the money's ready.

BAC   Very well, I'll stay. (*Phrygia pauses and then returns*)

SYR   And you'll get it at once.

BAC   As you like. I'm not pressing you for it, am I?

SYR   But do you know what I'd like you to do?

BAC   What?

SYR   Go over to Menedemus' house and take your maids with you.

BAC   What are you up to, you villain?

SYR   Me? I'm coining money to give to you.

BAC   Do you think I'm the sort of person to make a fool of?

SYR   There's a reason.

BAC   (*turning to go*) You've no other business for me here?

SYR   None at all. I'm just paying you what you're owed.

BAC   Let's go, then.

SYR   Follow me this way. (*he knocks at Menedemus' door*) Hey there, Dromo!

DRO   (*coming out*) Who wants me?

51 See note 22.

	SYR	Syrus.
	DRO	quid est rei?
	SYR	ancillas omnis Bacchidis transduce huc ad vos propere.
745	DRO	quam ob rem?
	SYR	ne quaeras. efferant quae secum huc attulerunt.
		sperabit sumptum sibi senex levatum esse harunc abitu:
		ne ille haud scit hoc paullum lucri quantum ei damnum
		apportet.
		tu nescis id quod scis, Dromo, si sapies.
	DRO	mutum dices.

IV. V: CHREMES. SYRUS.

	CHR	ita me di amabunt ut nunc Menedemi vicem
750		miseret me tantum devenisse ad eum mali.
		illancin mulierem alere cum illa familia!
		etsi scio, hosce aliquot dies non sentiet,
		ita magno desiderio fuit ei filius.
		verum ubi videbit tantos sibi sumptus domi
755		cotidianos fieri nec fieri modum,
		optabit rursum ut abeat ab se filius.
		Syrum optume eccum.
	SYR	cesso hunc adoriri?
	CHR	Syre!
	SYR	hem!
	CHR	quid est?
	SYR	te mihi ipsum iamdudum optabam dari.

---

52 It seems probable that this whole maneuver, for which Terence's play provides very little time, was covered by a choral ode in the Greek original. Clinia must also enter Menedemus' house at this point, after which he plays no further part in the play; it is surprising that Terence does not make more of his return home and his reconciliation with his father.

SYR Syrus.

DRO What's up?

SYR Bring all Bacchis' maids over here to your house, and look sharp about it.

DRO What for?

SYR Don't ask. See that they take everything they brought here with them. (*Dromo goes into Chremes' house*) The old man will expect his expenses to be reduced by their departure. Little does he know, believe me, how much loss that little gain will bring. (*Dromo reappears with maids and baggage*) If you've any sense, Dromo, you'll forget this whole business.

DRO Mum's the word. (*he ushers Bacchis, Phrygia, and all her other maids into Menedemus' house together with their belongings*)[52]

Enter CHREMES *from his house.*

CHR (*to himself*) As heaven is my witness, I'm sorry for Menedemus' sake that so much trouble has come his way. Fancy feeding that woman with all her household! Still, I'm sure he won't notice it for some days, he's been missing his son so much. But when he sees the expense mounting up in his house day after day and no end to it, he'll be wishing his son would go away again. (*seeing Syrus*) Excellent! There's Syrus.

SYR (*aside*) Time to approach him.

CHR Syrus!

SYR Oh, hello!

CHR How are things?

SYR I've been hoping to run into you for a while.

263

	CHR	videre egisse iam nescioquid cum sene.
760	SYR	de illo quid dudum? dictum factum reddidi.
	CHR	bonan fide?
	SYR	bona hercle.
	CHR	non possum pati

quin tibi caput demulceam. accede huc, Syre.
faciam boni tibi aliquid pro ista re ac lubens.

	SYR	at si scias quam scite in mentem venerit!
765	CHR	vah! gloriare evenisse ex sententia?
	SYR	non hercle vero. verum dico.
	CHR	dic quid est.
	SYR	tui Clitiphonis esse amicam hanc Bacchidem

Menedemo dixit Clinia, et ea gratia
secum adduxisse ne tu id persentisceres.

	CHR	probe!
770	SYR	dic sodes.
	CHR	nimium, inquam.
	SYR	immo si scias.

sed porro ausculta quod superest fallaciae.
sese ipse dicit tuam vidisse filiam;
eius sibi complacitam formam postquam aspexerit;
hanc cupere uxorem.

	CHR	modone quae inventast?
	SYR	eam.
775		et quidem iubebit posci.
	CHR	quam ob rem istuc, Syre?

nam prorsum nil intellego.

	SYR	vah! tardus es.
	CHR	fortasse.
	SYR	argentum dabitur ei ad nuptias,

aurum atque vestem qui—tenesne?

	CHR	comparet?

CHR I take it you've arranged something with the old man.

SYR What we talked about just now? No sooner said than done.

CHR Honestly?

SYR Yes, honestly, for god's sake.

CHR I can't resist giving you a pat on the head. Come here, Syrus. I'll do you a good turn for this, and gladly.

SYR If you only knew what a clever idea I thought of!

CHR Come on! Are you boasting that it all happened according to plan?

SYR Good god, no. I'm telling the truth.

CHR Tell me what's happening.

SYR Clinia told Menedemus that this Bacchis was the mistress of your Clitipho, and that *he* had brought her home himself just so that you wouldn't find this out.

CHR Well done!

SYR What's that again?

CHR Very well done, I said.

SYR (*aside*) If only you knew! (*to Chremes*) But let me explain the rest of the trick. Clinia said that he saw your daughter, fell for her beauty at first sight, and is eager to marry her.

CHR The one that's just been discovered?

SYR Yes, her. And he's going to arrange for a proposal.

CHR What's the point of this, Syrus? I don't understand at all.

SYR Oh! You're slow.

CHR Perhaps I am.

SYR He'll be given money for the wedding; there's jewellery and fine clothing—you get it?

CHR To purchase?

	SYR	id ipsum.
	CHR	at ego illi neque do neque despondeo.
780	SYR	non? quam ob rem?
	CHR	quam ob rem? me rogas? homini—
	SYR	ut lubet.

   non ego dicebam in perpetuom ut illam illi dares,
   verum ut simulares.

| | CHR | non meast simulatio. |

   ita tu istaec tua misceto ne me admisceas.
   egon, quoi daturus non sum, ut ei despondeam?

785	SYR	credebam.
	CHR	minume.
	SYR	scite poterat fieri,

   et ego hoc, quia dudum tu tanto opere iusseras,
   eo coepi.

| | CHR | credo. |
| | SYR | ceterum equidem istuc, Chreme, |

   aequi bonique facio.

| | CHR | atqui quam maxume |

   volo te dare operam ut fiat, verum alia via.

| 790 | SYR | fiat, quaeratur aliquid. sed illud quod tibi |

   dixi de argento quod ista debet Bacchidi,
   id nunc reddendumst illi. neque tu scilicet
   illuc confugies: "quid mea? num mihi datumst?
   num iussi? num illa oppignerare filiam

| 795 | | meam me invito potuit?" verum illuc, Chreme, |

   dicunt: "ius summum saepe summast malitia."

| | CHR | haud faciam. |

SYR Exactly.

CHR But I'm not giving him my daughter. I'm not agreeing to an engagement.

SYR No? Why not?

CHR Why not? Need you ask? To a man who—?

SYR (*unperturbed*) As you like. I wasn't suggesting that you should give her to him permanently, but just pretend.

CHR Pretence is not my way. You do your stirring but keep me out of the pot. Engage her to a man I don't intend to marry her to?

SYR I thought you might.

CHR Certainly not.

SYR It could have been managed quite cleverly. I only suggested it because you urged it so strongly just now.

CHR (*ironically*). I'm sure.

SYR However, I do see, Chremes, that your attitude is right and proper.

CHR Admittedly, I am very keen that you should bring it off, but in some other way.

SYR All right. I'll have to find something else. But about the money which I said the woman owes to Bacchis: it does need to be repaid now. You're not of course going to resort to arguments like "What's it to do with me? Was it given to me? Did I authorise it? Could she give my daughter as a security without my permission?" It's true what they say, Chremes: "More law, less justice."[53]

CHR I won't behave like that.

---

[53] A proverbial expression (literally "the greatest law is often the greatest wrong"), quoted also by Cicero, *On Duties* 1.33.

SYR   immo aliis si licet, tibi non licet.
      omnes te in lauta et bene parata re putant.
CHR   quin egomet iam ad eam deferam.
SYR   immo filium
800   iube potius.
CHR   quam ob rem?
SYR   quia enim in eum suspiciost
      translata amoris.
CHR   quid tum?
SYR   quia videbitur
      magis veri simile id esse, quom hic illi dabit;
      et simul conficiam facilius ego quod volo.
      ipse adeo adest. abi, effer argentum.
CHR   effero.

IV. vi: CLITIPHO. SYRUS.

805 CLIT   nullast tam facilis res quin difficilis siet,
      quam invitus facias. vel me haec deambulatio
      quam non laboriosa, ad languorem dedit.
      nec quicquam magis nunc metuo quam ne denuo
      miser aliquo extrudar hinc, ne accedam ad Bacchidem.
810   ut te quidem omnes di deae quantumst, Syre,
      cum istoc invento cumque incepto perduint!
      huius modi mihi res semper comminiscere
      ubi me excarnufices.
SYR   in' tu hinc quo dignus es?
      quam paene tua me perdidit protervitas!
815 CLIT   vellem hercle factum, ita meritu's.

<hr/>

798 *sic Fleckeisen,* in lauta et bene acta parte *codd. Eugr.,* in lauta
esse et bene acta re *Bentley*

SYR   No, others may get away with it, but you can't. Everybody regards you as a fine upstanding citizen.[54]

CHR   In fact, I'll take her the money myself.

SYR   No. Better tell your son to.

CHR   Why?

SYR   Because he's the one who's now supposed to be in love with her.

CHR   So?

SYR   Because the story will be more credible if it's he who gives her the money. And (*mysteriously*) at the same time I'll achieve what I want to achieve more easily. (*looking down the street*) But here he is. You go and bring out the money.

CHR   I will. (*he exits into his house*)

Enter CLITIPHO *from the left.*

CLIT (*to himself*) There's nothing so easy that it isn't difficult when you do it against your will. Take for example this stroll of mine: it wasn't at all strenuous, but it's tired me out. There is nothing I'm more afraid of now in my miserable state than to be pushed out of here again and denied access to Bacchis. (*seeing Syrus*) May all the gods and goddesses destroy you, Syrus, you and your plots and schemes! You're always thinking up things like this to torture me.

SYR   You go where you deserve. You nearly ruined me with your brazen behaviour.

CLIT I wish I had, by god; it would've served you right.

---

[54] This line is corrupt in the MSS but the general sense is clear.

SYR   meritus? quo modo?
        ne me istuc ex te prius audisse gaudeo
        quam argentum haberes quod daturus iam fui.

CLIT   quid igitur dicam tibi vis? abiisti, mihi
        amicam adduxti quam non licitumst tangere.

820 SYR   iam non sum iratus. sed scin ubi sit nunc tibi
        tua Bacchis?

CLIT   apud nos.

SYR   non.

CLIT   ubi ergo?

SYR   apud Cliniam.

CLIT   perii!

SYR   bono animo es. iam argentum ad eam deferes
        quod ei pollicitu's.

CLIT   garris. unde?

SYR   a tuo patre.

CLIT   ludis fortasse me?

SYR   ipsa re experibere.

825 CLIT ne ego homo sum fortunatus. deamo te, Syre.

SYR   sed pater egreditur. cave quicquam admiratu' sis
        qua causa id fiat; obsecundato in loco;
        quod imperabit facito; loquitor paucula.

       IV. vii: CHREMES. CLITIPHO. SYRUS.

CHR   ubi Clitipho hic est?

SYR   "eccum me" inque.

CLIT   eccum hic tibi.

830 CHR quid rei esset dixti huic?

SYR   Served me right? How? Believe me, I'm glad I heard you say that before I handed over the money which I was about to give you.

CLIT   So what do you want me to say? You went off, you brought my mistress here, and now you don't allow me to touch her.

SYR   I've got over my anger. But do you know where your Bacchis is now?

CLIT   At our place.

SYR   No.

CLIT   Where, then?

SYR   At Clinia's.

CLIT   I'm ruined!

SYR   Cheer up. You'll soon be delivering her the money you promised.

CLIT   You're joking. Where from?

SYR   Your father.

CLIT   I think you're making fun of me.

SYR   The facts will show.

CLIT   Then I'm a happy man. Syrus, I'm getting very fond of you.

SYR   (*as Chremes' door opens*) But your father's coming out. Mind you don't show yourself surprised or puzzled by his motives. Follow his lead where you can, do what he tells you, say very little.

Enter CHREMES from his house with a bag of money.

CHR   Where's Clitipho? (*Clitipho makes no response*)

SYR   (*to Clitipho*) Say "Here I am."

CLIT   (*to Chremes*) Here I am.

CHR   (*to Syrus*) Did you tell him what's going on?

271

SYR	dixi pleraque omnia.
CHR	cape hoc argentum ac defer.
SYR	i. quid stas, lapis?
	quin accipis?
CLIT	cedo sane.
SYR	sequere hac me ocius.

       tu hic nos dum eximus interea opperibere.
       nam nil est illic quod moremur diutius.

835 CHR minas quidem iam decem habet a me filia,
       quas hortamentis esse nunc duco datas.
       hasce ornamentis consequentur alterae.
       porro haec talenta dotis apposcunt duo.
       quam multa iniusta ac prava fiunt moribus!
840   mihi nunc relictis rebus inveniundus est
       aliquis, labore inventa mea quoi dem bona.

IV. viii: MENEDEMUS. CHREMES.

MEN	multo omnium nunc me fortunatissumum
	factum puto esse quom te, gnate, intellego
	resipisse.
CHR	ut errat!
MEN	te ipsum quaerebam, Chreme.

845   serva, quod in test, filium, me ac familiam.
CHR cedo, quid vis faciam?

---

836 hortamentis C^1p^2 *Eugr. gloss.*, ornamentis *codd. pl.*, pro alimentis F^2E^2

---

55 This is the meaning suggested by the commentator Eugraphius for the rare word *hortamentis,* which would normally mean "encouragement." Chremes is referring to the maintenance of his daughter by the Corinthian woman before she was recognised.

SYR   Yes, nearly everything.

CHR   (*holding out the money to Clitipho*). Take this money and deliver it. (*Clitipho again makes no response*)

SYR   (*to Clitipho*) Go on! What are you waiting for, you dolt? Why don't you take it?

CLIT   All right, give it to me. (*he takes the money from Chremes*)

SYR   (*to Clitipho*) Follow me this way and hurry up. (*to Chremes*) You wait here meanwhile until we come out. There's no reason why it should take us very long in there. (*he goes into Menedemus' house followed by Clitipho*)

CHR   (*to himself*) My daughter already has ten minas from me, which I regard as payment for her maintenance.[55] Another ten will follow these for her wardrobe. On top of this two talents will be needed for her dowry.[56] How perverse and unreasonable the demands of social convention are! I must now drop everything and find a son-in-law to bestow my hard-earned wealth on.

Enter MENEDEMUS *from his house.*

MEN   (*speaking back inside to Clinia*) I reckon I'm by far the happiest man in the world now that I see you've come to your senses, my son.

CHR   (*aside*) How wrong he is!

MEN   (*seeing Chremes*) I was looking for you, Chremes. So far as in you lies, save my son, myself, and my household.

CHR   Tell me, what do you want me to do?

[56] This is not a particularly generous amount for dowries in comedy: see *The Woman of Andros* note 54.

MEN   invenisti hodie filiam.

CHR   quid tum?

MEN   hanc uxorem sibi dari volt Clinia.

CHR   quaeso, quid tu hominis es?

MEN   quid?

CHR   iamne oblitus es
inter nos quid sit dictum de fallacia,
850   ut ea via abs te argentum auferretur?

MEN   scio.

CHR   ea res nunc agitur ipsa.

MEN   quid narras, Chreme?
immo haec quidem quae apud mest Clitiphonis est
amica.

CHR   ita aiunt; et tu credis omnia.
et illum aiunt velle uxorem ut, quom desponderim,
855   des qui aurum ac vestem atque alia quae opus sunt com-
        paret.

MEN   id est profecto; id amicae dabitur.

CHR   scilicet
daturum.

MEN   ah! frustra sum igitur gavisus miser.
quidvis tamen iam malo quam hunc amittere.
quid nunc renuntiem abs te responsum, Chreme,
860   ne sentiat me sensisse atque aegre ferat?

CHR   aegre? nimium illi, Menedeme, indulges.

MEN   sine.
inceptumst: perfice hoc mi perpetuo, Chreme.

CHR   dic convenisse, egisse te de nuptiis.

MEN   dicam. quid deinde?

CHR   me facturum esse omnia,
865   generum placere. postremo etiam, si voles,
desponsum quoque esse dicito.

MEN You've found a daughter today.

CHR What of it?

MEN Clinia requests her hand in marriage.

CHR For heaven's sake, what sort of a man are you?

MEN I beg your pardon.

CHR Have you already forgotten our conversation about a trick, as a way of getting money out of you?

MEN I remember.

CHR That's what's now happening.

MEN What are you saying, Chremes? You're mistaken. The girl who's in my house is *Clitipho's* mistress.

CHR That's what they say, and you believe it all! They're saying Clinia wants to get married simply so that, once I've agreed to the engagement, you'll give him money to purchase jewellery and fine clothing and the other requirements.

MEN That's it, without a doubt. The money will be given to the mistress!

CHR Of course it will.

MEN Oh! So my rejoicing was all for nothing, poor me! But I'd still prefer anything to losing him. What shall I tell him your response was, Chremes? I don't want him to realise that *I've* realised and be upset.

CHR Upset? You're far too soft on him, Menedemus.

MEN Let me be. I've made a beginning; help me to carry it through to the end, Chremes.

CHR Say that you've met me and discussed the marriage.

MEN I will. What next?

CHR Say that I'll go along with everything, I approve of him as son-in-law, and finally, if you like, even say that I've agreed to the engagement—

275

MEN   em, istuc volueram.

CHR tanto ocius te ut poscat et tu, id quod cupis,
     quam ocissume ut des.

MEN   cupio.

CHR   ne tu propediem,
     ut istanc rem video, istius obsaturabere.

870   sed, haec utut sunt, cautim et paulatim dabis
     si sapies.

MEN   faciam.

CHR   abi intro: vide quid postulet.
     ego domi ero si quid me voles.

MEN   sane volo.
     nam te scientem faciam quidquid egero.

ACTUS V

V. i: MENEDEMUS. CHREMES.

MEN ego me non tam astutum neque ita perspicacem esse id
     scio.

875   sed hic adiutor meus et monitor et praemonstrator
     Chremes
     hoc mihi praestat. in me quidvis harum rerum convenit
     quae sunt dicta in stulto: caudex, stipes, asinus, plum-
     beus.
     in illum nil potest: exsuperat eius stultitia haec omnia.

CHR ohe! iam desine deos, uxor, gratulando obtundere

880   tuam esse inventam gnatam, nisi illos ex tuo ingenio iudi-
     cas,

---

[57] The Roman performance was continuous; there will have been an
act break in the Greek original at this point to represent the passing of
time, which Terence has not attempted to cover.

MEN (*aside*) Good, that's what I wanted.

CHR —so that he'll ask for the money the sooner and you can give him it as soon you like, which is what you're so keen to do.

MEN Yes, I am.

CHR As I see it, you'll have had enough of this before very long, believe me. But, however that may be, if you've any sense, you'll pay up carefully and a little at a time.

MEN I will.

CHR Go in and see how much he asks for. I'll be at home if you need me.

MEN I'm sure I will. I'll keep you informed whatever I do. (*they go into their respective houses, leaving the stage empty*)

ACT FIVE

Enter MENEDEMUS *from his house, after a short interval.*[57]

MEN (*to himself*) I know that I am not a particularly clever or perceptive person. But this helper of mine and counsellor and guide, Chremes, is worse. You could apply to me any of the names that are applied to the stupid: blockhead, numskull, ass, nincompoop. But not to him: he's too stupid for any of them.

Enter CHREMES *from his house.*

CHR (*speaking back to Sostrata inside*) Hold on now! Stop deafening the gods with your thanksgiving for the discovery of your daughter—unless you judge them by your own standards and believe they don't understand any-

ut nil credas intellegere nisi idem dictumst centiens.
sed interim quid illic iamdudum gnatus cessat cum Syro?

MEN quos ais homines, Chreme, cessare?

CHR ehem, Menedeme, advenis?
dic mihi, Cliniae quae dixi nuntiastin?

MEN omnia.

885 CHR quid ait?

MEN gaudere adeo coepit quasi qui cupiunt nuptias.

CHR hahahae!

MEN quid risisti?

CHR servi venere in mentem Syri
calliditates.

MEN itane?

CHR voltus quoque hominum fingit scelus.

MEN gnatus quod se assimilat laetum id dicis?

CHR id.

MEN idem istuc mihi
venit in mentem.

CHR veterator!

MEN magis, si magis noris, putes
890 ita rem esse.

CHR ain tu?

MEN quin tu ausculta.

CHR mane. hoc prius scire expeto
quid perdideris. nam ubi desponsam nuntiasti filio,
continuo iniecisse verba tibi Dromonem scilicet,
sponsae vestem, aurum atque ancillas opus esse: argen-
tum ut dares.

MEN non.

CHR quid? non?

MEN non, inquam.

CHR neque ipse gnatus?

278

thing unless you've said the same thing a hundred times. (*to himself*) But meanwhile why's my son lingering so long in there with Syrus?

MEN (*going up to him*) Who do you say is lingering, Chremes?

CHR Oh hello, Menedemus. Are you back? Tell me, have you reported to Clinia what I said?

MEN Everything.

CHR What does he say?

MEN He was overcome with joy, just like a man eager to be married.

CHR Hahahahaha!

MEN What are you laughing at?

CHR I was thinking of the craftiness of my slave Syrus.

MEN Yes?

CHR He can train people's faces as well, the villain.

MEN You mean, my son's only pretending to be happy?

CHR Yes.

MEN The same thought occurred to me.

CHR The old rogue!

MEN If you knew more, you'd be even more inclined to believe it.

CHR Do you say so?

MEN Just you listen.

CHR Wait a minute! I'd like to know first how much it's cost you. When you reported to your son that I'd agreed to the engagement, I suppose Dromo immediately dropped hints that the bride needed dresses, jewellery, and maids, to get you to provide the money?

MEN No.

CHR What? No?

MEN No, I said.

CHR Nor your son himself?

279

	MEN	nil prorsum, Chreme.
895		magis unum etiam instare ut hodie conficiantur nuptiae.
	CHR	mira narras. quid Syrus meus? ne is quidem quicquam?
	MEN	nihil.
	CHR	quam ob rem, nescio.
	MEN	equidem miror, qui alia tam plane scias.

MEN   nil prorsum, Chreme.

895   magis unum etiam instare ut hodie conficiantur nuptiae.

CHR   mira narras. quid Syrus meus? ne is quidem quicquam?

MEN   nihil.

CHR   quam ob rem, nescio.

MEN   equidem miror, qui alia tam plane scias.

             sed ille tuom quoque servus idem mire finxit filium,

             ut ne paullulum quidem subolat esse amicam Cliniae.

900 CHR   quid agit?

MEN   mitto iam osculari atque amplexari. id nil puto.

CHR   quid est quod amplius simuletur?

MEN   vah!

CHR   quid est?

MEN   audi modo.

             est mihi ultimis conclave in aedibus quoddam retro.

             huc est intro latus lectus, vestimentis stratus est.

CHR   quid post hoc est factum?

MEN   dictum factum huc abiit Clitipho.

905 CHR   solus?

MEN   solus.

CHR   timeo.

MEN   Bacchis consecutast ilico.

CHR   sola?

MEN   sola.

CHR   perii!

MEN   ubi abiere intro, operuere ostium.

CHR   hem!

             Clinia haec fieri videbat?

MEN   quidni? mecum una simul.

CHR   filist amica Bacchis. Menedeme, occidi!

MEN   Not a word, Chremes. The only thing that he insisted on
       was that the wedding should take place today.

CHR   You amaze me. What about Syrus? Didn't he say any-
       thing either?

MEN   Nothing.

CHR   I've no idea why not.

MEN   (*teasing*) That's amazing, when you are so well informed
       on other things. Syrus has done a fantastic job on your
       son too: no one would ever suspect that Bacchis is Clinia's
       mistress.

CHR   What's he doing?

MEN   I'll say nothing of kisses and embraces. They're nothing.

CHR   He could hardly carry the pretence any further.

MEN   Huh!

CHR   What's the matter?

MEN   Just listen. There's a small room at the very back of my
       house. They took a bed in there and covered it with blan-
       kets.

CHR   Then what?

MEN   No sooner said than done, Clitipho went off there.

CHR   By himself?

MEN   By himself.

CHR   I'm beginning to be worried.

MEN   Bacchis followed at once.

CHR   By herself?

MEN   By herself.

CHR   I'm lost!

MEN   When they got inside, they closed the door.

CHR   What! Did Clinia see this going on?

MEN   Of course. He was with me all the time.

CHR   (*finally comprehending the situation*) So Bacchis is my
       son's mistress. Menedemus, I'm ruined!

281

	MEN	quam ob rem?
	CHR	decem dierum vix mist familia.
910	MEN	quid? istuc times quod ille operam amico dat suo?
	CHR	immo quod amicae.
	MEN	si dat.
	CHR	an dubium id tibist?

quemquamne animo tam comi esse aut leni putas
qui se vidente amicam patiatur suam—?

	MEN	ah!

quidni? quo verba facilius dentur mihi.

915	CHR	derides merito. mihi nunc ego suscenseo.

quot res dedere ubi possem persentiscere,
ni essem lapis! quae vidi! vae misero mihi!
at ne illud haud inultum, si vivo, ferent.
nam iam—

	MEN	non tu te cohibes? non te respicis?
920		non tibi exemplo satis sum?
	CHR	prae iracundia,

Menedeme, non sum apud me.

	MEN	tene istuc loqui!

nonne id flagitiumst te aliis consilium dare,
foris sapere, tibi non posse te auxiliarier?

	CHR	quid faciam?
	MEN	id quod me fecisse aiebas parum.
925		fac te patrem esse sentiat; fac ut audeat

tibi credere omnia, abs te petere et poscere,
ne quam aliam quaerat copiam ac te deserat.

	CHR	immo abeat multo malo quovis gentium
		quam hic per flagitium ad inopiam redigat patrem.
930		nam si illi pergo suppeditare sumptibus,

MEN   Why?

CHR   My estate will barely last ten days.

MEN   (*teasing*) What? Are you worried because he's lending a
      hand to his friend?

CHR   No. To his mistress.

MEN   If he is.

CHR   Can you doubt it? Do you reckon anyone could be so
      generous or easygoing that he would stand by and watch
      his mistress being—?

MEN   Oh! Why not? If it was all part of the plan to fool me.

CHR   You're mocking me and I deserve it. I'm furious now with
      myself. How many clues there were which would have
      led me to the truth, if I hadn't been such a dolt! The
      things I saw! Oh damn and blast! But, believe me, as sure
      as I live, they won't get away with this. I'll—

MEN   Control yourself! Think of your own position! Is my ex-
      ample not enough for you?

CHR   I'm beside myself with anger, Menedemus.

MEN   Fancy you saying that! Isn't it a disgrace that you should
      give advice to others, be so wise to outsiders, and be un-
      able to help yourself?

CHR   What shall I do?

MEN   What you kept telling me I failed to do.[58] Make him feel
      that you're his father. Give him the confidence to entrust
      all his secrets to you, and to come to you with his requests
      and demands, or else he'll look elsewhere for support
      and abandon you.

CHR   No, I'd much prefer he went away anywhere in the world
      than stay here and reduce his father to starvation by such
      disgraceful behaviour. If I continue to provide for his ex-

---

[58] See lines 151–157.

Menedeme, mihi illaec vere ad rastros res redit.

MEN quot incommoditates in hac re capies, nisi caves!
difficilem te esse ostendes et ignosces tamen
post, et id ingratum.

CHR ah! nescis quam doleam.

MEN ut lubet.

935 quid hoc quod rogo, ut illa nubat nostro? nisi quid est
quod magis vis.

CHR immo et gener et affines placent.

MEN quid dotis dicam te dixisse filio?
quid obticuisti?

CHR dotis?

MEN ita dico.

CHR ah!

MEN Chreme,
ne quid vereare, si minus. nil nos dos movet.

940 CHR duo talenta pro re nostra ego esse decrevi satis.
sed ita dictu opus est, si me vis salvom esse et rem et
filium,
me mea omnia bona doti dixisse illi.

MEN quam rem agis?

CHR id mirari te simulato et illum hoc rogitato simul
quam ob rem id faciam.

MEN quin ego vero quam ob rem id facias nescio.

945 CHR egone? ut eius animum, qui nunc luxuria et lascivia
diffluit, retundam, redigam, ut quo se vortat nesciat.

MEN quid agis?

---

59 That is, "I shall be reduced to labouring to earn my living." The
expression may be proverbial, though there is also a back-reference to
the opening scene. 60 Thus disinheriting Clitipho.

travagance, Menedemus, it really will be the hoe for me.[59]

MEN What a lot of problems you'll create for yourself over this, if you're not careful! You'll prove yourself a bad-tempered father, you'll still forgive him later, and you'll get no thanks for it.

CHR Oh! You don't know how I'm suffering.

MEN As you like. But what about my request that your daughter should marry my son? Unless you'd prefer some other arrangement.

CHR No, I'm very happy with the son-in-law and the family connection.

MEN How much dowry shall I tell my son you've offered? (*Chremes makes no reply*) Why the silence?

CHR (*deep in thought*) Dowry?

MEN That's what I said.

CHR Ah!

MEN Chremes, don't be afraid if it's rather small. The dowry doesn't concern us at all.

CHR I'd decided that two talents was a sufficient amount with regard to my wealth. But, if you want to save me and my fortunes and my son, what you must tell *him* is that I've offered my whole estate as her dowry.[60]

MEN What are you up to?

CHR Pretend that you're amazed, and at the same time ask my son why he thinks I'm doing this.

MEN In fact, I've no idea myself why you're doing this.

CHR Why? In order to beat some sense into a son who is going down the drain with his luxurious living and licentious behaviour and to reduce him to a state where he doesn't know which way to turn.

MEN What are you trying to do?

285

CHR   mitte. sine me in hac re gerere mihi morem.

MEN   sino.

itane vis?

CHR   ita.

MEN   fiat.

CHR   ac iam uxorem ut accersat paret.

hic ita ut liberos est aequom dictis confutabitur.

950   sed Syrum quidem egone si vivo adeo exornatum dabo,

adeo depexum, ut dum vivat meminerit semper mei,

qui sibi me pro deridiculo ac delectamento putat.

non, ita me di ament, auderet facere haec viduae mulieri

quae in me fecit.

V. ii: CLITIPHO. MENEDEMUS. CHREMES. SYRUS.

CLIT   itane tandem, quaeso, Menedeme, ut pater

955   tam in brevi spatio omnem de me eiecerit animum pa-
      tris?

quodnam ob facinus? quid ego tantum sceleris admisi
      miser?

volgo faciunt.

MEN   scio tibi esse hoc gravius multo ac durius,

quoi fit. verum ego haud minus aegre patior, id qui nescio

nec rationem capio, nisi quod tibi bene ex animo volo.

960 CLIT hic patrem astare aibas?

950 Syrum quidem egone A, Syrum. ME. quid eum? CH. egone
Σ *Don. ad Ad. 400*

---

61 See *The Woman of Andros* note 34.

62 Menedemus' exit is not marked in the text, but he needs to go in at this point if he is to reappear at line 954 having already explained Chremes' threat to Clitipho. The reading of manuscript A is thus pref-

CHR Never mind. Let me follow my own inclinations.

MEN All right. Is this what you want?

CHR It is.

MEN So be it.

CHR Now Clinia should prepare to fetch his wife.[61] (*Menedemus exits into his house*)[62] (*to himself*) I'll deal with my son by a good talking to, which is the proper way to deal with one's children. But as for Syrus, as sure as I live, I'll make him such a pretty sight[63] that he'll remember me as long as he lives. Treating me as an object of derision and amusement! Heaven help me, he wouldn't dare do to a poor widow what he's done to me!

Enter CLITIPHO *and* MENEDEMUS *from Menedemus' house, with* SYRUS *following.*

CLIT Tell me, please, Menedemus, has my father really lost all his fatherly feeling for me in so short a time? For what crime? What great misdeed have I committed, poor me? Everybody's doing it.

MEN I know that this is much more serious and difficult for you, since it's happening to you. But I'm just as upset myself, because I don't know or understand the reason, though I wish you well with all my heart.

CLIT (*looking around*) You said my father was waiting here?

erable to that of Σ, which in effect detains Menedemus onstage to the end of Chremes' speech.

⁶³ Literally, "adorned and combed"; the meaning is "I'll give him such a thrashing." For the metaphors compare Plautus, *The Rope* 661, 730.

MEN eccum.

CHR quid me incusas, Clitipho?
quidquid ego huius feci, tibi prospexi et stultitiae tuae.
ubi te vidi animo esse omisso et suavia in praesentia
quae essent prima habere neque consulere in longitudi-
nem,
cepi rationem ut neque egeres neque ut haec posses per-
dere.

965 ubi, quoi decuit primo, tibi non licuit per te mihi dare,
abii ad proxumum tibi qui erat; ei commisi et credidi.
ibi tuae stultitiae semper erit praesidium, Clitipho,
victus, vestitus, quo in tectum te receptes.

CLIT ei mihi!

CHR satius est quam te ipso herede haec possidere Bacchi-
dem.

970 SYR disperii! scelestus quantas turbas concivi insciens!

CLIT emori cupio.

CHR prius, quaeso, disce quid sit vivere.
ubi scies, si displicebit vita, tum istoc utitor.

SYR ere, licetne?

CHR loquere.

SYR at tuto.

CHR loquere.

SYR quae istast pravitas
quaeve amentiast, quod peccavi ego, id obesse huic?

---

64 This is another unmarked exit. When we next see Menedemus he
is coming out of his house (see line 1046).

MEN There he is. (*he withdraws into his house*)[64]

CHR (*going up to Clitipho*) Why are you blaming me, Clitipho? Whatever I have done in this matter, I have done out of consideration for you and your stupidity. When I saw that you were being irresponsible, putting the pleasures of the present first and taking no thought for the future, I conceived a plan whereby you should neither be in want nor be able to squander our assets. They should have been yours in the first place, but, when you made it impossible for me to give them to you, I had recourse to your closest relative[65] and entrusted them to him for safekeeping. In him you will always find protection against your own stupidity, Clitipho, and food and clothing, and a roof over your head.

CLIT Oh dear!

CHR This is a better way than for you to inherit them yourself and for Bacchis to take possession.

SYR (*aside*) Damn it all! What a wretch! What troubles I've unwittingly stirred up!

CLIT I want to die.

CHR First learn what it is to live, for heaven's sake. When you know that, if you don't like life, you can try the other way.

SYR (*to Chremes*) Master, may I?

CHR Speak.

SYR Safely?

CHR Speak.

SYR How can you be so perverse or out of your mind as to count against him a mistake which is mine?

[65] That is, to Clitipho's future brother-in-law Clinia, to whom Antiphila's dowry would pass as her legal guardian after her marriage.

289

CHR   ilicet.

975   ne te admisce. nemo accusat, Syre, te; nec tu aram tibi
           nec precatorem pararis.

SYR   quid agis?

CHR   nil suscenseo
           neque tibi nec tibi, nec vos est aequom quod facio mihi.

SYR   abiit? vah! rogasse vellem—

CLIT   quid?

SYR   —unde mi peterem cibum.
           ita nos alienavit. tibi iam esse ad sororem intellego.

980 CLIT adeon rem rediisse ut periclum etiam a fame mihi sit,
              Syre!

SYR   modo liceat vivere, est spes.

CLIT   quae?

SYR   nos esurituros satis.

CLIT irrides in re tanta neque me consilio quicquam adiuvas?

SYR   immo et ibi nunc sum et usque id egi dudum dum loqui-
              tur pater;
           et quantum ego intellegere possum—

CLIT   quid?

SYR   non aberit longius.

985 CLIT quid id ergo?

SYR   sic est: non esse horum te arbitror.

CLIT   quid istuc, Syre?
           satin sanus es?

SYR   ego dicam quod mihi in mentemst; tu diiudica.
          dum istis fuisti solus, dum nulla alia delectatio
          quae propior esset, te indulgebant, tibi dabant. nunc filia

CHR It's done. Don't you get mixed up in this. Nobody is accusing you, Syrus. You don't need to find an altar[66] or someone to plead for you.

SYR What are you doing?

CHR I'm not furious with you, nor (*turning to Clitipho*) with you; and you shouldn't be furious with me for what I'm doing. (*he goes into his house*)

SYR Has he gone? Blast! I wanted to ask him—

CLIT What?

SYR Where I should find some food, seeing that he's disowned us. I gather there's some for you at your sister's.

CLIT To think that it should get to the stage where I'm even in danger of starving, Syrus!

SYR Where there's life, there's hope.

CLIT What hope?

SYR Of enjoying a fair amount of hunger.

CLIT Can you joke at a time like this? Can't you give me some helpful advice?

SYR I can indeed. I'm working on it now and have been all the time that your father was talking. And as far as I can see—

CLIT What?

SYR —it won't be too long before it comes to me.

CLIT So what is it?

SYR It's this. I don't think you're their son.

CLIT What are you saying, Syrus? Are you in your right mind?

SYR I'll tell you what's occurred to me; you can decide for yourself. While you were all they had, while they had no other source of delight closer to them, they spoiled you,

---

[66] A traditional place of refuge, often used by slaves in comedy.

postquamst inventa vera, inventast causa qui te expelle-
rent.

990 CLIT est veri simile.

SYR   an tu ob peccatum hoc esse illum iratum putas?

CLIT non arbitror.

SYR   nunc aliud specta. matres omnes filiis
in peccato adiutrices, auxilio in paterna iniuria
solent esse; id non fit.

CLIT   verum dicis. quid ergo nunc faciam, Syre?

SYR suspicionem istanc ex illis quaere, rem profer palam.

995 si non est verum, ad misericordiam ambos adduces cito,
aut scibis quoius sis.

CLIT   recte suades. faciam.

SYR   sat recte hoc mihi
in mentem venit. nam quam maxume huic vera haec sus-
picio
erit, tam facillume patris pacem in leges conficiat suas.
etiam haud scio anne uxorem ducat. ac Syro nil gratiae!

1000 quid hoc autem? senex exit foras. ego fugio. adhuc quod
factumst,
miror non continuo arripi iusse. ad Menedemum hunc
pergam.
eum mihi precatorem paro. seni nostro fide nil habeo.

997 *sic scripsi:* namque adulescens maxime huic visa (vana?) haec
suspicio A^1, namque adulescens quam in minima spe situs Σ, nam cum
adulescens in minima spe situs *Eugr.*, nam quam maxume huic vana
haec suspicio *Geppert edd.*

1001 non continuo adripi iusse *Lindsay-Kauer*, continuo hunc
adripuisse A^1, non iusse me adripi A^2, non iussisse ilico adripi me Σ

they gave you things. But now that they've found a real daughter of their own, they've also found a reason to get rid of you.

CLIT It sounds plausible.

SYR Do you reckon it's this misbehaviour of yours that has made him angry?

CLIT I don't think so.

SYR Here's another point to consider. All mothers tend to stand by their sons when they misbehave and defend them against their fathers' ill-treatment. That's not happening.

CLIT You're right. So what shall I do now, Syrus?

SYR Ask them about your suspicion, bring the thing out into the open. If it's not true, you'll get instant sympathy from both of them; or else you'll find out whose son you are.

CLIT Good advice. I'll follow it. (*he goes into Chremes' house*)

SYR (*to himself*)That was a pretty good idea that occurred to me. The more genuine his suspicion is, the more easily he'll make peace with his father on his own terms. And, for all I know, he'll get himself a wife. But there'll be no thanks for Syrus! (*as Chremes' door opens*) But what's this? The old man's coming out. I'm off. After what's happened so far, I'm amazed he hasn't had me arrested on the spot. I'll go to Menedemus here, and get him to plead for me. I don't trust our old man a bit. (*he exits into Menedemus' house, leaving the stage empty*)

TERENCE

V. iii: SOSTRATA. CHREMES.

SOS profecto nisi caves tu homo, aliquid gnato conficies mali.
     idque adeo miror, quo modo
1005 tam ineptum quicquam tibi venire in mentem, mi vir,
         potuerit.
CHR oh! pergin mulier esse? nullamne ego rem umquam in
         vita mea
     volui quin tu in ea re mi fueris advorsatrix, Sostrata?
     at si rogem iam quid est quod peccem aut quam ob rem
         hoc faciam, nescias;
     in qua re nunc tam confidenter restas, stulta.
SOS   ego nescio?
1010 CHR immo scis, potius quam quidem redeat ad integrum ea-
         dem oratio.
SOS   oh!
     iniquos es qui me tacere de re tanta postules.
CHR non postulo iam. loquere. nihilo minus ego hoc faciam
         tamen.
SOS facies?
CHR   verum.
SOS   non vides quantum mali ex ea re excites?
     subditum se suspicatur.
CHR   "subditum" ain tu?
SOS   sic erit,
1015 mi vir.
CHR   confitere?
SOS   au, te obsecro, istuc inimicis siet.
     egon confitear meum non esse filium, qui sit meus?

     1008 faciam *A²Σ Eugr.*, facias *A¹*

294

Enter SOSTRATA and CHREMES from their house.

SOS If you're not careful, my good man, you'll do our son real harm, I can assure you. Indeed, I'm amazed that such a silly idea could have entered your head, my dear husband.

CHR Oh! Do you have to keep behaving like a woman? Is there nothing that I have ever wanted in my life on which you haven't contradicted me, Sostrata? If I asked you now what I am doing wrong or why I am doing this, you wouldn't have any idea, and yet you oppose me so confidently, you fool.

SOS I have no idea?

CHR All right, you have, anything to stop this argument starting again from the beginning.

SOS Oh! It's not fair of you to expect me to say nothing when it's so important.

CHR I don't expect it any more. Have your say. But I'll carry out my plan none the less.

SOS You will?

CHR Yes.

SOS Don't you see how much trouble you're creating by it? He suspects he's not our son.[67]

CHR Did you say "not our son"?

SOS That's it, my dear husband.

CHR Do you admit it?

SOS Oh, for heaven's sake, leave that to our enemies. Should I admit he's not my son, when he is?

---

[67] Literally "supposititious"; the reference is to the practice of smuggling in a substitute baby and passing it off as the mother's.

CHR   quid? metuis ne non, quom velis, convincas esse illum
       tuom?

SOS   quod filiast inventa?

CHR   non. sed, quo magis credundum siet,
       quod est consimilis moribus.

1020   convinces facile ex te natum; nam tui similist probe.
       nam illi nil vitist relictum quin siet itidem tibi.
       tum praeterea talem nisi tu nulla pareret filium.
       sed ipse egreditur, quam severus! rem quom videas cen-
       seas.

V. iv: CLITIPHO. SOSTRATA. CHREMES.

CLIT   si umquam ullum fuit tempus, mater, quom ego voluptati
       tibi

1025   fuerim, dictus filius tuos vostra voluntate, obsecro
       eius ut memineris atque inopis nunc te miserescat mei,
       quod peto aut volo, parentes meos ut commonstres mihi.

SOS   obsecro, mi gnate, ne istuc in animum inducas tuom,
       alienum esse te.

CLIT   sum.

SOS   miseram me! hocin quaesisti, obsecro?

1030   ita mihi atque huic sis superstes ut ex me atque ex hoc
       natus es.
       at cave posthac, si me amas, umquam istuc verbum ex te
       audiam.

CHR   at ego, si me metuis, mores cave in te esse istos sentiam.

CLIT   quos?

CHR   si scire vis, ego dicam. gerro, iners, fraus, helluo,
       ganeo's, damnosus. crede, et nostrum te esse credito.

1035 CLIT   non sunt haec parentis dicta.

CHR Well, you needn't be afraid that you can't prove him yours any time you like.

SOS (*puzzled*) Because I've found my daughter?

CHR No. Something which will make it more credible: because he's similar in character. You'll easily be able to prove that he's your son; he's exactly similar to you. He has every single one of your vices. And besides, no woman could bear such a son but you. (*as Chremes' door opens*) But he's coming out. What a solemn look! You can make up your mind when you've seen how things are.

Enter CLITIPHO *from Chremes' house.*

CLIT (*to Sostrata, solemnly*) If there was ever any time, mother, when I was a source of pleasure to you, when you both willingly called me your son, I implore you to remember that time, have pity on me now in my plight, and grant me what I ask and want: show me my true parents.

SOS I implore you, my dear son, not to entertain the idea that you are someone else's son.

CLIT I am.

SOS (*to Chremes*) Misery me, is that what you wanted, for heaven's sake? (*to Clitipho*) As I pray you'll outlive him and me, you are my son and his. And, if you love me, make sure that I don't ever again hear such a thing from you.

CHR And, if you fear *me*, make sure that I don't ever see such behaviour in you again.

CLIT What behaviour?

CHR If you want to know, I'll tell you. You're a useless, good-for-nothing, two-faced, profligate, debauched reprobate. Believe that, and believe that you're our son.

CLIT Those are not a father's words.

297

CHR   non, si ex capite sis meo
       natus, item ut aiunt Minervam esse ex Iove, ea causa
           magis
       patiar, Clitipho, flagitiis tuis me infamem fieri.
SOS   di istaec prohibeant!
CHR   deos nescio: ego, quod potero, sedulo.
       quaeris id quod habes, parentes. quod abest non quaeris,
           patri
1040   quo modo obsequare et ut serves quod labore invenerit.
       non mihi per fallacias adducere ante oculos—pudet
       dicere hac praesente verbum turpe. at te id nullo modo
       facere puduit.
CLIT   eheu! quam nunc totus displiceo mihi!
       quam pudet! neque quod principium incipiam ad pla-
          candum scio.

     V. V: MENEDEMUS. CHREMES. SOSTRATA. CLITIPHO.

1045 MEN   enimvero Chremes nimis graviter cruciat adulescentu-
          lum
       nimisque inhumane. exeo ergo ut pacem conciliem.
          optume
       ipsos video.
CHR   ehem, Menedeme, quor non accersi iubes
       filiam et quot dotis dixi firmas?
SOS   mi vir, te obsecro
       ne facias.
CLIT   pater, obsecro me ignoscas.
MEN   da veniam, Chreme.
1050   sine te exorem.

---

[68] According to the Greek myth, Athena (Minerva) had no mother
but sprang fully armed from the head of her father Zeus (Jupiter).

CHR Not even if you were born from my own head, as they say Minerva was from Jupiter's,[68] would I any more for that reason, Clitipho, allow your disgraceful behaviour to destroy my reputation.

SOS May heaven forbid!

CHR I don't know about heaven, but *I*'ll do my best. You're looking for what you have, parents; you're not looking for what you don't have, the will to obey your father and preserve what he has earned by hard toil. As for playing tricks on me and bringing in before my very eyes a—I'm ashamed to say so vile a word in my wife's presence, but you weren't at all ashamed to do the deed.

CLIT (*aside*) Oh dear! How utterly annoyed I now am with myself! How ashamed I am! But I don't know how to begin to win back his favour.

Enter MENEDEMUS *from his house.*

MEN (*to himself*) Chremes really is too harsh and inhuman; he's tormenting the poor lad. So I'm coming out to make peace between them. (*seeing them*) Excellent! There they are.

CHR Oh hello, Menedemus! Why don't you send for my daughter and confirm the dowry that I offered?[69]

SOS My dear husband, I implore you, don't do it.

CLIT Father, I implore you, forgive me.

MEN Pardon him, Chremes. Let me persuade you.

Chremes' point is that, even if he were solely responsible for bringing Clitipho into the world and thus had both paternal and maternal feelings for him, he would not tolerate his misbehaviour.

[69] That is, his whole estate (see line 942).

CHR   egon mea bona ut dem Bacchidi dono sciens?
non faciam.

MEN   at id nos non sinemus.

CLIT   si me vivom vis, pater,
ignosce.

SOS   age, Chreme mi.

MEN   age, quaeso, ne tam offirma te, Chreme.

CHR quid istic? video non licere ut coeperam hoc pertendere.

MEN facis ut te decet.

CHR   ea lege hoc adeo faciam, si facit

1055   quod ego hunc aequom censeo.

CLIT   pater, omnia faciam. impera.

CHR uxorem ut ducas.

CLIT   pater!

CHR   nil audio.

SOS   ad me recipio:
faciet.

CHR   nil etiam audio ipsum.

CLIT   perii!

SOS   an dubitas, Clitipho?

CHR immo, utrum volt.

SOS   faciet omnia.

MEN   haec dum incipias, gravia sunt,
dumque ignores. ubi cognoris, facilia.

CLIT   faciam, pater.

1060 SOS gnate mi, ego pol tibi dabo illam lepidam, quam tu facile
     ames,
filiam Phanocratae nostri.

CLIT   rufamne illam virginem,
caesiam, sparso ore, adunco naso? non possum, pater.

CHR heia! ut elegans est! credas animum ibi esse.

SOS   aliam dabo.

CHR Am I to make a gift of my property to Bacchis knowingly?
I won't do it.

MEN But we won't allow that to happen.

CLIT If you want me to go on living, father, forgive me.

SOS Go on, Chremes dear.

MEN Go on, please; don't be so stubborn, Chremes.

CHR All right, then. I see I'm not allowed to persist in my intention.

MEN Now you're doing what you should.

CHR I'll do it on one conditon, that he does what I consider right and proper.

CLIT Father, I'll do anything. Just give me my orders.

CHR You must take a wife.

CLIT Father!

CHR I'm not hearing an answer.

SOS I'll take this on myself. He'll do it.

CHR I'm still not hearing an answer from him.

CLIT (*aside*) Damnation!

SOS Are you hesitating, Clitipho?

CHR No, let him choose which he prefers.

SOS He'll do everything you say.

MEN (*to Clitipho*) These things are difficult at the beginning when you're unfamiliar with them. When you get to know them, they're easy.

CLIT I'll do it, father.

SOS Heavens, my son, I'll get you a nice girl, one you'll find it easy to love, the daughter of our friend Phanocrates.

CLIT That red-haired girl, with the green eyes, freckled face, and hooked nose? I can't, father.

CHR Well, well! How choosy he is! You'd think he'd studied these things!

SOS I'll find you another girl.

CLIT immo, quandoquidem ducendast, egomet habeo prope-
          modum
1065   quam volo.

CHR   nunc laudo, gnate.

CLIT   Archonidi huius filiam.

SOS perplacet.

CLIT   pater, hoc nunc restat.

CHR   quid?

CLIT   Syro ignoscas volo
          quae mea causa fecit.

CHR   fiat.

Ω   vos valete et plaudite.

1065 nunc laudo gnate *Chremeti dat* A, *Sostratae* Σ

CLIT No. Since I've got to marry, I have one in mind myself who suits me pretty well.

CHR Now I approve of you, my son.

CLIT The daughter of our neighbour Archonides.

SOS An excellent choice.

CLIT Father, there's one more thing.

CHR What?

CLIT I want you to forgive Syrus for what he did on my behalf.

CHR Very well.

ALL *(to the audience)* Farewell and give us your applause.[70]

---

[70] See *The Woman of Andros* note 55.

THE EUNUCH

INTRODUCTORY NOTE

The Eunuch was Terence's most successful play in his own lifetime. It is said to have been staged twice in one day and to have earned the highest fee ever paid for a comedy. It is the product of a "contamination" to which Terence freely admits in the prologue; the play is based on Menander's *The Eunuch,* but Terence has added the characters of the swaggering soldier and the flattering "parasite" (or hanger-on) from a second play of Menander's called *The Flatterer.* It seems that Terence had learned from the failure of his *Mother-in-Law (Hecyra)* two years before that the Roman audience wanted more than the sophisticated comedy of manners which appealed to Terence himself and to the tastes of his immediate literary circle. For *The Eunuch,* therefore, he chose as his primary model a play which already included an audacious eunuch substitution by which an ebullient young man gained access to his girl and raped her; and to this he added two colourful stock characters from a second Greek original. The result was a play which in its general tone bore a closer resemblance to Plautus and the rest of the Roman comic tradition than did any other of Terence's plays.

The plot is centred on the affairs of two young brothers. The elder brother Phaedria is in love with the courtesan Thais, who has asked him to withdraw for a couple of days

307

while she secures from the soldier Thraso the gift of a young slave girl, who, unknown to Thraso, had been brought up as Thais' sister in their home on Rhodes and had subsequently been sold into slavery. Thais believes the girl to be of Athenian citizen parentage and is hoping to gain protection for herself as a foreigner in Athens by restoring her to her family. But the younger brother Chaerea sees the girl in the street and is captivated by her beauty; and, when the family slave Parmeno suggests that he could gain access to the girl in Thais' house by changing places with a eunuch being given to Thais by Phaedria as a present, Chaerea eagerly takes up the suggestion. Meanwhile, Thais herself attends a dinner party at Thraso's house, from which she returns with news of a quarrel and of the imminent arrival of Thraso intent on taking the girl back. After the attack of Thraso and his "army" of cooks and slaves has been turned back, Thais learns of Chaerea's rape of the girl and agrees to allow him to marry her. Thais has now lost hope of gaining support from the girl's family but instead persuades Chaerea's father to take her under his protection. All is now set for a resumption of the affair between Thais and Phaedria and for the banishment of Thraso, but by a surprise twist Thraso's hanger-on Gnatho persuades Phaedria that Thais should also keep Thraso on as a harmless dupe who will continue to pay for her extravagant tastes.

The ending of the play has given rise to much critical discussion. To many it has seemed strange that Thais, who has appeared throughout as a strong and independent woman well able to manage the menfolk with whom she has to deal, should have her affairs arranged for her behind her back. It also seems unlikely that Phaedria, who has been portrayed as a jealous lover unhappy to think of Thais spending time with a rival, should so easily agree to her keeping Thraso. Nor is Gnatho the endearing kind of parasite (like Phormio in Terence's *Phormio*) with whose final victory the audience is likely to empathise. There are two approaches to this question. One is to look for some deeper meaning in the play which the ending is designed to underline. The simplest moral is that an affair with a courtesan, in contrast to an affair with a citizen, can never be permanent or exclusive, but this is a point which scarcely requires a contrived or controversial ending. Rather more subtly, the triumph of the hanger-on has been seen as a pointer to dependence on others as a key factor in human affairs or indeed to selfishness as a prime human motive; but neither of these attitudes to life seems to be characteristic of Terence. The other approach is simply to assume that Terence has sacrificed consistency for dramatic effect; on this view the ending is merely an amusing tailpiece designed to send the audience away in good humour. In any case, Terence has chosen to modify the ending of Menander's *The Eunuch* by including the two characters taken over from *The Flatterer*, and it may be that he substituted the ending of the latter for the original *Eunuch* ending. The courtesan in *The Flatterer* was not an independent woman like Thais but a slave girl in the hands of a pimp, whose affairs could more reasonably have been settled without her being consulted.

The Eunuch is a play of colourful characters and vivid incident. Apart from the vain but cowardly Thraso and the slick self-serving Gnatho, Thais stands out as the most sympathetically drawn courtesan in Roman comedy; if not quite the "good courtesan" of the ancient commentator

Donatus, she combines self-interest with some genuine feeling both for Phaedria and for her supposed sister, and she handles Chaerea with the right mixture of humanity and reproof. Parmeno is also notable as another would-be tricky slave who turns out as a bungling slave; so far from bringing the affairs of his two younger masters to a successful conclusion, he tries vainly to withdraw his suggestion of the eunuch substitution, and is in the end fooled by Thais' vindictive maid Pythias into blurting out the truth to Chaerea's father. The most striking scene is the "siege" scene, in which Thraso and Gnatho, coming to recover the girl with a motley army of cooks and slaves, are repulsed by Thais; also good are the early dialogue in which Gnatho shamelessly flatters Thraso, the narrative of the rape by the exuberant Chaerea to his friend Antipho, and the bullying interrogation of the real eunuch by Phaedria which reveals the truth of the substitution.

SELECT BIBLIOGRAPHY

Editions and Commentaries

Barsby, J. (Cambridge, 1999).
Fabia, P. (Paris, 1895).
Tromara, L. (Thessaloniki, 1991; Hildesheim, 1994).

Criticism

Bader, B. "Terenz, *Eunuchus* 46–57." *Rheinisches Museum* 116 (1973): 54–59.
Barsby, J. A. "Problems of Adaptation in the *Eunuchus* of Terence," in N. W. Slater and B. Zimmermann, eds.,

Intertextualität in der Griechisch-römischen Komödie. Stuttgart, 1993: 160–179.

Goldberg, S. M. *"Contaminatio,"* in *Understanding Terence.* Princeton, 1986: 105–122.

Konstan, D. "Love in Terence's *Eunuch:* the Origins of Erotic Subjectivity." *American Journal of Philology* 107 (1986): 369–393.

——— *"Eunuch"* in *Greek Comedy and Ideology.* New York, 1995: 131–140.

Lowe, J. C. B. "The *Eunuchus:* Terence and Menander." *Classical Quarterly* 33 (1983): 428–444.

Ludwig, W. "Von Terenz zu Menander." *Philologus* 103 (1959): 1–38. Reprinted with addenda in E. Lefèvre (ed.), *Die römische Komödie: Plautus und Terenz.* Darmstadt, 1969: 354–408.

Martin, R. H. "A Not-so-minor Character in Terence's *Eunuchus." Classical Philology* 90 (1995): 135–151.

Rand, E. K. "The Art of Terence's *Eunuchus." Transactions of the American Philological Association* 63 (1932): 54–72.

DIDASCALIA

INCIPIT TERENTI EVNVCHVS
ACTA LVDIS MEGALENSIBVS
L. POSTVMIO ALBINO L. CORNELIO MERVLA AEDILIBVS
CVRVLIBVS
EGERE L. AMBIVIVS TVRPIO L. ATILIVS PRAENESTINVS
MODOS FECIT FLACCVS CLAVDI TIBIIS DVABVS DEXTRIS
GRAECA MENANDRV
FACTA II M. VALERIO C. FANNIO COS.

C. SVLPICI APOLLINARIS PERIOCHA

sororem falso dictitatam Thaidis
id ipsum ignorans miles advexit Thraso
ipsique donat. erat haec civis Attica.
eidem eunuchum quem emerat tradi iubet
Thaidis amator Phaedria ac rus ipse abit,
Thrasoni oratus biduom concederet.
ephebus frater Phaedriae puellulam
cum deperiret dono missam Thaidi,
ornatu eunuchi induitur (suadet Parmeno);
introiit, vitiat virginem. sed Atticus
civis repertus frater eius collocat
vitiatam ephebo. Phaedriam exorat Thraso.

PRODUCTION NOTICE

Here begins the Eunuch of Terence, acted at the Ludi Megalenses in the curule aedileship of L. Postumius Albinus and L. Cornelius Merula. The producers were L. Ambivius Turpio and L. Atilius of Praeneste. Music composed by Flaccus, slave of Claudius, for two right-hand pipes. Greek original by Menander. The author's second play, performed in the consulship of M. Valerius and C. Fannius.[1]

SYNOPSIS BY C. SULPICIUS APOLLINARIS

A girl wrongly regarded as the sister of Thais is brought by the soldier Thraso, who is unaware of her identity, and presented to Thais. The girl was in fact an Athenian citizen. Phaedria, the lover of Thais, orders a eunuch whom he has bought to be handed over to Thais, and departs himself for the country, having been persuaded to give way to Thraso for two days. Phaedria's brother, who is serving as an ephebe, falls in love with the girl given as a present to Thais, and, at Parmeno's suggestion, dresses up in the eunuch's clothes, enters the house and rapes the girl. But her brother, an Athenian citizen, is found, and he betrothes her, no longer a virgin, to the ephebe. Thraso persuades Phaedria to let him stay.

[1] That is, in 161 B.C., which makes *The Eunuch* Terence's third play, after *The Woman of Andros* (166) and *The Self-Tormentor* (163).

313

PERSONAE

PHAEDRIA adulescens
PARMENO servus
THAIS meretrix
GNATHO parasitus
CHAEREA adulescens
THRASO miles
PYTHIAS ancilla
CHREMES adulescens
ANTIPHO adulescens
DORIAS ancilla
DORUS eunuchus
SANGA servos
SOPHRONA nutrix
SENEX

Scaena: Athenis

CHARACTERS

PHAEDRIA, a young man, lover of Thais
PARMENO, slave of Phaedria's family
THAIS, a courtesan
GNATHO, hanger-on of Thraso
CHAEREA, a young man, brother of Phaedria, lover of
  Pamphila
THRASO, a soldier, another lover of Thais
PYTHIAS, a maid of Thais
CHREMES, a young man, brother of Pamphila
ANTIPHO, a young man, friend of Chaerea
DORIAS, another maid of Thais
DORUS, a eunuch
SANGA, a cook, slave of Thraso
SOPHRONA, a nurse of Pamphila's family
OLD MAN, **FATHER** (unnamed) of Phaedria and Chaerea

Staging

The stage represents a street in Athens. On it are two houses,
that of Thais to the audience's left and that of Phaedria and
Chaerea to their right. The exit on the right leads to the forum
and the house of Thraso; that on the left leads to the harbour, in
which direction lies Antipho's house, and to the country, where
Phaedria's family's farm is situated.[2]

---

[2] The location of the various houses is conjectural.

EUNUCHUS

si quisquamst qui placere se studeat bonis
quam plurumis et minume multos laedere,
in his poeta hic nomen profitetur suom.
tum si quis est qui dictum in se inclementius
5   existumavit esse, sic existumet:
responsum non dictum esse, quia laesit prior.
qui bene vortendo et easdem scribendo male ex
Graecis bonis Latinas fecit non bonas.
idem Menandri Phasma nuper perdidit,
10   atque in Thesauro scripsit causam dicere
prius unde petitur aurum qua re sit suom
quam illic qui petit unde is sit thesaurus sibi
aut unde in patrium monumentum pervenerit.
dehinc ne frustretur ipse se aut sic cogitet
15   "defunctus iam sum: nil est quod dicat mihi,"
is ne erret moneo et desinat lacessere.
habeo alia multa quae nunc condonabitur,
quae proferentur post si perget laedere
ita ut facere instituit. quam nunc acturi sumus

---

3 The reference is to Luscius of Lanuvium (see Introduction).
4 This seems to be a complaint about over-literal translation.

THE EUNUCH

PROLOGUE

If there're any who are eager to please as many worthy citizens as possible and to offend as few as possible, the playwright wishes to enrol in their number.

Further, if there's anyone[3] who believes that he has been attacked with undue harshness, let him also believe that this is a response not an attack: he struck the first blow. By translating well but at the same time writing poorly he has made bad Latin plays out of good Greek ones.[4] He recently ruined Menander's "Apparition," and in his "Treasure"[5] represented the defendant as putting his case for the possession of the gold *before* the plaintiff explained how the treasure belonged to *him* and how it came to be in his father's tomb.[6]

From now on, in case he deludes himself and imagines that he is done with this and I have nothing more to say, I warn him not to misjudge the situation or continue to provoke me. I have many other charges which he shall be spared for the moment, but they will be brought up later if he persists in attacking me as he has set out to do.

The play which we are about to perform is Menander's

[5] Apparently also based on Menander, though we know of six Greek plays of this title by different authors.

[6] The point is that, in a court of law, the plaintiff usually speaks first.

317

20   Menandri Eunuchum, postquam aediles emerunt,
        perfecit sibi ut inspiciundi esset copia.
        magistratus quom ibi adesset, occeptast agi.
        exclamat furem non poetam fabulam
        dedisse, et nil dedisse verborum tamen.
25   Colacem esse Naevi et Plauti veterem fabulam:
        parasiti personam inde ablatam et militis.
        si id est peccatum, peccatum imprudentiast
        poetae, non quo furtum facere studuerit.
        id ita esse vos iam iudicare poteritis.
30   Colax Menandrist, in east parasitus colax
        et miles gloriosus. eas se non negat
        personas transtulisse in Eunuchum suam
        ex Graeca. sed eas fabulas factas prius
        Latinas scisse sese, id vero pernegat.
35   quod si personis isdem huic uti non licet,
        qui magis licet currentem servom scribere,
        bonas matronas facere, meretrices malas,
        parasitum edacem, gloriosum militem,
        puerum supponi, falli per servom senem,
40   amare, odisse, suspicari? denique
        nullumst iam dictum quod non dictum sit prius.
        qua re aequomst vos cognoscere atque ignoscere
        quae veteres factitarunt si faciunt novi.
        date operam, cum silentio animum attendite,
45   ut pernoscatis quid sibi Eunuchus velit.

33 eas fabulas *codd.*, eas ab aliis *Ritchl,* ea ex fabula *Fleckeisen*

---

7 The aediles were the state officials in charge of the public games. This is our only record of a preview performance.

8 The Latin here could refer to a single play of joint authorship ("a

"Eunuch." After the aediles purchased it, he contrived for himself an opportunity to examine the play, and, when the official arrived, the performance began.[7] He shouted that the play was the work of a thief, not a playwright, but that the attempt to deceive had not worked. There was, he claimed, a "Flatterer" by Naevius and an old play by Plautus,[8] and the character of the parasite and the soldier had been stolen from these.

If that was an offence, the offence was due to the inadvertence of the playwright; he had no intention of committing plagiarism.[9] You can judge the truth of this for yourselves. There is a "Flatterer" of Menander, in which there is a flattering parasite and a swaggering soldier. The playwright does not deny that he has imported these characters into his "Eunuch" from the Greek play. But he does most definitely deny any knowledge of the prior existence of the Latin versions.

But in any case, if he is not permitted to use the same characters again, how is it any more permissible to present a running slave or good matrons or wicked courtesans or a greedy parasite or a boastful soldier or babies being substituted or an old man being deceived by his slave or love or hate or suspicions? In the end nothing is said now which has not been said before. So it's only fair that you should examine the facts and pardon the new playwrights if they do what the old have always done. Pay attention and listen carefully in silence, so that you may understand what "The Eunuch" has to say.

'Flatterer' of Naevius and Plautus, an old play"), but the ancient sources preserve quotations both from a "Flatterer" of Naevius and from a "Flatterer" of Plautus, and it is more likely that there were two separate plays. Line 33 below, as it stands, refers to two Latin plays; the emendations of Ritschl and Fleckeisen were designed to make it refer to two *characters* taken from a single play.

[9] On plagiarism or "theft" (Latin *furtum*) see Introduction.

ACTUS I

I. i: PHAEDRIA. PARMENO.

PHAE   quid igitur faciam? non eam ne nunc quidem
     cum accersor ultro? an potius ita me comparem
     non perpeti meretricum contumelias?
     exclusit, revocat: redeam? non si me obsecret.

50   siquidem hercle possis, nil prius neque fortius.
     verum si incipies neque pertendes gnaviter
     atque ubi pati non poteris, cum nemo expetet,
     infecta pace ultro ad eam venies, indicans
     te amare et ferre non posse, actumst, ilicet,

55   peristi; eludet ubi te victum senserit.
     proin tu, dumst tempus, etiam atque etiam cogita.

PAR   ere, quae res in se neque consilium neque modum
     habet ullum, eam consilio regere non potes.
     in amore haec omnia insunt vitia: iniuriae,

60   suspiciones, inimicitiae, indutiae,
     bellum, pax rursum. incerta haec si tu postules
     ratione certa facere, nihilo plus agas
     quam si des operam ut cum ratione insanias.
     et quod nunc tute tecum iratus cogitas

65   "egon illam, quae illum, quae me, quae non—! sine
       modo,
     mori me malim, sentiet qui vir siem,"
     haec verba una mehercle falsa lacrimula,
     quam oculos terendo misere vix vi expresserit,

50–6 *Phaedriae continuant AC¹D¹P¹ Don., 50–5 Parmenoni 56
Phaedriae dant cett., 50–6 Parmenoni dant edd.*

---

[10] Lines 50–55 are given to Parmeno by a number of the MSS, influ-

THE EUNUCH

ACT ONE

Enter PHAEDRIA *from his house with* PARMENO.

PHAE So what am I to do? Should I not go, not even now, when
she invites me of her own accord? Should I rather take
myself in hand and refuse to endure the insults of courte-
sans? She shut me out, she calls me back: shall I go? No,
not if she implores me. (*arguing with himself*)[10] If only
you could, by god, this would be the best course, and the
bravest. But if you start on it and haven't the strength to
carry it through, and, when you can't endure it, when no-
body wants you, you go to her of your own accord with no
terms negotiated, making it quite clear that you love her
and can't bear it—you've had it, it's all over, you're done
for; she'll toy with you once she sees you beaten. So,
while there's time, think and think again.

PAR Master, when a thing has no logic to it and no means
of control, you can't rule it by logic. A love affair has
all these symptoms: wrongs, suspicions, quarrels, truces,
war, peace again. If you try to impose certainty on uncer-
tainty by reason, you'd achieve no more than if you set
about going insane by reason. And as for your present
angry thoughts—"I—her? when she—him? when she—
me? when she won't—? Just let it be, I'd prefer to die,
she shall realise what sort of man I am"—god knows
she'll quell that sort of talk with one tiny little false tear,
which she's just managed to squeeze out by rubbing her

---

enced no doubt by the change to second person in line 50. Editors tend
to give line 56 also ("So . . . again:") to Parmeno, making a continuous
speech for him from line 50 to line 70 (to "pays the penalty").

321

restinguet, et te ultro accusabit, et dabis
70   ultro supplicium.
PHAE   o indignum facinus! nunc ego
    et illam scelestam esse et me miserum sentio.
    et taedet et amore ardeo, et prudens sciens
    vivos vidensque pereo nec quid agam scio.
PAR   quid agas? nisi ut te redimas captum quam queas
75   minumo; si nequeas paullulo, at quanti queas.
    et ne te afflictes.
PHAE   itane suades?
PAR   si sapis,
    neque praeterquam quas ipse amor molestias
    habet addas, et illas quas habet recte feras.
    sed eccam ipsa egreditur, nostri fundi calamitas;
80   nam quod nos capere oportet haec intercipit.

I. ii: THAIS. PHAEDRIA. PARMENO.

THA   miseram me! vereor ne illud gravius Phaedria
    tulerit neve aliorsum atque ego feci acceperit,
    quod heri intro missus non est.
PHAE   totus, Parmeno,
    tremo horreoque, postquam aspexi hanc.
PAR   bono animo es:
85   accede ad ignem hunc, iam calesces plus satis.
THA   quis hic loquitur? ehem! tun hic eras, mi Phaedria?
    quid hic stabas? quor non recta intro ibas?
PAR   ceterum
    de exclusione verbum nullum.
THA   quid taces?

eyes all pathetically; and she'll turn the accusation back
on you, and you'll be the one who pays the penalty.

PHAE What an outrageous way to behave! Now I realise that
she's a scoundrel and I'm in misery. I'm fed up with her,
but I'm on fire with love. I'm going to my ruin awake and
aware, alive and with my eyes open. And I've no idea
what to do.

PAR What to do? What else but ransom yourself from your
captivity at the lowest possible price? If you can't do it at
a trivial cost, then do it for what you can; and don't dis-
tress yourself.

PHAE Is that what you advise?

PAR If you've any sense, you won't add more troubles to those
love brings anyway, and you'll bear the ones it does bring
philosophically. (*as Thais' door opens*) But here she
comes, that blight on our estate: she takes the profits that
should come to us.

Enter THAIS *from her house.*

THA (*to herself*) Oh dear! I'm afraid Phaedria's taken my
refusal to let him in yesterday too much to heart and
interpreted it in a different way from what I intended.

PHAE (*to Parmeno*) I'm trembling and shivering all over, Par-
meno, at the sight of her.

PAR (*to Phaedria*) Don't worry. Just go near the fire (*indicat-
ing Thais*), and you'll be more than warm enough.

THA Who's that speaking? Oh hello! It's you, my dear Phae-
dria! Why are you waiting here? Why don't you come
straight inside?

PAR (*aside*) Not a word about shutting him out!

THA Why no reply?

323

PHAE sane quia vero haec mihi patent semper fores
90   aut quia sum apud te primus.

THA   missa istaec face.

PHAE quid "missa"? o Thais, Thais, utinam esset mihi
       pars aequa amoris tecum ac pariter fieret
       ut aut hoc tibi doleret itidem ut mihi dolet
       aut ego istuc abs te factum nihili penderem!

95 THA ne crucia te, obsecro, anime mi, mi Phaedria.
       non pol quo quemquam plus amem aut plus diligam
       eo feci; sed ita erat res, faciendum fuit.

PAR credo, ut fit, misera prae amore exclusti hunc foras.

THA sicin agis, Parmeno? age; sed huc qua gratia
100   te accersi iussi, ausculta.

PHAE   fiat.

THA   dic mihi
       hoc primum, potin est hic tacere?

PAR   egon? optume.
       verum heus tu, hac lege tibi meam astringo fidem.
       quae vera audivi taceo et contineo optume;
       sin falsum aut vanum aut fictumst, continuo palamst:
105   plenus rimarum sum, hac atque illac perfluo.
       proin tu, taceri si vis, vera dicito.

THA Samia mihi mater fuit. ea habitabat Rhodi.

PAR potest taceri hoc.

THA   ibi tum matri parvolam
       puellam dono quidam mercator dedit
110   ex Attica hinc abreptam.

PHAE   civemne?

---

110 civemne? *Phaedriae dant codd. pl., Parmenoni ADE*

PHAE (*with bitter irony*) It must be because in fact these doors
      are always open to me and because I come first in your
      affections.

THA   Forget all that.

PHAE How do you mean "forget"? Oh Thais, Thais, if only our
      love were evenly matched and we both felt the same, so
      that either this hurt you as much as it does me or I didn't
      care a damn about what you've done!

THA   Don't torment yourself, I implore you, my darling, my
      Phaedria. Heaven knows, I didn't do it because I love or
      care for anyone more than you; but the situation was
      such, I had to do it.

PAR   (*ironically*) I suppose you shut him out through love,
      poor woman. It does happen.

THA   Must you, Parmeno? Come on! (*to Phaedria*) But let me
      tell you why I invited you here.

PHAE (*without much enthusiasm*) All right.

THA   Tell me this first, can he (*indicating Parmeno*) keep a
      secret?

PAR   Me? Very well. But mark my words, I make you this
      promise on one condition. The truths I hear I keep se-
      cret; I contain them very well. But if anything's false or
      fanciful or fictional, it's out at once: I'm full of cracks, I
      leak all over. So, if you want your secrets kept, tell the
      truth.

THA   I had a Samian mother; she lived in Rhodes.

PAR   That can be kept secret.

THA   (*ignoring Parmeno's remark*) While she was there, a mer-
      chant gave my mother a little girl as a present. She had
      been kidnapped from here, from Attica.

PHAE An Athenian citizen?

THA   arbitror.
certum non scimus. matris nomen et patris
dicebat ipsa. patriam et signa cetera
neque scibat neque per aetatem etiam potis erat.
mercator hoc addebat: e praedonibus
115 unde emerat se audisse abreptam e Sunio.
mater ubi accepit, coepit studiose omnia
docere, educere, ita uti si esset filia.
sororem plerique esse credebant meam.
ego cum illo quocum tum uno rem habebam hospite
120 abii huc, qui mihi reliquit haec quae habeo omnia.
PAR utrumque hoc falsumst: effluet.
THA   qui istuc?
PAR   quia
neque tu uno eras contenta neque solus dedit.
nam hic quoque bonam magnamque partem ad te attulit.
THA itast. sed sine me pervenire quo volo.
125 interea miles qui me amare occeperat
in Cariamst profectus. te interea loci
cognovi. tute scis postilla quam intumum
habeam te et mea consilia ut tibi credam omnia.
PAR ne hoc quidem tacebit Parmeno.
PHAE   oh! dubiumne id est?
130 THA hoc agite, amabo. mater mea illic mortuast
nuper. eius frater aliquantum ad remst avidior.

[129] *priorem partem versus Parmenoni alteram Phaedriae dat
Thomas, priorem Phaedriae alteram Parmenoni codd. Don., priorem
Parmenoni alteram Thaidi Fleckeisen*

---

[11] A coastal village at the southern tip of Attica, about 25 miles from
Athens, with a prominent temple of Poseidon.

THA I believe so. We don't know for sure. She could tell us herself the names of her father and mother. But she knew nothing of her country of birth or other things which would identify her, nor indeed could she at her age. The merchant did add that he had heard from the pirates who sold her to him that she had been kidnapped from Sunium.[11] When my mother received her, she set about teaching and educating her as devotedly as if she were her own daughter. Most people believed she was my sister. As for me, I came to Athens with a visitor with whom I was then having an affair, my only one. It was he who left me everything I now have.

PAR Two falsehoods. They'll both leak out.

THA How do you mean?

PAR You were not content with one man, nor was he the only one who gave you gifts. He too (*indicating Phaedria*) has made a handsome contribution.

THA That's true. But let me complete my story. After this a soldier fell in love with me. He left for Caria,[12] and while he was away I got to know you. You know yourself how close we have been since then and how I confide all my plans to you.

PAR Parmeno won't keep that secret either.

PHAE (*with heavy irony*) Oh! Is there some doubt, then?

THA Do me a favour and pay attention. My mother recently died over there. She has a brother who is rather too greedy where money's concerned. When he saw that the

[12] An area in what is now the southwest corner of Turkey, which figured in the squabbles of the Macedonian generals after the death of Alexander the Great and is mentioned several times in comedy as a scene of fighting for mercenary soldiers.

is ubi esse hanc forma videt honesta virginem
et fidibus scire, pretium sperans ilico
producit, vendit. forte fortuna adfuit
135 hic meus amicus. emit eam dono mihi
imprudens harum rerum ignarusque omnium.
is venit. postquam sensit me tecum quoque
rem habere, fingit causas ne det sedulo.
ait, si fidem habeat se iri praepositum tibi
140 apud me ac non id metuat ne ubi acceperim
sese relinquam, velle se illam mihi dare;
verum id vereri. sed ego quantum suspicor,
ad virginem animum adiecit.

PHAE   etiamne amplius?

THA nil; nam quaesivi. nunc ego eam, mi Phaedria,
145 multae sunt causae quam ob rem cupiam abducere:
primum quod soror est dicta, praeterea ut suis
restituam ac reddam. sola sum: habeo hic neminem
neque amicum neque cognatum. quam ob rem, Phae-
    dria,
cupio aliquos parere amicos beneficio meo.
150 id amabo adiuta me. quo id fiat facilius,
sine illum priores partis hosce aliquot dies
apud me habere. nil respondes?

PHAE   pessuma,
egon quicquam cum istis factis tibi respondeam?

PAR eu, noster, laudo. tandem perdoluit. vir es.

155 PHAE aut ego nescibam quorsum tu ires? "parvola
hinc est abrepta; eduxit mater pro sua;

---

13 The reference is probably to the cithara, a guitar-like instrument

girl was good-looking and could play the lute,[13] he put
her up for sale on the spot, hoping for a good price, and
sold her. By a lucky chance this friend of mind was there,
and he bought her as a gift for me, in complete and utter
ignorance of all the circumstances. He then came back
here. Once he realised that I was having an affair with
you as well, he constantly invented reasons for not giving
me the girl. He said that, if he was convinced he would be
preferred to you in my eyes and if he wasn't afraid I
would abandon him once I'd got the girl, he was willing to
give her to me; but, he said, he was afraid of this. Anyway,
I've a suspicion he's taken a fancy to the girl.

PHAE Has he done more than that?

THA No; I've inquired. Now, my dear Phaedria, there are
many reasons why I am keen to get her away from him.
First, because she's called my sister; and, besides, I want
to restore her to her family. I'm alone. I have no friend
here or relative, and so, Phaedria, I'm keen to gain some
friends by doing a good turn of my own. Be a darling
and help me with this. To make things easier for me, let
him have the first place with me for the next few days.
(*Phaedria remains silent*) You don't reply?

PHAE Damn you, do you expect a reply when you treat me as
you do?

PAR (*to Phaedria*) Well done, master, good for you! At last
she's provoked you; you're a man.

PHAE Or do you think I didn't know what you were driving
at? "She was kidnapped from here as a small child; my
mother brought her up as her own; she was called my sis-

held on the knee, rather than to the lyre, which sat on the floor like a
harp.

soror dictast; cupio abducere, ut reddam suis."
nempe omnia haec nunc verba huc redeunt denique:
ego excludor, ille recipitur. qua gratia?

160 nisi illum plus amas quam me et istam nunc times
quae advectast ne illum talem praeripiat tibi.

THA ego id timeo?

PHAE   quid te ergo aliud sollicitat? cedo:
num solus ille dona dat? num ubi meam
benignitatem sensisti intercludier?

165 nonne ubi mi dixti cupere te ex Aethiopia
ancillulam, relictis rebus omnibus
quaesivi? porro eunuchum dixti velle te,
quia solae utuntur his reginae: repperi.
heri minas viginti pro ambobus dedi.

170 tamen contemptus abs te haec habui in memoria;
ob haec facta abs te spernor.

THA   quid istic, Phaedria?
quamquam illam cupio abducere atque hac re arbitror
id fieri posse maxume, verum tamen
potius quam te inimicum habeam faciam ut iusseris.

175 PHAE utinam istuc verbum ex animo ac vere diceres:
"potius quam te inimicum habeam"! si istuc crederem
sincere dici, quidvis possem perpeti.

PAR labascit victus uno verbo quam cito!

---

14 The Greeks and Romans envisaged the Ethiopians as living right
across Africa from west to east. Dark-skinned slaves were fashionable in
Greece from the time of Alexander's conquests and continued to be so
in the Roman period.

15 Eunuchs were employed at the courts of the Persian kings and
also by Alexander the Great. In the context of the play the eunuch is an
exotic and extravagant gift.

ter; I want to get her away from him to restore her to her family." The fact is, all these fine words in the end come down to this: I'm shut out, he's let in. Why? Unless you love him more than me and you're afraid now that this girl who has been brought here will snatch your splendid soldier from you.

THA Me afraid of that?

PHAE Well, what else worries you? Tell me, is he the only one who gives you gifts? Is there any respect in which you have seen my generosity falter? When you told me that you wanted a slave girl from Ethiopia,[14] didn't I leave everything and find you one? On top of that you said you wanted a eunuch,[15] because only royal women have them. I found one, and yesterday I paid twenty minas for the pair.[16] Though you treated me with contempt, I didn't forget; and in return for all this you scorn me.

THA All right, then, Phaedria. Although I'm keen to get possession of her and I judge this is the best way to do it, even so, rather than lose your friendship, I'll do as you suggest.

PHAE "Rather than lose your friendship"? If only you spoke that sentence truthfully and from the bottom of your heart! If I believed you spoke it sincerely, I could endure anything.

PAR (aside) How soon he wavers, overcome by a single sentence!

---

[16] In real-life Athens a skilled adult slave cost only three to five minas; in comedy young men are willing to pay up to 40 minas to buy their girls from slave dealers.

	THA	ego non ex animo misera dico? quam ioco
180		rem voluisti a me tandem quin perfeceris?
		ego impetrare nequeo hoc abs te, biduom
		saltem ut concedas solum.

PHAE   siquidem biduom;

        verum ne fiant isti viginti dies.

THA   profecto non plus biduom aut—

PHAE   "aut" nil moror.

185 THA non fiet; hoc modo sine te exorem.

PHAE   scilicet

        faciundumst quod vis.

THA   merito te amo, bene facis.

PHAE rus ibo. ibi hoc me macerabo biduom.

        ita facere certumst, mos gerundust Thaidi.

        tu, Parmeno, huc fac illi adducantur.

PAR   maxume.

190 PHAE in hoc biduom, Thais, vale.

THA   mi Phaedria,

        et tu. numquid vis aliud?

PHAE   egone quid velim?

        cum milite isto praesens absens ut sies;

        dies noctisque me ames, me desideres,

        me somnies, me exspectes, de me cogites,

195   me speres, me te oblectes, mecum tota sis;

        meus fac sis postremo animus, quando ego sum tuos.

THA   me miseram, fors sit an hic mi parvam habeat fidem

        atque ex aliarum ingeniis nunc me iudicet.

        ego pol, quae mihi sum conscia, hoc certo scio,

200   neque me finxisse falsi quicquam neque meo

        cordi esse quemquam cariorem hoc Phaedria.

        et quidquid huius feci, causa virginis

THA   Oh dear, do I not speak from the bottom of my heart? Tell me, what have you asked from me even in jest, which you haven't obtained? Yet I can't prevail upon you to do me the favour of going away for a mere two days.

PHAE If it is two days. But make sure they don't become twenty.

THA   I assure you, not more than two days, or—

PHAE "Or"? I don't like the sound of that.

THA   It won't happen. Just grant me this one thing.

PHAE (*reluctantly*) Evidently I have to do what you want.

THA   No wonder I love you. You're very kind.

PHAE (*to himself*) I'll go to the farm and stew in misery there for two days. I've made up my mind: I must let Thais have her way. (*to Parmeno, nodding towards his house*) Parmeno, have those two brought across.

PAR   Certainly. (*he exits into the house*)

PHAE For these two days, Thais, farewell.

THA   You too, my dear Phaedria. Is there anything else I can do for you?

PHAE Do for me? When you're with that soldier, be absent from him. Day and night love me, miss me, dream of me, look for me, think of me, hope for me, delight in me, be entirely with me. In short, be my heart as I am yours. (*he exits into his house, leaving Thais alone on stage*)

THA   (*to herself*) Oh dear! It looks as if he has little trust in me and is judging me by the character of other women. As for me, knowing myself as I do, I'm quite sure I've not invented any falsehood and nobody is dearer to me than Phaedria. Whatever I've done in this matter, I've done

feci. nam me eius spero fratrem propemodum
iam repperisse, adulescentem adeo nobilem;
205   et is hodie venturum ad me constituit domum.
concedam hinc intro atque exspectabo dum venit.

ACTUS II

II. i: PHAEDRIA. PARMENO.

PHAE fac, ita ut iussi, deducantur isti.
PAR   faciam.
PHAE   at diligenter.
PAR   fiet.
PHAE   at mature.
PAR   fiet.
PHAE   satin hoc mandatumst tibi?
PAR   ah!
rogitare quasi difficile sit!
210   utinam tam aliquid invenire facile possis, Phaedria,
quam hoc peribit!
PHAE   ego quoque una pereo, quod mist carius.
ne istuc tam iniquo patiare animo.
PAR   minume, qui effectum dabo.
sed numquid aliud imperas?
PHAE munus nostrum ornato verbis, quod poteris, et istum ae-
           mulum,
215   quod poteris, ab ea pellito.
PAR   memini, tam etsi nullus moneas.
PHAE   ego rus ibo atque ibi manebo.
PAR censeo.
PHAE   sed heus tu!
PAR   quid vis?

for the girl's sake. I think I've now just about identified her brother, a young man of a very good family; and he's agreed to come and see me at home today. I'll go inside and wait until he comes. (*she exits into her house, leaving the stage empty*)

ACT TWO

Enter PHAEDRIA from his house with PARMENO.

PHAE Have them brought across, as I told you.

PAR I will.

PHAE But be sure.

PAR It will be done.

PHAE But quickly.

PAR It will be done.

PHAE Are my instructions quite clear?

PAR Oh! Why keep asking, as if it were difficult? If only you could find a way to make a profit, Phaedria, as easily as you'll make a loss here!

PHAE I am lost myself at the same time, which I care about more; so don't be so unreasonable about it.

PAR I'm not being unreasonable; I'll get it done. Is there anything else?

PHAE Say what you can in praise of my gift, and do what you can to chase that rival away.

PAR I have that in mind even without you prompting me.

PHAE I'll go to the farm and stay there.

PAR I think you should.

PHAE But listen.

PAR What do you want?

PHAE   censen posse me offirmare et
perpeti ne redeam interea?

PAR   tene? non hercle arbitror;
nam aut iam revortere aut mox noctu te adiget horsum
    insomnia.

220 PHAE opus faciam, ut defetiger usque, ingratiis ut dormiam.

PAR vigilabis lassus: hoc plus facies.

PHAE   abi, nil dicis, Parmeno.
eicienda hercle haec est mollities animi. nimis me indul-
    geo.
tandem non ego illam caream, si sit opus, vel totum tri-
    duom?

PAR   hui!
universum triduom? vide quid agas.

PHAE   stat sententia.

225 PAR di boni! quid hoc morbist? adeon homines immutarier
ex amore ut non cognoscas eundem esse! hoc nemo fuit
minus ineptus, magis severus quisquam nec magis conti-
    nens.
sed quis hic est qui huc pergit? attat! hicquidemst parasi-
    tus Gnatho
militis. ducit secum una virginem dono huic. papae,
230 facie honesta! mirum ni ego me turpiter hodie hic dabo
cum meo decrepito hoc eunucho. haec superat ipsam
    Thaidem.

II. ii: GNATHO. PARMENO.

GNA di immortales! homini homo quid praestat? stulto intel-
    legens
quid interest? hoc adeo ex hac re venit in mentem mihi.

PHAE Do you suppose I can be resolute and hold out without coming back meanwhile?

PAR You? No, I don't, for god's sake. Either you'll return at once, or presently when night comes insomnia will drive you back.

PHAE I'll work on the farm until I'm so utterly exhausted that I sleep in spite of myself.

PAR You'll lie awake weary; that's all you'll achieve.

PHAE Come on, Parmeno, you're talking nonsense. (*to himself*) By god, I must banish this softness of heart; I'm being too easy on myself. Couldn't I in the end do without her for a whole three days if I had to?

PAR Wow! A whole three days? Be careful!

PHAE My mind's made up. (*he exits left in the direction of the farm, leaving Parmeno onstage alone*)

PAR (*to himself*) Good gods, what kind of a disease is this? To think that people can be so changed by love that you wouldn't recognise them as the same person! Nobody was less irresponsible than Phaedria or more serious or more sober-minded. (*looking down the street*) But who's this coming this way? Oh no! It's the soldier's parasite Gnatho. He's bringing the girl with him to present to her (*pointing to Thais' house*). Gosh, what a beauty! It looks like I'm going to cut a sorry figure today with this decrepit eunuch of mine. This girl surpasses Thais herself.

Enter GNATHO right from the direction of the forum with Pamphila and a maid.

GNA (*to himself*) Ye immortal gods! How one man excels another! What a difference there is between an intelligent man and a fool! I'll tell you how this thought occurred to

337

conveni hodie adveniens quendam mei loci hinc atque
    ordinis,

235   hominem haud impurum, itidem patria qui abligurrierat
    bona.

video sentum, squalidum, aegrum, pannis annisque obsi-
    tum. "oh!

quid istuc" inquam "ornatist?" "quoniam miser quod ha-
    bui perdidi, em

quo redactus sum. omnes noti me atque amici deserunt."

hic ego illum contempsi prae me: "quid, homo" inquam
    "ignavissume?

240   itan parasti te ut spes nulla relicua in te sit tibi?

simul consilium cum re amisti? viden me ex eodem or-
    tum loco?

qui color, nitor, vestitus, quae habitudost corporis!

omnia habeo neque quicquam habeo; nil quomst, nil
    defit tamen."

245   "at ego infelix neque ridiculus esse neque plagas pati

possum." "quid? tu his rebus credis fieri? tota erras via.

olim isti fuit generi quondam quaestus apud saeclum
    prius.

hoc novomst aucipium; ego adeo primus inveni viam.

est genus hominum qui esse primos se omnium rerum
    volunt

nec sunt. hos consector; hisce ego non paro me ut ri-
    deant,

250   sed eis ultro arrideo et eorum ingenia admiror simul.

quidquid dicunt laudo; id rursum si negant, laudo id
    quoque.

negat quis, nego; ait, aio. postremo imperavi egomet
    mihi

omnia assentari. is quaestus nunc est multo uberrimus."

me. On my way here today I met a person of my own rank
and station, a decent enough fellow, who had, like me,
guzzled away his inheritance. He looked unkempt, dirty,
sick, shabbily dressed, and senile. "Oh!" I said, "What
sort of a get-up is that?" "I've lost what I had, unfortu-
nately, and look what I'm reduced to. I'm abandoned by
all my friends and acquaintances." I was full of contempt
for him compared with myself. "What!" I said, "you
spineless fellow! Have you managed your life in such a
way as to leave yourself without hope? Have you lost your
wits along with your wealth? I've come from the same
background: look at me, my complexion, my style, my
clothes, my physical condition. I have everything and
I have nothing; no possessions but nothing lacking." "But
in my unhappy state I can't play the buffoon or take
a beating." "What? Is that how you suppose it's done?
You're on quite the wrong track. Once upon a time, long
ago, in a previous generation, that was the way our type
earned a living. Now there's a new way to catch our prey,
and I am the original inventor. There is a type of men
who want to be the first in everything but aren't. I track
these down. I don't set out to make them laugh at me; I
laugh at them instead while at the same time expressing
admiration for their wit. Whatever they say, I praise it; if
they then say the opposite, I praise that too. They deny, I
deny; they affirm, I affirm. In short it's my self-imposed
rule to agree to everything. It's by far the most profitable
way to earn a living these days."

PAR   scitum hercle hominem! hic homines prorsum ex stultis
      insanos facit.

255 GNA   dum haec loquimur, interea loci ad macellum ubi adven-
         tamus,
      concurrunt laeti mi obviam cuppedenarii omnes,
      cetarii, lanii, coqui, fartores, piscatores,
      quibus et re salva et perdita profueram et prosum saepe.
      salutant, ad cenam vocant, adventum gratulantur.
260   ille ubi miser famelicus videt mi esse tantum honorem et
      tam facile victum quaerere, ibi homo coepit me obse-
         crare
      ut sibi liceret discere id de me. sectari iussi,
      si potis est, tamquam philosophorum habent disciplinae
         ex ipsis
      vocabula, parasiti ita ut Gnathonici vocentur.
265 PAR   viden otium et cibus quid facit alienus?
    GNA   sed ego cesso
      ad Thaidem hanc deducere et rogare ad cenam ut veniat?
      sed Parmenonem ante ostium hic astare tristem video,
      rivalis servom. salva res est! nimirum homines frigent.
      nebulonem hunc certumst ludere.
    PAR   hisce hoc munere arbitrantur
270   suam Thaidem esse.
    GNA   pluruma salute Parmenonem
      summum suom impertit Gnatho. quid agitur?
    PAR   statur.
    GNA   video.
      numquidnam hic quod nolis vides?

---

[267] ostium hic astare *Fabia,* ostium Thainis *Don. in comm.,* ostium
Thaidis *codd.*

PAR (*aside*) A smart fellow indeed! Turns fools into madmen just like that!

GNA In the course of this conversation we arrived at the market. Everybody ran up delighted to see me, the snack sellers, the fishmongers, the butchers, the cooks, the poulterers, the spratsellers, men who had profited by me in good times and in bad and often still do. They greeted me, invited me to dinner, congratulated me on my safe return. When the starving wretch saw me held in such respect and earning my living so easily, he began to implore me to let him learn the technique from me. I told him to enrol as my pupil, in the hope that, just as philosophical schools take their names from their founders, so parasites may be called Gnathonists.

PAR (*aside*) Do you see what a life of idleness, and other people's food, does for a person?

GNA But I must hurry up and deliver this girl to Thais and ask her to come to dinner. (*turning towards Thais' house*) But I see our rival's slave Parmeno standing by the door looking gloomy. All's well. Unless I'm mistaken, they're getting a cool reception. I've a mind to to make fun of this good-for-nothing.

PAR (*aside*) These people think that with this gift Thais is theirs.

GNA Gnatho offers his warmest greetings to his most esteemed friend Parmeno. How are you doing?

PAR I'm standing.

GNA So I see. Is there anything here (*indicating the girl*) which you would rather not see?

PAR   te.

GNA   credo. at numquid aliud?

PAR quidum?

GNA   quia tristi's.

PAR   nil quidem.

GNA   ne sis. sed quid videtur
hoc tibi mancupium?

PAR   non malum hercle.

GNA   uro hominem.

PAR   ut falsus animist!

275 GNA quam hoc munus gratum Thaidi arbitrare esse?

PAR   hoc nunc dicis
eiectos hinc nos. omnium rerum, heus, vicissitudost.

GNA sex ego te totos, Parmeno, hos mensis quietum reddam,
ne sursum deorsum cursites neve usque ad lucem vigiles.
ecquid beo te?

PAR   men? papae!

GNA   sic soleo amicos.

PAR   laudo.

280 GNA detineo te. fortasse tu profectus alio fueras.

PAR nusquam.

GNA   tum tu igitur paullulum da mi operae. fac ut admittar
ad illam.

PAR   age modo, i. nunc tibi patent fores haec quia istam ducis.

GNA numquem evocari hinc vis foras?

PAR   sine biduom hoc praetereat:
qui mihi nunc uno digitulo fores aperis fortunatus,

285   ne tu istas faxo calcibus saepe insultabis frustra.

PAR You.

GNA Quite so. But anything else?

PAR How do you mean?

GNA You're looking gloomy.

PAR Not at all.

GNA You mustn't be. But what do you think of this piece of goods (*indicating the girl*)?

PAR Not bad, for god's sake.

GNA (*aside*) He's smarting.

PAR (*aside*) How mistaken he is!

GNA How do you think Thais will like this gift?

PAR What you're saying is that with this gift we're now shut out of here. All things are subject to change, you mark my words.

GNA I'll give you six whole months of peace, Parmeno: no running up and down all the time and staying awake until dawn. Doesn't that make you happy?

PAR Me? Oh yes!

GNA This is what I do for my friends.

PAR (*ironically*) Congratulations.

GNA I'm keeping you. Perhaps you were on your way somewhere else.

PAR Nowhere.

GNA Then give me a tiny bit of help. Get me admitted to her. (*indicating Thais' house*)

PAR Come off it! Go in! These doors are open to you now that you are bringing her. (*indicating the girl*)

GNA (*gloating*) Is there anyone you would like sent out? (*he exits into Thais' house with Pamphila and her maid*)

PAR (*shouting after him*) Just let these two days pass. Now, when your luck's in, you can open these doors with your little finger; but, believe me, I'll have you kicking at them in the future with no success, however often you try.

343

GNA etiamnunc tu hic stas, Parmeno? eho, numnam hic relic-
tu's custos,
ne quis forte internuntius clam a milite ad istam curset?
PAR facete dictum! mira vero militi qui placeat!
sed video erilem filium minorem huc advenire.
290 miror quid ex Piraeo abierit. nam ibi custos publicest
nunc.
non temerest, et properans venit. nescioquid circum-
spectat.

II. iii: CHAEREA. PARMENO.

CHAE occidi!
neque virgost usquam neque ego, qui illam a conspectu
amisi meo.
ubi quaeram, ubi investigem, quem perconter, quam in-
sistam viam,
295 incertus sum. una haec spes est: ubi ubist, diu celari non
potest.
o faciem pulchram! deleo omnis dehinc ex animo mulie-
res.
taedet cotidianarum harum formarum.
PAR   ecce autem alterum!
nescioquid de amore loquitur. o infortunatum senem!
hic vero est qui si occeperit
300 ludum iocumque dices fuisse illum alterum,
praeut huius rabies quae dabit.
CHAE ut illum di deaeque senium perdant qui me hodie remo-
ratus est,
meque adeo qui ei restiterim, tum autem qui illum flocci
fecerim.
sed eccum Parmenonem. salve.

GNA (*emerging from Thais' house*) Are you still standing here, Parmeno? Hey, were you left here on guard in case some messenger from the soldier called on her secretly? (*he exits right in the direction of the forum, leaving Parmeno on stage alone*)

PAR (*to himself*) Very witty! Quite surprising for a soldier's hanger-on! (*looking down the street*) But I see the master's younger son approaching. I wonder why he's left the Piraeus;[17] he's on guard duty there.[18] There must be a reason. And he's in a hurry: he's looking around for something.

Enter CHAEREA *left from the harbour in military uniform with cloak, cap, and sword.*

CHAE (*to himself*) Damnation! The girl's lost; and so am I, now I've lost sight of her. I just don't know where to look, where to search, whom to question, which way to take. There's only one hope: wherever she is, she can't be hidden for long. What gorgeous looks! From now on I banish all other women from my mind. I've had enough of these everyday beauties.

PAR (*aside*) Now look, here's the other one, muttering something about love! The poor old master! If this one gets going, you'll say the other was only fun and games, compared with the effects of this one's passions.

CHAE (*to himself*) May all the gods and goddesses destroy the old fool who delayed me today, and me too for stopping and taking any notice of him! (*catching sight of Parmeno*) But there's Parmeno. Good day.

---

[17] The port of Athens, about four miles southwest of the city.
[18] See *The Woman of Andros* note 9.

PAR   quid tu's tristis? quidve es alacris?

305   unde is?

CHAE   egone? nescio hercle,

       neque unde eam neque quorsum eam; ita prorsus sum oblitus mei.

PAR   qui, quaeso?

CHAE   amo.

PAR   hem!

CHAE   nunc, Parmeno, ostendes te qui vir sies.

       scis te mihi saepe pollicitum esse "Chaerea, aliquid inveni

       modo quod ames; in ea re utilitatem ego faciam ut cognoscas meam,"

310   quom in cellulam ad te patris penum omnem congerebam clanculum.

PAR   age, inepte.

CHAE   hoc hercle factumst. fac sis nunc promissa appareant,

       si adeo digna res est ubi tu nervos intendas tuos.

       haud similis virgost virginum nostrarum quas matres student

       demissis umeris esse, vincto pectore, ut gracilae sient.

315   si quaest habitior paullo, pugilem esse aiunt, deducunt cibum.

       tam etsi bonast natura, reddunt curatura iunceam.

       itaque ergo amantur.

PAR   quid tua istaec?

CHAE   nova figura oris.

PAR   papae!

CHAE color verus, corpus solidum et suci plenum.

PAR   anni?

CHAE   anni? sedecim.

PAR Why so gloomy? Why so agitated? Where've you been?

CHAE Me? I've no idea where I've been or where I'm going.
      I've lost myself completely.

PAR How so, if I may ask?

CHAE I'm in love.

PAR What!

CHAE Now, Parmeno, you shall show what sort of man you are.
      You know, when I used to bring my father's whole larder
      to your room in secret, you often made me a promise:
      "Chaerea, just find someone to love, and I'll make you
      aware how useful I can be in that regard."

PAR Come off it, don't be silly!

CHAE Well, it's happened, for god's sake. Now kindly make
      good your promises, always supposing this is a matter
      worth exerting your powers on. This girl is quite different
      from those local girls whose mothers want them to round
      their shoulders and strap up their chests to make them
      look slim. If one's a bit plump, they say she looks like a
      boxer, and put her on a diet. However well endowed she
      is by nature, the treatment makes her as thin as a reed.
      And they still find lovers!

PAR Well, what about this girl of yours?

CHAE A quite unusual face.

PAR Gosh!

CHAE Natural complexion, body firm and juicy.

PAR Age?

CHAE Age? Sixteen.

PAR flos ipse.

CHAE nunc hanc tu mihi vel vi vel clam vel precario
320 fac tradas. mea nil refert dum potiar modo.

PAR quid? virgo quoiast?

CHAE nescio hercle.

PAR undest?

CHAE tantundem.

PAR ubi habitat?

CHAE ne id quidem.

PAR ubi vidisti?

CHAE in via.

PAR qua ratione amisisti?

CHAE id equidem adveniens mecum stomachabar modo
nec quemquam ego esse hominem arbitror quoi magis
bonae
325 felicitates omnes advorsae sient.

PAR quid hoc est sceleris?

CHAE perii!

PAR quid factumst?

CHAE rogas?
patris cognatum atque aequalem Archidemidem
novistin?

PAR quidni?

CHAE is, dum hanc sequor, fit mi obviam.

PAR incommode hercle.

CHAE immo enimvero infeliciter;
330 nam incommoda alia sunt dicenda, Parmeno.
illum liquet mihi deierare his mensibus
sex septem prorsum non vidisse proxumis,
nisi nunc quom minume vellem minumeque opus fuit.
eho, nonne hoc monstri similest? quid ais?

348

THE EUNUCH

PAR The very flower of youth!

CHAE Now get her delivered to me, by force or stealth or entreaty. I don't mind how, so long as I get possession of her.

PAR What? Who does she belong to?

CHAE I've no idea.

PAR Where's she from?

CHAE Nor that.

PAR Where does she live?

CHAE Nor that either.

PAR Where did you see her?

CHAE In the street.

PAR How did you lose her?

CHAE That is what I was fuming about when I arrived here just now. I don't think there's a man alive whose good fortunes all turn to bad like mine.

PAR What sort of calamity is this?

CHAE I'm ruined!

PAR What happened?

CHAE Well may you ask! My father's friend and relative Archidemides—you know him?

PAR Of course.

CHAE He ran into me while I was following the girl.

PAR Rather inconvenient.

CHAE Positively disastrous, you mean. Other things deserve to be called inconvenient, Parmeno. I can swear in all honesty that I haven't set eyes on the fellow in the past six or seven months, except now, when it was the last thing I could want and the last thing I needed. Hey, isn't this monstrous? What do you say?

---

326 quid hoc est sceleris? *Parmenoni dat Σ, Chaereae continuat A*

PAR   maxume.

335 CHAE continuo accurrit ad me, quam longe quidem,
incurvos, tremulus, labiis demissis, gemens.
"heus, heus, tibi dico, Chaerea" inquit. restiti.
"scin quid ego te volebam?" "dic." "cras est mihi
iudicium." "quid tum?" "ut diligenter nunties

340 patri, advocatus mane mi esse ut meminerit."
dum haec dicit, abiit hora. rogo numquid velit.
"recte" inquit. abeo. quom huc respicio ad virginem,
illaec se interea commodum huc advorterat
in hanc nostram plateam.

PAR   mirum ni hanc dicit, modo

345 huic quae datast dono.

CHAE   huc quom advenio, nulla erat.

PAR comites secuti scilicet sunt virginem?

CHAE verum: parasitus cum ancilla.

PAR   ipsast. ilicet,
desine, iam conclamatumst.

CHAE   alias res agis.

PAR istuc ago equidem.

CHAE   nostin quae sit, dic mihi, aut

350 vidistin?

PAR   vidi, novi, scio quo abducta sit.

CHAE eho, Parmeno mi, nostin? et scis ubi siet?

PAR huc deductast ad meretricem Thaidem; ei dono datast.

CHAE quis is est tam potens cum tanto munere hoc?

PAR   miles Thraso,
Phaedriae rivalis.

CHAE   duras fratris partis praedicas.

---

343 illaec se *Grant metri gratia*, illa sese *codd.*

PAR Absolutely.

CHAE He ran straight up to me, from quite a way off, stooping, shaking, lips sagging, wheezing. "Hey, hey, I say, you there! Chaerea!" he said. I stopped. "Do you know what I want you for?" "Tell me." "I've a court case tomorrow." "So what?" "Make sure you remind your father to come and support me first thing." While he was saying this, an hour passed. I asked him if there was anything else. "No, thanks," he said. I was off. When I looked this way for the girl, she had that very moment turned down here into our street.

PAR (*aside*) It looks as if he's talking about the girl who's just been presented to Thais.

CHAE When I got here, she was nowhere to be seen.

PAR I suppose there were some companions to escort the girl?

CHAE Yes. A sponger and a maid.

PAR (*aside*) It's the very girl. (*to Chaerea*) It's all over, forget it, it's dead and buried.

CHAE You're talking about something else.

PAR I'm talking about your problem.

CHAE (*eagerly*) Do you know who she is? Tell me, have you seen her?

PAR Seen her, know her, know where she's been taken.

CHAE (*excitedly*) Hey, my dear Parmeno, you know her? You know where she is?

PAR She was delivered to the courtesan Thais as a present.

CHAE What man has the means to give a gift like that?

PAR The soldier Thraso, Phaedria's rival.

CHAE This means my brother will have a hard part to play.

355 PAR   immo enim si scias quod donum huic dono contra comparet,
        magis id dicas.

CHAE   quodnam, quaeso hercle?

PAR   eunuchum.

CHAE   illumne, obsecro,
        inhonestum hominem, quem mercatus est heri, senem
        mulierem?

PAR   istunc ipsum.

CHAE   homo quatietur certe cum dono foras.
        sed istam Thaidem non scivi nobis vicinam.

PAR   haud diust.

360 CHAE perii! numquamne etiam me illam vidisse! ehodum, dic
        mi
        estne, ut fertur, forma?

PAR   sane.

CHAE   at nil ad nostram hanc?

PAR   alia res.

CHAE obsecro hercle, Parmeno, fac ut potiar.

PAR   faciam sedulo ac
        dabo operam, adiuvabo. numquid me aliud?

CHAE   quo nunc is?

PAR   domum,
        ut mancupia haec, ita uti iussit frater, ducam ad Thaidem.

365 CHAE o fortunatum istum eunuchum quiquidem in hanc detur
        domum!

PAR   quid ita?

CHAE   rogitas? summa forma semper conservam domi

        videbit, conloquetur, aderit una in unis aedibus,

THE EUNUCH

PAR Yes indeed, and, if you knew what gift he is offering in competition, you'd say so all the more.

CHAE Tell me, what gift?

PAR A eunuch.

CHAE Not that repulsive fellow he bought yesterday, for goodness' sake, that woman of a man?

PAR The very one.

CHAE He'll be thrown out for sure, gift and all. But I didn't know Thais was a neighbour of ours.

PAR She hasn't been for long.

CHAE Damn it! To think that I've never yet set eyes on her! Hey, tell me, is she the beauty she's made out to be?

PAR Very much so.

CHAE But nothing compared to my girl?

PAR No, she's something different.

CHAE Parmeno, I implore you, help me to get possession of her.

PAR I'll do my best, I'll attend to it, I'll help you. Now is there anything else? (*he makes to leave*)

CHAE Where are you off to?

PAR Home, to take those goods to Thais, as your brother told me to.

CHAE Oh the lucky eunuch, to be taken into that house as a gift!

PAR How do you mean?

CHAE You ask? He'll have this gorgeous fellow slave at home all the time to look at and talk to. He'll live together in the

cibum nonnumquam capiet cum ea, interdum propter
   dormiet.
PAR   quid si nunc tute fortunatus fias?
CHAE   qua re, Parmeno?
370   responde.
PAR   capias tu illius vestem.
CHAE   vestem? quid tum postea?
PAR   pro illo te ducam.
CHAE   audio.
PAR   te esse illum dicam.
CHAE   intellego.
PAR   tu illis fruare commodis quibus tu illum dicebas modo:
       cibum una capias, adsis, tangas, ludas, propter dormias,
       quandoquidem illarum neque te quisquam novit neque
          scit qui sies.
375   praeterea forma et aetas ipsast facile ut pro eunucho pro-
       bes.
CHAE dixisti pulchre. numquam vidi melius consilium dari.
       age eamus intro nunciam; orna me, abduc, duc quantum
          potest.
PAR   quid agis? iocabar equidem.
CHAE   garris.
PAR   perii! quid ego egi miser?
       quo trudis? perculeris iam tu me. tibi equidem dico,
          mane!
380 CHAE eamus.
PAR   pergin?
CHAE   certumst.
PAR   vide ne nimium calidum hoc sit modo.
CHAE non est profecto. sine.
PAR   at enim istaec in me cudetur faba.

same house, he'll sometimes eat with her, and from time
to time he'll sleep next to her.

PAR What if you now became the lucky one?

CHAE In what way? (*eagerly*) Answer me.

PAR You could put on his clothes.

CHAE Clothes? And then what?

PAR I could take you instead of him.

CHAE I'm listening.

PAR I could say you were him.

CHAE I begin to see.

PAR You could enjoy the benefits which you were just saying
would be his—eat with her, live with her, touch her, play
with her, sleep next to her. None of the women recog-
nises you or knows who you are. Besides, you're so young
and good-looking, you could easily pass as a eunuch.

CHAE It's a brilliant idea. I've never known better advice. (*ea-
gerly*) Come on then, let's go in now. Dress me up and
take me across as quick as you can.

PAR What are you thinking of? I was only joking.

CHAE Nonsense!

PAR Damn it! Oh, what have I done? (*Chaerea pushes him
towards the house*) Stop shoving me. You'll knock me
down. I'm warning you, stop it!

CHAE Let's go.

PAR Are you going through with this?

CHAE My mind's made up.

PAR Be careful. This may turn out too hot to hold.

CHAE It won't, I'm sure. Let me.

PAR But I'm the one who'll pay for it.[19]

---

[19] Literally "your bean will be threshed on me," evidently a prover-
bial expression.

CHAE   ah!

PAR flagitium facimus.

CHAE   an id flagitiumst si in domum meretriciam
     deducar et illis crucibus, quae nos nostramque adules-
        centiam
     habent despicatam et quae nos semper omnibus cruciant
        modis,

385   nunc referam gratiam atque eas itidem fallam ut ab eis
        fallimur?
     an potius haec patri aequomst fieri ut a me ludatur dolis?
     quod qui rescierint culpent; illud merito factum omnes
        putent.

PAR quid istic? si certumst facere, facias. verum ne post
     conferas
     culpam in me.

CHAE   non faciam.

PAR   iubesne?

CHAE   iubeam? cogo atque impero.

390   numquam defugiam auctoritatem. sequere.

PAR   di vortant bene!

ACTUS III

III. i: THRASO. GNATHO. PARMENO.

THR magnas vero agere gratias Thais mihi?

GNA ingentis.

THR   ain tu, laetast?

GNA   non tam ipso quidem
     dono quam abs te datum esse. id vero serio
     triumphat.

PAR   hoc proviso ut ubi tempus siet

395   deducam. sed eccum militem.

CHAE (*impatiently*) Oh!

PAR We're committing an outrage.

CHAE Is it an outrage if I'm taken into a courtesan's house and pay back those tormentors, who hold us young men in contempt and torture us in every possible way? If I cheat them in the same way that they cheat us? Is it a more proper thing to play tricks on my father? Anyone who caught me doing that would blame me, but everybody can see that this is perfectly justified.

PAR (*reluctantly*) All right. If your mind's made up, do it. But don't you put the blame on me afterwards.

CHAE I won't.

PAR Are you telling me to do it?

CHAE Telling you? I'm insisting, it's an order. I'll accept the responsibility, I promise. Come along. (*he turns towards the house*)

PAR May the gods grant us a happy outcome! (*he follows Chaerea into the house, leaving the stage empty*)

ACT THREE

Enter THRASO *and* GNATHO *right from the direction of the forum.*

THR So Thais really sent me many thanks?

GNA Profuse.

THR What do you say? Is she delighted?

GNA Not so much with the gift itself but with the fact it comes from you. That really and truly is a triumph for her.

PAR (*entering from the house, to himself*) I'm coming out to see if the time's right to deliver the gifts. (*seeing Thraso*) But there's the soldier.

357

THR   est istuc datum
profecto ut grata mihi sint quae facio omnia.

GNA   advorti hercle animum.

THR   vel rex semper maxumas
mihi agebat quidquid feceram, aliis non item.

GNA   labore alieno magno partam gloriam

400   verbis saepe in se transmovet qui habet salem;
quod in test.

THR   habes.

GNA   rex te ergo in oculis—

THR   scilicet.

GNA   —gestare.

THR   vero. credere omnem exercitum,
consilia.

GNA   mirum!

THR   tum sicubi eum satietas
hominum aut negoti si quando odium ceperat,

405   requiescere ubi volebat, quasi—nostin?

GNA   scio:
quasi ubi illam exspueret miseriam ex animo.

THR   tenes.
tum me convivam solum abducebat sibi.

GNA   hui!
regem elegantem narras.

THR   immo sic homost,
perpaucorum hominum.

GNA   immo nullorum arbitror,

410   si tecum vivit.

THR   invidere omnes mihi,
mordere clanculum. ego non flocci pendere.
illi invidere misere, verum unus tamen

THR I assure you, it's a gift of mine that everything I do wins me favour.

GNA (*ironically*) So I've noticed, by god.

THR The king,[20] for example, used to thank me effusively for whatever I'd done, but not others.

GNA It often happens that a man endowed with wit can appropriate by words the glory that others have won by hard work. As in your case.

THR You have it.

GNA So the king always held you

THR (*butting in eagerly*) Of course.

GNA —in his gaze.[21]

THR True. He entrusted his whole army to me, and his plans.

GNA Amazing!

THR Moreover, when he was weary of company and tired of work, when he wanted to rest, as if—you know?

GNA I know: as if to cast out the troubles from his mind.

THR You've got it. Then he would take me aside as his sole companion.

GNA Wow! You're talking about a most discriminating king.

THR No, that's how he is. He's a man of very few friends.

GNA (*aside*) None at all, if he spends his life with you.

THR They were all envious, and criticised me behind my back. I didn't care a damn. They were all terribly envious, and one of them desperately so, the man who was in charge of

[20] Soldiers in comedy tend to be serving as mercenaries to the Hellenistic kings who came into power after the death of Alexander the Great in 323 B.C.

[21] Gnatho comically conflates two Latin expressions, *in oculis habere* ("keep in one's sight") and *in sinu habere* ("hold in one's bosom").

359

impense, elephantis quem Indicis praefecerat.
is ubi molestus magis est, "quaeso," inquam "Strato,
415   eon es ferox quia habes imperium in beluas?"
GNA   pulchre mehercle dictum et sapienter. papae,
iugularas hominem! quid ille?
THR   mutus ilico.
GNA   quidni esset?
PAR   di vostram fidem! hominem perditum
miserumque et illum sacrilegum!
THR   quid illud, Gnatho?
420   quo pacto Rhodium tetigerim in convivio,
numquam tibi dixi?
GNA   numquam; sed narra, obsecro.
plus miliens audivi.
THR   una in convivio
erat hic quem dico Rhodius adulescentulus.
forte habui scortum. coepit ad id alludere
425   et me irridere. "quid ais," inquam "homo impudens?
lepus tute's: pulpamentum quaeris?"
GNA   hahahae!
THR   quid est?
GNA   facete, lepide, laute, nil supra.
tuomne, obsecro te, hoc dictum erat? vetus credidi.
THR   audieras?
GNA   saepe, et fertur in primis.
THR   meumst.

---

[22] Elephants formed an important part of the armies of the Hellenistic monarchs. The Seleucid kings from Syria cornered the market in Indian elephants, leaving the Ptolemies from Egypt to look to African elephants from Ethiopia.

the Indian elephants.[22] When he was being particularly offensive, I said: "Tell me, Strato, is it being in charge of wild animals that makes you ferocious?"

GNA Brilliant, by god! And profound! Gosh! You had your sword at his throat! What did he say?

THR Struck dumb on he spot.

GNA Of course he was.

PAR (*aside*) Heaven help us! What a hopeless wretch! And the other one's a scoundrel!

THR And what about the hit I scored on the Rhodian at the dinner party—did I never tell you?

GNA Never. But do tell me, I implore you. (*aside*) I've heard it more than a thousand times.

THR This Rhodian youth I'm talking about was with me at a dinner party. As it happened I had a woman with me. He began to flirt with her and make fun of me. "Answer me this," I said, "you impudent fellow: being a hare yourself, do you hunt for game?"[23]

GNA (*laughing uproariously*) Hahahahaha!

THR (*slightly taken aback*) What's the matter?

GNA Witty, clever, neat, couldn't be better! Was that *your* witticism, for goodness' sake? I thought it was an old one.

THR Had you heard it?

GNA Often. It's known as one of the best.

THR It's mine.

---

23 A well known old saying, which apparently occurred in the comedies of Livius Andronicus in the 3rd century B.C. The point, according to Donatus, is that, just as a hare is game itself and should not be hunting game, so the sexually desirable young man should not be making sexual advances to girls.

430	GNA	dolet dictum imprudenti adulescenti et libero.
	PAR	at te di perdant!
	GNA	quid ille, quaeso?
	THR	perditus.
		risu omnes qui aderant emoriri. denique
		metuebant omnes iam me.
	GNA	haud iniuria.
	THR	sed heus tu, purgon ego me de istac Thaidi,
435		quod eam me amare suspicatast?
	GNA	nil minus.
		immo auge magis suspicionem.
	THR	quor?
	GNA	rogas?
		scin, si quando illa mentionem Phaedriae
		facit aut si laudat, te ut male urat?
	THR	sentio.
	GNA	id ut ne fiat haec res solast remedio:
440		ubi nominabit Phaedriam, tu Pamphilam
		continuo. si quando illa dicet "Phaedriam
		intromittamus comissatum," Pamphilam
		cantatum provocemus. si laudabit haec
		illius formam, tu huius contra. denique
445		par pro pari referto quod eam mordeat.
	THR	siquidem me amaret, tum istuc prodesset, Gnatho.
	GNA	quando illud quod tu das exspectat atque amat,
		iamdudum te amat, iamdudum illi facile fit
		quod doleat. metuit semper quem ipsa nunc capit
450		fructum ne quando iratus tu alio conferas.
	THR	bene dixti, ac mihi istuc non in mentem venerat.
	GNA	ridiculum! non enim cogitaras. ceterum
		idem hoc tute melius quanto invenisses, Thraso!

GNA I'm sorry for the poor youth you aimed it at, just for being a bit careless and not holding his tongue.

PAR (*aside*) May the gods destroy you!

GNA What did he say, if I may ask?

THR He was finished. Everyone there died of laughter. They've all been afraid of me ever since.

GNA And rightly so.

THR But listen, about this girl, do I rid Thais of her suspicion that I'm in love with her?

GNA Absolutely not. On the contrary, make her more suspicious.

THR Why?

GNA Need you ask? You know how, if ever she mentions Phaedria or praises him, it pains you terribly?

THR And I feel it.

GNA There's only one way to prevent this happening. When she names Phaedria, you must immediately name Pamphila. If she ever says: "Let's invite Phaedria to join the party," you say: "Let's summon Pamphila to sing." If she praises his good looks, you praise hers. In short pay her back tit for tat with something that will annoy her.

THR (*with a sigh*) If she loved me, then that might work, Gnatho.

GNA Since she looks forward to your presents and loves them, she's loved you all this time, and all this time there's been an easy way of hurting her. She's always been afraid that you might one day in anger transfer elsewhere the income that she now derives from you.

THR Quite right. That hadn't occurred to me.

GNA Ridiculous! You just hadn't thought about it. Otherwise you'd have come up with the same idea yourself far more easily, Thraso!

III. ii: THAIS. THRASO. GNATHO. PARMENO. PYTHIAS.

THA   audire vocem visa sum modo militis;
455   atque eccum. salve, mi Thraso.

THR   o Thais mea,
    meum savium, quid agitur? ecquid nos amas
    de fidicina istac?

PAR   quam venuste! quod dedit
    principium adveniens!

THA   plurumum merito tuo.

GNA   eamus ergo ad cenam. quid stas?

PAR   em alterum.
460   ex homine hunc natum dicas?

THA   ubi vis, non moror.

PAR   adibo atque assimulabo quasi nunc exeam.
    ituran, Thais, quopiam's?

THA   ehem, Parmeno!
    bene fecisti; hodie itura—

PAR   quo?

THA   quid? hunc non vides?

PAR   video et me taedet. ubi vis, dona adsunt tibi
465   a Phaedria.

THR   quid stamus? quor non imus hinc?

PAR   quaeso hercle ut liceat, pace quod fiat tua,
    dare huic quae volumus, convenire et colloqui.

THR   perpulchra credo dona aut nostri similia.

PAR   res indicabit. heus, iubete istos foras
470   exire quos iussi ocius. procede tu huc.

---

459 eamus . . . stas *Gnathoni dant codd.*, Thrasoni *Fraenkel*

Enter THAIS *from her house.*

THA I thought I heard the soldier's voice. (*seeing Thraso*)
There he is. Good day, my dear Thraso.

THR Oh my dear Thais, the object of my kisses, how are you?
Do you love me a little bit in return for the music girl?

PAR (*aside*) How charming! On his arrival! What a way to be-
gin!

THA Very much, as you deserve.

GNA (*to Thais*) Let's go to dinner, then. What are you waiting
for?

PAR (*aside*) Now the other one. Would you say he had a
human being for a father?

THA When you like. I'm ready.

PAR (*aside*) I'll go up and pretend I've just come out. (*to
Thais*) Are you going somewhere, Thais?

THA Oh hello, Parmeno! Good of you to come. But today I'm
off—

PAR Where?

THA (*lowering her voice*) What! Don't you see him? (*pointing
to Thraso*)

PAR (*aside to Thais*) I see him and it makes me sick. (*aloud*)
When you're ready, there are some gifts for you from
Phaedria.

THR What are we waiting for? Why don't we go?

PAR (*to Thraso*) I should like, if I may, with your permission,
to give Thais what we want to give her, and have a few
words with her in private.

THR (*sarcastically*) Superb gifts, I suppose, a match for mine!

PAR That remains to be seen. (*calling into the house*) Hey, tell
those two I told you about to come out at once. (*as the
Ethiopian slave girl emerges*) You step forward here. (*to*

365

ex Aethiopiast usque haec.

THR   hic sunt tres minae.

GNA vix.

PAR   ubi tu's, Dore? accede huc. em eunuchum tibi!
quam liberali facie, quam aetate integra!

THA ita me di ament, honestust.

PAR   quid tu ais, Gnatho?
475   numquid habes quod contemnas? quid tu autem, Thra-
so?

tacent: satis laudant. fac periclum in litteris,
fac in palaestra, in musicis. quae liberum
scire aequomst adulescentem, sollertem dabo.

THR ego illum eunuchum, si opus sit, vel sobrius—

480 PAR atque haec qui misit non sibi soli postulat
te vivere et sua causa excludi ceteros,
neque pugnas narrat neque cicatrices suas
ostentat neque tibi obstat, quod quidam facit;
verum ubi molestum non erit, ubi tu voles,

485   ubi tempus tibi erit, sat habet si tum recipitur.

THR apparet servom hunc esse domini pauperis
miserique.

GNA   nam hercle nemo posset, sat scio,
qui haberet qui pararet alium, hunc perpeti.

PAR tace tu, quem ego esse infra infumos omnis puto

490   homines. nam qui huic animum assentari induxeris,
e flamma petere te cibum posse arbitror.

THR iamne imus?

Thais) All the way from Ethiopia!

THR Worth three minas.

GNA Barely.

PAR (*calling into the house*) Where are you, Dorus? Come over here. (*as Chaerea emerges in the eunuch costume*) Here's the eunuch for you. With the looks of a gentleman and in the bloom of youth!

THA Heaven help me, he is good looking!

PAR What do you say, Gnatho? Can you see anything to disparage? What about you, Thraso? (*there is no reply*) Their silence is praise enough. (*to Thais*) Test him on literature, athletics, music. I'll prove him an expert in everything a well educated young gentleman should know.

THR (*aside*) I know what I'd do to that eunuch, even when sober, if it came to it!

PAR And moreover, the man who sent these presents doesn't demand that you live for him alone and shut out all others for his sake. He doesn't narrate his battles or parade his scars, or get in your way, as a certain person does. He's content to be invited in when it's convenient, when it suits you, when you have the time.

THR This is obviously the slave of a wretched poverty-stricken master.

GNA Yes. I'm quite sure nobody would put up with such a slave if he had the means to get himself another one.

PAR You shut up! I judge you to be the lowest of the low. If you can bring yourself to flatter someone like him, I reckon you could steal food from a funeral pyre.[24]

THR Are we going now?

---

[24] A proverbial expression, alluding to the stealing from the ashes of food that was burned with the bodies of the dead.

THA   hos prius intro ducam et quae volo
simul imperabo. poste continuo exeo.

THR ego hinc abeo; tu istanc opperire.

PAR   haud convenit

495   una ire cum amica imperatorem in via.

THR quid tibi ego multa dicam? domini similis es.

GNA hahahae!

THR   quid rides?

GNA   istuc quod dixti modo,
et illud de Rhodio dictum quom in mentem venit.
sed Thais exit.

THR   abi prae, cura ut sint domi

500   parata.

GNA   fiat.

THA   diligenter, Pythias,
fac cures, si Chremes hoc forte advenerit,
ut ores primum ut maneat; si id non commodumst,
ut redeat; si id non poterit, ad me adducito.

PYTH ita faciam.

THA   quid? quid aliud volui dicere?

505   ehem! curate istam diligenter virginem;
domi adsitis facite.

THR   eamus.

THA   vos me sequimini.

---

493 poste *gloss.*, post, postea, post hoc *codd.*
499 cura *Paumier,* curre *codd. Don.*

THA I'll take these inside first and give instructions for what I want to be done. I'll come straight out afterwards. (*she exits into her house with Chaerea and the Ethiopian slave girl*)

THR (*to Gnatho*) I'm off. You wait for her.

PAR (*sneering*) It's not proper for a commander-in-chief to be seen in the street with his mistress. (*he exits left down the street*)

THR (*shouting after him*) Why should I waste words on you? You take after your master.

GNA Hahahahaha!

THR (*suspiciously*) What are you laughing at?

GNA What you just said—and the one about the Rhodian, when I think of it. But here comes Thais.

THR You go first and make sure everything's ready at home.

GNA All right. (*he exits right in the direction of Thraso's house*)

THA (*entering from her house with Pythias and two other maids*) Make sure you don't forget, Pythias; if Chremes by any chance arrives here, first beg him to stay; if that's not convenient, ask him to return later; and if he can't do that, bring him to me.

PYTH Very well. (*she exits into Thais' house*)

THA (*for Thraso's benefit*) Well, then, what else did I mean to say? (*calling back into the house*) You there, look after that girl with the greatest care. Don't leave the house.

THR (*impatiently*) Let's go.

THA (*to her maids*) You follow me. (*Thraso exits right in the direction of his house, followed by Thais and her maids, leaving the stage empty*)

III. iii: CHREMES. PYTHIAS.

CHR profecto quanto magis magisque cogito,
      nimirum dabit haec Thais mi magnum malum:
      ita me ab ea astute video labefactarier,
510   iam tum quom primum iussit me ad se accersier.
      roget quis "quid tibi cum illa?": ne noram quidem.
      ubi veni, causam ut ibi manerem repperit;
      ait rem divinam fecisse et rem seriam
      velle agere mecum. iam tum erat suspicio
515   dolo malo haec fieri omnia. ipsa accumbere
      mecum, mihi sese dare, sermonem quaerere.
      ubi friget, huc evasit, quam pridem pater
      mihi et mater mortui essent: dico, iamdiu.
      rus Sunii ecquod habeam et quam longe a mari:
520   credo ei placere hoc; sperat se a me avellere.
      postremo, ecqua inde parva periisset soror,
      ecquis cum ea una, quid habuisset quom perit,
      ecquis eam posset noscere. haec quor quaeritet?
      nisi si illa forte, quae olim periit parvola
525   soror, hanc se intendit esse, ut est audacia.
      verum ea si vivit annos natast sedecim,
      non maior; Thais quam ego sum maiusculast.
      misit porro orare ut venirem serio.
      aut dicat quid volt aut molesta ne siet;
530   non hercle veniam tertio. heus, heus, ecquis hic?
      ego sum Chremes.
PYTH   o capitulum lepidissumum!

---

[25] Effectively an invitation to dinner. Sacrifices were regularly followed by a meal at which the meat from the sacrifical victim would be eaten, and it was common practice for visitors to be invited to join in.

Enter CHREMES *left.*

CHR (*to himself*) Without a doubt, the more and more I think about it, unless I'm very much mistaken, this Thais is going to cause me a lot of trouble. I can see how cleverly she's been working on me ever since she first sent for me. If anyone wonders what my relationship is with her, I hadn't even met her before. When I arrived, she invented an excuse for keeping me there. She said she had been carrying out a sacrifice[25] and had some serious business to discuss with me. Even at that stage I had a suspicion that there was some ulterior motive behind all this. She sat next to me on the couch, put herself at my disposal, and started to make conversation. When this dried up, she came to the point. "How long ago had my father and mother died?" "Long since," I said. "Did I have a farm at Sunium? How far was it from the sea?" I think she's set her heart on it and is hoping to get it off me. Finally, "Had I lost a little sister from there? Was there anyone with her? What did she have on her when she disappeared? Was there anyone who could recognise her?" Why should she keep asking these questions? Unless perhaps she wants to claim that *she* is the little sister who disappeared long ago; she's brazen enough. But if the girl's alive, she's sixteen years old, no more; and Thais is a bit older than I am. On top of all this she's now sent an urgent request for me to come. She must say what she wants or stop pestering me. I'm not coming a third time, by god. (*knocking on the door*) Hello! Hello! Anyone here? It's Chremes.

PYTH (*coming out and speaking in alluring tones*) Oh you lovely little man!

CHR   dico mi insidias fieri.

PYTH   Thais maxumo
      te orabat opere ut cras redires.

CHR   rus eo.

PYTH   fac amabo.

CHR   non possum, inquam.

PYTH   at tu apud nos hic mane
535   dum redeat ipsa.

CHR   nil minus.

PYTH   quor, mi Chremes?

CHR   malam rem hinc ibis?

PYTH   si istuc ita certumst tibi,
      amabo ut illuc transeas ubi illast.

CHR   eo.

PYTH   abi, Dorias, cito hunc deduce ad militem.

III. iv: ANTIPHO.

ANT   heri aliquot adulescentuli coimus in Piraeo
540   in hunc diem ut de symbolis essemus. Chaeream ei rei
      praefecimus; dati anuli; locus, tempus constitutumst.
      praeteriit tempus. quo in loco dictumst parati nil est;
      homo ipse nusquamst neque scio quid dicam aut quid
      coniectem.
      nunc mi hoc negoti ceteri dedere ut illum quaeram,
545   idque adeo visam si domist. quisnam hinc ab Thaide exit?
      is est an non est? ipsus est. quid hoc hominist? qui hic
      ornatust?

---

[26] Clubbing together for dinner was a common Greek practice. Rings were given by the participants to the organiser as a guarantee that each would pay his share.

CHR (*aside*) I told you it was a trap.

PYTH Thais begs you most earnestly to come back tomorrow.

CHR I'm off to the country.

PYTH Go on! Be a darling!

CHR I tell you, I can't.

PYTH Well, wait here with us (*suggestively*) until she returns.

CHR Out of the question.

PYTH Why, my dearest Chremes? (*putting her hand on his arm*)

CHR Kindly go to hell.

PYTH If you won't agree to that, darling, go over to where she is.

CHR I'll go.

PYTH (*calling back inside the house*) Dorias, run along and take this gentleman to the soldier's. (*Dorias emerges from the house and goes off right with Chremes in the direction of Thraso's house, leaving the stage empty*)

Enter ANTIPHO *left from the direction of the harbour in military dress.*

ANT (*to himself*) Yesterday several of the lads got together at the Piraeus and arranged to club together for dinner today. We put Chaerea in charge of arrangements, handed over our rings,[26] and settled a place and time. The time has passed, and there is no sign of any preparations at the place we said. Chaerea himself is nowhere to be seen, and I don't know what to say or how to explain it. Now the others have given me the job of finding him, and that's why I'm coming to see if he's at home. (*as Thais' door opens*) Who's this coming out of Thais' house? Is it him or isn't it? It is, the very man. (*looking again at Chaerea's costume*) But what kind of a man is this? What's this get-

373

quid illud malist? nequeo satis mirari neque conicere;
nisi, quidquid est, procul hinc lubet prius quid sit scisci-
tari.

III. v: CHAEREA. ANTIPHO.

CHAE numquis hic est? nemost. numquis hinc me sequitur?
nemo homost.

550   iamne erumpere hoc licet mi gaudium? pro Iuppiter,
nunc est profecto interfici quom perpeti me possum,
ne hoc gaudium contaminet vita aegritudine aliqua.
sed neminemne curiosum intervenire nunc mihi,
qui me sequatur quoquo eam, rogitando obtundat, eni-
cet

555   quid gestiam aut quid laetus sim, quo pergam, unde
emergam, ubi siem
vestitum hunc nanctus, quid mi quaeram, sanus sim anne
insaniam!

ANT adibo atque ab eo gratiam hanc quam video velle inibo.
Chaerea, quid est quod sic gestis? quid sibi hic vestitus
quaerit?
quid est quod laetus es? quid tibi vis? satine sanu's? quid
me aspectas?

560   quid taces?

CHAE   o festus dies! amice, salve. hominum omnium
nemost quem ego nunciam magis cuperem videre quam
te.

ANT narra istuc quaeso quid sit.

---

560 *sic Dziatzko,* o festus dies hominis amice salve *codd. Don.*
561 *sic A¹,* nemost hominum quem ego nunc magis *A²,* nemost om-
nium quem ego nunc magis *Σ*

up? What the hell is going on? I'm pretty well baffled; I can't even hazard a guess. Whatever the explanation is, I think I'll pursue it first from a distance. (*he stands aside so that Chaerea doesn't see him*)

Enter CHAEREA *from Thais' house in the eunuch's costume.*

CHAE (*to himself*) Is there anyone here? Nobody. Anyone following me? Not a soul. Can I now let my joy burst out? By Jupiter, at this moment without a doubt I'd rather face death than have this joy spoiled by any of life's sorrows. But fancy there being no busybody here to intrude upon me, pursuing me wherever I go, battering my ears and plaguing me to death with questions—why I'm excited and happy, where I'm going, where I've come from, where I got this clothing, what I'm up to, whether I'm sane or insane!

ANT (*to himself*) I'll go up and do him the favour I see he wants. (*approaching Chaerea*) Chaerea, how come you're so excited? What's the reason for this clothing? How come you're so happy? What are you up to? Are you out of your mind? (*as Chaerea stares at him blankly*) Why are you staring at me? Why don't you say something?

CHAE (*hugging him*) Oh glorious day! Greetings, my friend! There's no one in the whole world I'd rather see right now than you.[27]

ANT May I ask you what's going on?

---

[27] The text of this speech is confused in the MSS but the general sense is clear.

CHAE   immo ego te obsecro hercle ut audias.
       nostin hanc quam amat frater?

ANT   novi. nempe, opinor, Thaidem.

CHAE istam ipsam.

ANT   sic commemineram.

CHAE   quaedam hodiest ei dono data

565   virgo. quid ego eius tibi nunc faciem praedicem aut lau-
      dem, Antipho,
      quom ipsum me noris quam elegans formarum spectator
      siem?
      in hac commotus sum.

ANT   ain tu?

CHAE   primam dices, scio, si videris.
      quid multa verba? amare coepi. forte fortuna domi
      erat quidam eunuchus quem mercatus frater fuerat
      Thaidi,

570   neque is deductus etiamdum ad eam. submonuit me Par-
      meno
      ibi servos quod ego arripui.

ANT   quid id est?

CHAE   tacitus citius audies:
      ut vestem cum illo mutem et pro illo iubeam me illoc
      ducier.

ANT   pro eunuchon?

CHAE   sic est.

ANT   quid ex ea re tandem ut caperes commodi?

CHAE rogas? viderem, audirem, essem una quacum cupiebam,
      Antipho,

575   num parva causa aut prava ratiost? traditus sum mulieri.
      illa ilico, ubi me accepit, laeta vero ad se abducit domum,
      commendat virginem.

CHAE God knows I'm only too keen for you to hear. You know this woman my brother's in love with? (*indicating Thais' house*)

ANT I do indeed. You mean Thais, I presume.

CHAE The very one.

ANT I thought I remembered.

CHAE A girl was given to her today as a present. I don't need to describe her beauty to you or praise it, Antipho. You know what a connoisseur I am of the female form. I was swept off my feet.

ANT You don't say!

CHAE You'll give her top marks, if you see her, I'm sure. To put it briefly, I fell in love. By a lucky chance there was a eunuch at home whom my brother had bought for Thais, and he hadn't yet been delivered to her house. At this point our slave Parmeno dropped me a suggestion which I snatched up.

ANT What was that?

CHAE You'll hear all the quicker if you keep quiet. To exchange clothes with him and have myself taken there in his place.

ANT In place of the eunuch?

CHAE That's right.

ANT And what would you achieve by that, if I may ask?

CHAE What a question! I would look at, listen to, and live together with the girl I wanted, Antipho. Was that a minor objective or a miscalculation? I was handed over to the woman, and, as soon as she received me, she took me into her house with great delight, and entrusted the girl to my care.

---

575 prava *Paumier,* parva *codd. Don.*

ANT   quoi? tibine?

CHAE   mihi.

ANT   satis tuto tamen?

CHAE edicit ne vir quisquam ad eam adeat et mihi ne abscedam
       imperat,

in interiore parte ut maneam solus cum sola. adnuo

580   terram intuens modeste.

ANT   miser!

CHAE   "ego" inquit "ad cenam hinc eo."

abducit secum ancillas; paucae quae circum illam essent
       manent

noviciae puellae. continuo haec adornant ut lavet.

adhortor properent. dum apparatur, virgo in conclavi se-
       det

suspectans tabulam quandam pictam. ibi inerat pictura
       haec, Iovem

585   quo pacto Danaae misisse aiunt quondam in gremium
       imbrem aureum.

egomet quoque id spectare coepi; et, quia consimilem lu-
       serat

iam olim ille ludum, impendio magis animus gaudebat
       mihi,

deum sese in hominem convortisse atque in alienas tegu-
       las

venisse clanculum per impluvium fucum factum mulieri.

590   at quem deum, qui templa caeli summa sonitu concutit!

588 in hominem *codd. Don.*, in imbrem *Fabia*
589 per impluvium *codd. Don.*, per pluviam *Bentley*

---

28 In a Greek house the women's quarters were in the back, separate
from the men's.   29 Danae was the daughter of Acrisius, king of

ANT Whose? Yours?

CHAE Mine.

ANT (*ironically*) Was that quite safe?

CHAE (*ignoring Antipho's remark*) She gave me instructions that no man was to approach the girl and ordered me not to leave her side. I was to stay in the inner quarters[28] alone with her. I nodded, keeping my eyes modestly on the ground.

ANT You poor thing!

CHAE "I'm off to a dinner party" she said, and took her maids with her. A few young ones stayed behind to attend the girl. Presently they made preparations for her bath. I urged them to hurry. While things were being got ready, the girl sat in the room, looking up at a painting; it depicted the story of how Jupiter sent a shower of gold into Danae's bosom.[29] I began to look at it myself, and the fact that he had played a similar game long ago made me all the more excited: a god had turned himself into human shape, made his way by stealth on to another man's roof, and come through the skylight[30] to play a trick on a woman. And what a god! The one who shakes the lofty vaults of heaven with his thunder![31] Was I, a mere mortal,

Argos, who, in response to an oracle that he would be killed by Danae's son, imprisoned her in an underground chamber (or, in some versions of the legend, in a tower) to prevent her becoming pregnant. Zeus, however, visited Danae as a shower of gold, and Danae duly bore a son, Perseus, who eventually killed Acrisius. [30] The *atrium* of a Roman house had a rectangular opening in the roof (*compluvium*) and a similarly shaped basin underneath to catch rainwater (*impluvium*). Here Terence is using *impluvium* to refer to the aperture.

[31] According to Donatus this is a quotation from the early Roman poet Ennius.

ego homuncio hoc non facerem? ego illud vero ita feci ac
  lubens.

dum haec mecum reputo, accersitur lavatum interea
  virgo.
iit, lavit, rediit. deinde eam in lecto illae collocarunt.
sto exspectans si quid mi imperent. venit una. "heus tu,"
  inquit, "Dore,

595 cape hoc flabellum, ventulum huic sic facito, dum lava-
    mus.
ubi nos laverimus, si voles, lavato." accipio tristis.

ANT tum equidem istoc os tuom impudens videre nimium
    vellem,
qui esset status, flabellulum tenere te asinum tantum.

CHAE vix elocutast hoc, foras simul omnes proruont se,

600 abeunt lavatum, perstrepunt, ita ut fit domini ubi absunt.
interea somnus virginem opprimit. ego limis specto
sic per flabellum clanculum. simul alia circumspecto,
satin explorata sint. video esse. pessulum ostio obdo.

ANT quid tum?

CHAE   quid "quid tum," fatue?

ANT   fateor.

CHAE   an ego occasionem

605 mi ostentam, tantam, tam brevem, tam optatam, tam
    insperatam
amitterem? tum pol ego is essem vero qui simulabar.

ANT sane hercle ut dicis. sed interim de symbolis quid ac-
    tumst?

CHAE paratumst.

---

[32] Chaerea here uses the word *pol* (translated "for heaven's sake"),
which is normally a female speech marker in Terence.

not to do the same? I did just that—and gladly.

    While I was thinking over all this, the girl was summoned to take her bath. She went, bathed, returned. Then the maids laid her down on the bed. I stood waiting to see if they had any orders for me. One of them came up and said, "Hey you, Dorus, take this fan and make a nice little breeze for her, like this (*making fanning motions*), while we take a bath. When we've done so, if you like, you can take one." I accepted the fan with a scowl.

ANT How I wish I had seen your impudent expression, and your posturing, and you holding your little fan, you great ass.

CHAE She had scarcely uttered these words and they all rushed out of the room to take their baths, chattering away, as happens when the master is absent. Meanwhile the girl fell asleep. I looked at her sideways through the fan, like this (*posturing*), and at the same time had a good look round to make sure that the coast was clear. I saw it was, and bolted the door.

ANT What then?

CHAE How do you mean "What then," you idiot?

ANT Sorry.

CHAE Was I going to let slip the opportunity when it was offered to me, so great, so fleeting, so desired, so unexpected? If I had, I would actually have been what I pretended to be, (*putting on a female voice*) for heaven's sake.[32]

ANT Quite. As you say. But meanwhile what's happened about the dinner?

CHAE It's ready.

ANT	frugi's. ubi? domin?
CHAE	immo apud libertum Discum.
ANT	perlongest, sed tanto ocius properemus. muta vestem.

610 CHAE ubi mutem? perii! nam domo exsulo nunc. metuo fra-
trem
ne intus sit, porro autem pater ne rure redierit iam.

ANT eamus ad me. ibi proxumumst ubi mutes.

CHAE recte dicis.
eamus, et de istac simul, quo pacto porro possim
potiri, consilium volo capere una tecum.

ANT fiat.

ACTUS IV

IV. i: DORIAS.

615 DORI ita me di ament, quantum ego illum vidi, non nil timeo
misera
ne quam ille hodie insanus turbam faciat aut vim Thaidi.
nam postquam iste advenit Chremes adulescens, frater
virginis,
militem rogat ut illum admitti iubeat. ill' continuo irasci
neque negare audere. Thais porro instare ut hominem
invitet.

620 id faciebat retinendi illius causa, quia illa quae cupiebat
de sorore eius indicare ad eam rem tempus non erat.
invitat tristis. mansit. ibi illa cum illo sermonem ilico.

miles vero sibi putare adductum ante oculos aemulum.

---

33 Discus is either a freedman of Chaerea's father's who is willing to

ANT   Good man! But where? At your place?

CHAE No. At the freedman Discus'.[33]

ANT   That's a very long way away. All the more need to hurry.
      Change your clothes.

CHAE Where can I? Damn it! I'm banished from home now. I'm
      afraid my brother may be in the house and, what's more,
      my father may already have returned from the farm.

ANT   Let's go to my house. That's the nearest place for you to
      change.

CHAE You're right. Let's go, and on the way I want to take your
      advice on how I can secure possession of the girl for the
      future.

ANT   All right. (*they exit left in the direction of Antipho's
      house, leaving the stage empty*)

ACT FOUR

Enter DORIAS right from the direction of Thraso's house.

DORI (*to herself*) Oh dear, heaven help us, from what I've seen
      of him I'm very much afraid that madman will stir up trou-
      ble or do Thais an injury today. After young Chremes,
      the girl's brother, arrived, she asked the soldier to have
      him admitted. He flew into a temper but didn't dare re-
      fuse. Thais kept insisting he should be invited in. She did
      this to keep him there, since the time wasn't right to tell
      him what she wanted about his sister. Thraso grudgingly
      invited him, and he stayed. Thais struck up a conversa-
      tion with him at once. But the soldier thought that a rival

play host to a party for the younger son of the family, or some uncon-
nected freedman who owns a cookshop (*popina*).

voluit facere contra huic aegre: "heus," inquit "puere,
   Pamphilam
625   accerse ut delectet hic nos." illa "minume gentium.
   in convivium illam?" miles tendere. inde ad iurgium.
   interea aurum sibi clam mulier demit; dat mi ut auferam.
   hoc est signi: ubi primum poterit, se illinc subducet, scio.

IV. ii: PHAEDRIA. (DORIAS.)

PHAE dum rus eo, coepi egomet mecum inter vias
630   ita ut fit ubi quid in animost molestiae,
   aliam rem ex alia cogitare et ea omnia in
   peiorem partem. quid opust verbis? dum haec puto,
   praeterii imprudens villam. longe iam abieram
   quom sensi. redeo rursum male me vero habens.
635   ubi ad ipsum veni devorticulum, constiti.
   occepi mecum cogitare "hem! biduom hic
   manendumst soli sine illa? quid tum postea?
   nil est. quid "nil"? si non tangendi copiast,
   eho, ne videndi quidem erit? si illud non licet,
640   saltem hoc licebit. certe extrema linea
   amare haud nil est." villam praetereo sciens.
   sed quid hoc quod timida subito egreditur Pythias?

IV. iii: PYTHIAS. PHAEDRIA. DORIAS.

PYTH ubi ego illum scelerosum misera atque impium inve-
   niam? aut ubi quaeram?
   hocin tam audax facinus facere esse ausum!

---

[34] Literally "from the furthest line"; it is not clear what metaphor is
intended.

had been brought in under his very nose, and decided to spite her in return. "Hey, slave," he said, "go and fetch Pamphila to entertain us." "Not in this world," said Thais; "That girl? At a dinner party?" The soldier persisted, and there was an argument. Presently Thais took off her jewellery in secret and gave it to me to take away. I'm sure this is a sign that, as soon as she can, she'll steal away. (*she stands aside as Phaedria approaches*)

Enter PHAEDRIA *left from the direction of the country.*

PHAE (*to himself*) While I was on my way to the farm, as happens when there is some trouble on your mind, I began to ponder one thing after another, seeing the worse side of everything. To put it briefly, while engrossed in my thoughts, I went past our farmhouse by mistake. I was a long way past before I realised, and I retraced my steps in a bad mood. When I came to the actual turning, I stopped and began to think: "What! You've got to stay here for two days alone without her? Then what? Nothing. How do you mean 'nothing'? If I'm not allowed to touch her, hey, won't I even be allowed to look at her? If I can't do one, I shall at least be able to do the other. To love from a distance[34] is better than nothing." This time I passed the farmhouse on purpose. (*as Thais' door opens*) But why on earth is Pythias rushing out all of a sudden looking so upset?

Enter PYTHIAS *from Thais' house in a state of great agitation.*

PYTH (*to herself*) Oh dear, where can I find that god-forsaken criminal? Where can I look? To think that he dared do such a brazen deed!

385

PHAE   perii! hoc quid sit vereor.

645 PYTH quin etiam insuper scelus, postquam ludificatust virgi-
         nem,

         vestem omnem miserae discidit, tum ipsam capillo con-
         scidit.

PHAE hem!

PYTH   qui nunc si detur mihi,

         ut ego unguibus facile illi in oculos involem venefico!

PHAE nescioquid profecto absente nobis turbatumst domi.

650   adibo. quid istuc? quid festinas? aut quem quaeris, Py-
         thias?

PYTH ehem, Phaedria! egon quem quaeram? in' hinc quo dig-
         nu's cum donis tuis

         tam lepidis?

PHAE   quid istuc est rei?

PYTH rogas me? eunuchum quem dedisti nobis quas turbas
         dedit!

         virginem quam erae dono dederat miles vitiavit.

PHAE   quid ais?

655 PYTH perii!

PHAE   temulenta's.

PYTH   utinam sic sint qui mihi male volunt!

DORI au obsecro, mea Pythias, quid istuc nam monstri fuit?

PHAE insanis. qui istuc facere eunuchus potuit?

PYTH   ego illum nescio

         qui fuerit. hoc quod fecit res ipsa indicat.

         virgo ipsa lacrumat neque quom rogites quid sit audet
         dicere.

660   ille autem bonus vir nusquam apparet. etiam hoc misera
         suspicor,

         aliquid domo abeuntem abstulisse.

PHAE (*aside*) Damn it! I'm afraid to think what this is about.

PYTH Why, on top of it all, after he'd had his fun and games with the poor girl, the villain ripped her whole dress and tore her hair.

PHAE (*aside*) What!

PYTH If I get my hands on him, I can't wait to fly at his face with my nails, the poisonous wretch!

PHAE (*aside*) There's obviously been some sort of trouble at home in my absence. I'll go up to her. (*to Pythias*) What's the matter? What's the panic? Who are you looking for, Pythias?

PYTH (*coldly*) Oh it's you, Phaedria! Who am I looking for? You go where you deserve and take your charming gifts with you.

PHAE What are you talking about?

PYTH A fine question! That eunuch you gave us, what trouble he's caused! He's raped the girl the soldier gave to my mistress as a present.

PHAE What are you saying?

PYTH I'm ruined.

PHAE You're drunk.

PYTH If only my enemies were in the same state!

DORI (*coming forward*) Oh for goodness' sake, my dear Pythias, what sort of an unnatural deed is this?

PHAE (*to Pythias*) You're crazy. How could a eunuch do it?

PYTH I don't know who he was, but what he did is clear from the facts. The girl is crying and doesn't dare say what happened when you ask her. And that fine fellow is nowhere to be seen. Oh dear, I suspect that he also took something from the house when he left.

PHAE   nequeo mirari satis
        quo ille abire ignavos possit longius, nisi si domum
        forte ad nos rediit.

PYTH   vise amabo num sit.

PHAE   iam faxo scies.

DORI perii, obsecro! tam infandum facinus, mea tu, ne audivi
        quidem.

665 PYTH at pol ego amatores audieram mulierum esse eos maxu-
           mos,
        sed nil potesse. verum miserae non in mentem venerat.
        nam illum aliquo conclusissem neque illi commisissem
        virginem.

          IV. iv: PHAEDRIA. DORUS. PYTHIAS. DORIAS.

PHAE exi foras, sceleste. at etiam restitas,
        fugitive? prodi, male conciliate.

DORU   obsecro.

PHAE   oh!

670   illud vide, os ut sibi distorsit carnufex!
        quid huc tibi reditiost? quid vestis mutatio?
        quid narras? paullum si cessassem, Pythias,
        domi non offendissem, ita iam ornarat fugam.

PYTH haben hominem, amabo?

PHAE   quidni habeam?

PYTH   o factum bene!

675 DORI istuc pol vero bene!

PYTH   ubist?

PHAE   rogitas? non vides?

PYTH videam? obsecro, quem?

PHAE   hunc scilicet.

PYTH   quis hic est homo?

PHAE qui ad vos deductus hodiest.

PHAE I'd be very surprised if the useless creature has got too far, unless perhaps he's gone back to our place.

PYTH Be a darling and go and see if he's there.

PHAE I'll let you know in a moment. (*he exits into his house*)

DORI Damn it! For goodness' sake! I've never even heard of such an unspeakable act, my dear.

PYTH I'd heard that they were great lovers of women, for heaven's sake, but couldn't do it. Oh dear, the thought never even occurred to me. Otherwise I would have shut him in somewhere and never put him in charge of the girl.

Enter PHAEDRIA *from his house, dragging a reluctant* DORUS.

PHAE Come outside, you villain! Don't you resist me, you vaga-bond! Come out, you waste of money! (*he kicks him*)

DORU (*cowering*) Don't, please!

PHAE Oh! Look at that! What a face he's pulled, the gallows-bird! What do you mean by returning here? Why this change of clothes? What's your explanation? (*to Pythias*) If I'd left it any longer, Pythias, I wouldn't have caught him at home. He was all prepared to run away.

PYTH Have you got the fellow, darling?

PHAE Of course I've got him.

PYTH Well done!

DORI Yes, well done indeed!

PYTH (*looking around*) Where is he?

PHAE What a question! Don't you see him?

PYTH See him? For goodness' sake, who?

PHAE (*indicating Dorus*) Him.

PYTH Who's he?

PHAE The one who was delivered to you today.

389

PYTH   hunc oculis suis
        nostrarum numquam quisquam vidit, Phaedria.
PHAE non vidit?
PYTH   an tu hunc credidisti esse, obsecro,
680   ad nos deductum?
PHAE   namque alium habui neminem.
PYTH   au!
        ne comparandus hicquidem ad illumst. ille erat
        honesta facie et liberali.
PHAE   ita visus est
        dudum, quia varia veste exornatus fuit.
        nunc tibi videtur foedus, quia illam non habet.
685 PYTH tace, obsecro. quasi vero paullum intersiet.
        ad nos deductus hodiest adulescentulus,
        quem tu videre vero velles, Phaedria.
        hic est vietus, vetus, veternosus senex,
        colore mustelino.
PHAE   hem! quae haec est fabula?
690   eo rediges me ut quid egerim egomet nesciam?
        eho tu, emin ego te?
DORU   emisti.
PYTH   iube mi denuo
        respondeat.
PHAE   roga.
PYTH   venisti hodie ad nos? negat.
        at ille alter venit annos natus sedecim,
        quem secum adduxit Parmeno.
PHAE   agedum, hoc mi expedi
695   primum: istam quam habes unde habes vestem? taces?
        monstrum hominis, non dicturu's?
DORU   venit Chaerea.

PYTH None of us has ever set eyes on this man, Phaedria.

PHAE Not set eyes on him?

PYTH For goodness' sake, did you suppose this was the one delivered to us?

PHAE (*wrily*) Well, I didn't have another one.

PYTH Oh! There's no comparison between them. The other one was good-looking, a handsome fellow.

PHAE He seemed to be then, because he was wearing colorful clothes. Now he looks ugly, because he hasn't got them.

PYTH Come on, for goodness' sake! There's a huge difference between them. The one delivered to us today was a young lad who you yourself, Phaedria, might well want to look at. This one is a shrivelled, lethargic, senile old man with the colour of a weasel.[35]

PHAE Hey! What's this nonsense? Are you trying to tell me I don't know what I did myself? (*to Dorus*) Here you, did I buy you?

DORU You did.

PYTH Tell him to answer me as well.

PHAE Go ahead.

PYTH (*to Dorus*) Did you come over to us today? (*to Phaedria, as Dorus shakes his head*) He denies it. But that other one did, the sixteen-year-old, who Parmeno brought with him.

PHAE (*to Dorus*) Come on then, explain this first. Those clothes you are wearing—where did you get them? No answer? You monstrosity of a man, aren't you going to say?

DORU (*still cowering*) Chaerea came.

[35] Donatus tells us that Terence here mistranslated the Greek original, which compared the eunuch to a lizard ($\gamma\alpha\lambda\epsilon\acute{\omega}\tau\eta\varsigma$), not to a weasel ($\gamma\alpha\lambda\hat{\eta}$).

PHAE fraterne?
DORU   ita.
PHAE   quando?
DORU   hodie.
PHAE   quam dudum?
DORU   modo.
PHAE quicum?
DORU   cum Parmenone.
PHAE   norasne eum prius?
DORU non, nec quis esset umquam audieram dicier.
700 PHAE unde igitur fratrem meum esse scibas?
DORU   Parmeno
      dicebat eum esse. is dedit mi hanc vestem.
PHAE   occidi!
DORU meam ipse induit. post una ambo abierunt foras.

PYTH iam satis credis sobriam esse me et nil mentitam tibi?
      iam satis certumst virginem vitiatam esse?
PHAE   age nunc, belua,
705   credis huic quod dicat?
PYTH   quid isti credam? res ipsa indicat.
PHAE concede istuc paullulum. audin? etiamnunc paullum. sat
      est.
      dic dum hoc rursum: Chaerea tuam vestem detraxit tibi?
DORU factum.
PHAE   et eamst indutus?
DORU   factum.
PHAE   et pro te huc deductust?
DORU   ita.

PHAE My brother?

DORU Yes.

PHAE When?

DORU Today.

PHAE How long ago?

DORU Just now.

PHAE Who with?

DORU With Parmeno.

PHAE Did you know him before?

DORU No. I'd never even heard about him.

PHAE So how did you know he was my brother?

DORU Parmeno said he was. It was he who gave me these clothes.

PHAE Damnation!

DORU He put on mine, then the two of them left the house together.

PYTH (*coming forward, to Phaedria*) Now are you satisfied I'm sober and haven't been making it all up? Now do you believe the girl has been raped?

PHAE Come on now, you dumb creature, you don't believe what *he* says?

PYTH There's no need to believe *him*. The facts speak for themselves.

PHAE (*to Dorus*) Move over there a bit. Do you hear me? A bit more. That's enough. (*he pushes Dorus out of earshot of the maids*). Now tell me this again. Did Chaerea take your clothes from you?

DORU He did.

PHAE And put them on himself?

DORU He did.

PHAE And was brought over here in place of you?

DORU Yes.

PHAE Iuppiter magne! o scelestum atque audacem hominem!

PYTH   vae mihi!

710   etiamnunc non credis indignis nos irrisas modis?

PHAE mirum ni tu credas quod iste dicat. quid agam nescio.

     heus, negato rursum. possumne ego hodie ex te exscul-
        pere

     verum? vidistine fratrem Chaeream?

DORU   non.

PHAE   non potest

     sine malo fateri, video. sequere hac. modo ait, modo
     negat.

715   ora me.

DORU   obsecro te vero, Phaedria.

PHAE   i intro nunciam.

DORU oiei.

PHAE   alio pacto honeste quo modo hinc abeam nescio.

     actumst, siquidem tu me hic etiam, nebulo, ludificabere.

PYTH Parmenonis tam scio esse hanc techinam quam me vi-
     vere.

DORI sic est.

PYTH   inveniam pol hodie parem ubi referam gratiam.

720   sed nunc quid faciendum censes, Dorias?

DORI   de istac rogas
     virgine?

PYTH   ita, utrum praedicemne an taceam?

DORI   tu pol, si sapis,

     quod scis nescis neque de eunucho neque de vitio virgi-
     nis.

---

36 Phaedria's "What a bare-faced villain!" is a reflection on Chae-
rea's behaviour, but Pythias takes it as a reaction to Dorus' story and an
indication that Phaedria does not believe it.

PHAE Almighty Jupiter! What a bare-faced villain!

PYTH (*overhearing*) Oh dear, oh dear! Do you still not believe that we've been made fools of? It's outrageous.[36]

PHAE (*scornfully*) No doubt you'd believe anything this fellow said. (*to himself*) I've no idea what to do. (*to Dorus*) Hey, change your story. (*aloud, for Pythias' benefit*) Can I drag the truth out of you now? Did you see my brother Chaerea?

DORU (*trying his best to cooperate*) No.

PHAE He can't tell the truth without a beating, I see. (*to Dorus, turning towards his house*) You come with me. (*to Pythias*) First he admits it, then he denies it. (*aside to Dorus*) Start begging.

DORU I beseech you, truly, Phaedria.

PHAE You go inside for now.

DORU (*as Phaedria kicks him*) Ouch! (*he exits into the house*)

PHAE (*to himself*) I don't know any other way to get out of this without losing face. (*shouting to Dorus inside the house*) You've had it if you make a fool of me again, you good-for-nothing! (*he exits into the house*)

PYTH (*to Dorias*) As sure as I live, I know this is one of Parmeno's tricks.

DORI Quite right.

PYTH Heaven knows I'll find a way to pay him back in kind today. But what do you suggest I should do now, Dorias?

DORI You mean about the girl?

PYTH Yes. Shall I tell what has happened or keep it quiet?

DORI If you've any sense, for heaven's sake, you've forgotten all you know both about the eunuch and about the rape

hac re et te omni turba evolves et illi gratum feceris.

id modo dic, abisse Dorum.

PYTH ita faciam.

DORI sed videon Chremem?

725 Thais iam aderit.

PYTH quid ita?

DORI quia, quom inde abeo, iam tum occeperat

turba inter eos.

PYTH tu aufer aurum hoc. ego scibo ex hoc quid siet.

IV. v: CHREMES. PYTHIAS.

CHR attat! data hercle verba mihi sunt: vicit vinum quod bibi.

at dum accubabam quam videbar mi esse pulchre so-
brius!

postquam surrexi neque pes neque mens satis suom

officium facit.

730 PYTH Chremes!

CHR quis est? ehem, Pythias! vah! quanto nunc formosior

videre mihi quam dudum!

PYTH certe tuquidem pol multo hilarior.

CHR verbum hercle hoc verum erit: "sine Cerere et Libero

friget Venus."

sed Thais multon ante venit?

PYTH an abiit iam a milite?

CHR iamdudum, aetatem. lites factae sunt inter eos maxumae.

735 PYTH nil dixit tu ut sequerere sese?

CHR nil, nisi abiens mi innuit.

PYTH eho, nonne id sat erat?

---

[37] The Latin is ambiguous and could also mean "him." It is most
probable that Pamphila is meant: her chances of an honourable mar-
riage would be ruined if it was known that she had lost her virginity.

of the girl. That way you'll extricate yourself from this
whole mess and you'll be doing her[37] a favour. Just say
Dorus has disappeared.

PYTH I'll do that.

DORI (*looking down the street*) But is that Chremes I see?
Thais will be here soon.

PYTH Why so?

DORI Because, when I left, a row had already broken out be-
tween them.

PYTH You put that jewellery away. I'll find out from him what's
happening. (*Dorias exits into Thais' house*)

Enter CHREMES *right from the direction of Thraso's house,
rather drunk.*

CHR Help! I've been led astray. The wine I've drunk has done
me in, though when I was reclining at the table I seemed
beautifully sober. Since I got up, neither foot nor mind
has been functioning as it should.

PYTH Chremes!

CHR Who is it? Oh hello, Pythias! Wow! How much more
beautiful you look now than you did a while ago! (*he tries
to embrace her*)

PYTH Well, you certainly look a good deal more cheerful.

CHR The proverb turns out to be true: "Without food and wine
love is cold." But did Thais get back much before me?

PYTH Has she left the soldier's already?

CHR Long ago, ages. There was a terrible argument between
them.

PYTH Didn't she suggest you should follow her?

CHR No, except that she nodded to me as she left.

PYTH Hey, wasn't that enough?

397

CHR   at nescibam id dicere illam, nisi quia
correxit miles quod intellexi minus; nam me extrusit fo-
    ras.
sed eccam ipsam. miror ubi ego huic antevorterim.

IV. vi: THAIS. CHREMES. PYTHIAS.

THA credo equidem illum iam adfuturum esse ut illam a me
    eripiat. sine veniat.
740 atqui si illam digito attigerit uno, oculi ilico effodientur.
usque adeo ego illius ferre possum ineptiam et magnifica
    verba,
verba dum sint. verum enim si ad rem conferentur vapu-
    labit.

CHR Thais, ego iamdudum hic adsum.

THA   o mi Chremes, te ipsum exspectabam.
scin tu turbam hanc propter te esse factam? et adeo ad te
    attinere hanc
745 omnem rem?

CHR   ad me? qui, quaeso, istuc?

THA   quia, dum tibi sororem studeo
reddere ac restituere, haec atque huius modi sum multa
    passa.

CHR ubi east?

THA   domi apud me.

CHR   hem!

THA   quid est?
educta ita uti teque illaque dignumst.

CHR   quid ais?

THA   id quod res est.
hanc tibi dono do neque repeto pro illa quicquam abs te
    preti.

745 quaeso *Bentley,* quasi *codd. Don.*

THE EUNUCH

CHR   Well, I didn't know what she meant, but the soldier set
      me straight by throwing me out. (*looking down the street*)
      But here she is. I wonder where I got ahead of her.

Enter THAIS *right from the direction of Thraso's house with her
maids.*

THA   (*to herself*) I suppose he'll be here in a minute to steal the
      girl from me. Let him come! If he lays a finger on her, I'll
      gouge out his eyes on the spot. I can put up with his stu-
      pidity and boastful words so long as they *are* just words.
      But if they turn into actions, he'll get a thrashing.

CHR   (*coming forward*) Thais, I've been here some time.

THA   Oh, my dear Chremes, I was looking out for you. You
      realise that this dispute is on your account? And indeed
      that this whole business is your business?

CHR   Mine? How so, if I may ask?

THA   Because it's through my eagerness to restore your sister
      to your keeping that I've suffered this treatment and
      much more like it.

CHR   Where is she?

THA   In my house.

CHR   (*pulling a face*) Really!

THA   What's the matter? She's been brought up in a manner
      appropriate both to you and to herself.

CHR   What are you saying?

THA   It's the truth. I'm giving her to you as a present and I'm
      not asking any reward from you in return.

750 CHR et habetur et referetur, Thais, ita uti merita's gratia.

THA at enim cave ne prius quam hanc a me accipias amittas,
Chreme.

nam haec east quam miles a me vi nunc ereptum venit.

abi tu, cistellam, Pythias, domo ecfer cum monumentis.

CHR viden tu illum, Thais—

PYTH ubi sitast?

THA in risco. odiosa cessas.

755 CHR —militem secum ad te quantas copias adducere?
attat!

THA num formidulosus, obsecro, es, mi homo?

CHR apage sis!

egon formidulosus? nemost hominum qui vivat minus.

THA atqui ita opust.

CHR ah! metuo qualem tu me esse hominem existumes.

THA immo hoc cogitato. quicum res tibist peregrinus est,

760 minus potens quam tu, minus notus, minus amicorum
hic habens.

CHR scio istuc. sed tu quod cavere possis stultum admitterest.

malo ego nos prospicere quam hunc ulcisci accepta iniu-
ria.

tu abi atque obsera ostium intus, dum ego hinc transcur-
ro ad forum.

volo ego adesse hic advocatos nobis in turba hac.

THA mane.

765 CHR melius est.

THA omitte.

CHR iam adero.

765 THA. omitte. CHR. iam adero A, THA. mane. CHR. omitte, iam
adero Σ

400

CHR I'm grateful to you, Thais, and I'll repay you as you deserve.

THA But mind you don't lose her before you even get her from me, Chremes. She's the one the soldier's now coming to steal from me by force. (*to Pythias*) Pythias, you run indoors and fetch the box with the tokens. (*Pythias exits into the house*)

CHR (*looking down the street*) Do you see the soldier, Thais—?

PYTH (*appearing at the door, to Thais*) Where is it?

THA (*to Pythias*) In the chest. You're a nuisance to be so slow.

CHR —and what a large army he's bringing with him? Help!

THA You're not frightened, for goodness' sake, my dear fellow?

CHR Get away with you! Me frightened? There's not a man living who's less so.

THA Well, we need some courage.

CHR Oh! I'm afraid you don't think much of me.

THA Never mind that; look at it this way. The man you have to deal with is a foreigner, less influential than you, less well known, and with fewer friends here.

CHR I'm aware of that. But it's stupid to let something happen when you could prevent it. I'd prefer us to take action beforehand rather than seek redress when the injury's been done. You go and bolt the door from inside, while I run off to the forum. I'd like to have some people to support me in this dispute. (*he makes to leave right*)

THA (*restraining him*) Wait.

CHR It's better.

THA Forget it.

CHR I'll soon be back.

THA   nil opus est istis, Chreme.
hoc modo dic, sororem illam tuam esse et te parvam vir-
    ginem
amisisse, nunc cognosse. signa ostende.

PYTH   adsunt.

THA   cape.
si vim faciet, in ius ducito hominem. intellextin?

CHR   probe.

THA   fac animo haec praesenti dicas.

CHR   faciam.

THA   attolle pallium.

770   perii! huic ipsist opus patrono quem defensorem paro.

IV. vii: THRASO. GNATHO. SANGA. THAIS. CHREMES.

THR   hancine ego ut contumeliam tam insignem in me acci-
    piam, Gnatho?
mori me satiust. Simalio, Donax, Syrisce, sequimini.
primum aedis expugnabo.

GNA   recte.

THR   virginem eripiam.

GNA   probe.

THR   male mulcabo ipsam.

GNA   pulchre.

THR   in medium huc agmen cum vecti, Donax;

775   tu, Simalio, in sinistrum cornum; tu, Syrisce, in dexte-
    rum.
cedo alios. ubi centuriost Sanga et manipulus furum?

SAN   eccum adest.

THR   quid, ignave? peniculon pugnare, qui istum huc portes,
    cogitas?

THA We don't need them, Chremes. Just tell him that she's your sister, that you lost her as a small girl, and that you've now confirmed her identity. Show him the tokens.

PYTH (*returning with the box*) Here they are.

THA (*to Chremes*) Take them. If he uses violence, take him to court. You understand?

CHR Perfectly.

THA Be firm when you speak to him.

CHR I will.

THA Gird yourself for action. (*aside*) Damn it! The man I'm setting up as my defender needs a champion himself. (*they take up their positions in front of Thais' house*)

Enter THRASO *and* GNATHO *right from the direction of Thraso's house with a motley army of household slaves, including* SANGA.

THR The very idea that I should put up with such a palpable insult, Gnatho! I'd rather die. (*to the slaves*) Simalio, Donax, Syriscus, follow me. First I'll storm the house.

GNA Right!

THR I'll carry off the girl.

GNA Excellent!

THR I'll give the mistress a good thrashing.

GNA Brilliant!

THR Donax, in the centre of the line with your crowbar. You, Simalio, on the left wing. You, Syriscus, on the right. Bring on the others. Where is centurion Sanga and his company of thieves?

SAN (*coming forward*) Present.

THR What, you useless creature? Are you proposing to fight with a sponge? I see you're carrying one with you.

403

SAN egon? imperatoris virtutem noveram et vim militum:
     sine sanguine hoc non posse fieri. qui abstergerem volne-
          ra?
780 THR ubi alii?
GNA   qui malum "alii"? solus Sannio servat domi.
THR tu hosce instrue. ego hic ero post principia: inde omnibus
     signum dabo.
GNA illuc est sapere: ut hosce instruxit, ipse sibi cavit loco.
THR idem hoc iam Pyrrhus factitavit.
CHR   viden tu, Thais, quam hic rem agit?
     nimirum consilium illud rectumst de occludendis aedi-
     bus.
785 THA sane, quod tibi nunc vir videatur esse hic, nebulo magnus
     est.
     ne metuas.
THR   quid videtur?
GNA   fundam tibi nunc nimis vellem dari,
     ut tu illos procul hinc ex occulto caederes: facerent fu-
     gam.

THR sed eccam Thaidem ipsam video.
GNA   quam mox irruimus?
THR   mane.
     omnia prius experiri quam armis sapientem decet.
790 qui scis an quae iubeam sine vi faciat?
GNA   di vostram fidem!
     quantist sapere! numquam accedo quin abs te abeam
     doctior.

---

⁷⁸³ idem . . . factitavit *Thrasoni dat* A, *Gnathoni* Σ

404

SAN   Me? I knew the valour of the general and the violence of the soldiers. This operation cannot take place without blood. How else was I to wipe the wounds?

THR   (*to Gnatho*) Where are the others?

GNA   What others, damn it? There's only Sannio and he's on duty at home.

THR   You draw up these. I'll be here behind the front line.[38] I'll give the signal to everybody from there.

GNA   (*aside*) There's a wise man for you. He's drawn up the troops to protect himself.

THR   Pyrrhus did the same before me.[39]

CHR   (*to Thais*) Thais, do you see what he's doing? It was surely a good idea to bolt the door.

THA   (*to Chremes*) The truth is, though he may seem now to you a real man, he's a great fairy. Don't be afraid.

THR   (*to Gnatho*) What do you think?

GNA   I only wish you had a sling, so that you could cut them down in hiding from a distance. That would put them to flight.

THR   But look, there's Thais.

GNA   (*mischievously*) How soon do we attack?

THR   Wait! The wise man should try everything before resorting to arms. For all you know, she will do what I tell her without force.

GNA   (*ironically*) Heaven help us! What it is to be wise! I never come near you without going away the wiser.

---

[38] Literally "behind the *principia*," the prime troops who in fact fought in the second of the three lines of the Roman army formation.

[39] Pyrrhus, king of Epirus in northwest Greece, invaded Italy in 280 B.C. to help the Greek cities of southern Italy against the Romans; there is no historical basis for the suggestion that he led his army from behind.

THR Thais, primum hoc mihi responde. quom tibi do istam virginem,
dixtin hos dies mihi soli dare te?

THA   quid tum postea?

THR rogitas, quae mi ante oculos coram amatorem adduxti tuom?

795 THA quid cum illoc agas?

THR   et cum eo clam te subduxti mihi?

THA lubuit.

THR   Pamphilam ergo huc redde, nisi vi mavis eripi.

CHR tibi illam reddat aut tu eam tangas, omnium—?

GNA   ah! quid agis? tace!

THR quid tu tibi vis? ego non tangam meam?

CHR   tuam autem, furcifer?

GNA cave sis. nescis quoi maledicas nunc viro.

CHR   non tu hinc abis?

800 scin tu ut tibi res se habeat? si quicquam hodie turbae coeperis,
faciam ut huius loci dieique meique semper memineris.

GNA miseret tui me qui hunc tantum hominem facias inimicum tibi.

CHR diminuam ego caput tuom hodie, nisi abis.

GNA   ain vero, canis?
sicin agis?

THR   quis tu homo's? quid tibi vis? quid cum illa rei tibist?

805 CHR scibis. principio eam esse dico liberam.

THR (*to Thais*) Thais, first answer me this. When I gave you the girl, didn't you say you would keep these next days for me alone?

THA What of it?

THR You ask? When you brought in your lover right under my nose?

THA What's he to you?

THR And stole away with him in secret?

THA I wanted to.

THR Well, give Pamphila back here, unless you prefer her to be taken by force.

CHR (*to Thraso*) Give Pamphila back? You lay hands on her? Of all the—!

GNA (*to Chremes*) Watch it! Hold your tongue!

THR (*to Chremes*) How do you mean? Not lay hands on my own girl?

CHR Your girl indeed? You rascal!

GNA (*to Chremes*) Kindly be careful. You don't realise what sort of a man you're abusing.

CHR (*to Gnatho*) You keep out of this. (*to Thraso*) Do you realise your situation here? If you cause the slightest trouble, I'll make sure you always remember this place, this day, and me.

GNA (*to Chremes*) I'm sorry for you, making yourself an enemy of such a man.

CHR (*to Thraso*) I'll bash your brains out, if you don't go away.

GNA (*to Chremes*) Do you say so, you cur? Is that your attitude?

THR (*to Chremes*) Who do you think you are? What are you after? What's your connection with the girl?

CHR I'll tell you. In the first place, I declare that she's a free woman.

THR		hem!
CHR		civem Atticam.
THR		hui!
CHR	meam sororem.	
THR		os durum!
CHR		miles, nunc adeo edico tibi

ne vim facias ullam in illam. Thais, ego eo ad Sophronam
nutricem, ut eam adducam et signa ostendam haec.

THR		tun me prohibeas

meam ne tangam?

CHR	prohibebo inquam.	
GNA		audin tu? furti se alligat.

810 CHR sat hoc tibist?

THR	idem hoc tu, Thais?	
THA		quaere qui respondeat.
THR	quid nunc agimus?	
GNA		quin redeamus? iam haec tibi aderit supplicans

ultro.

THR	credin?	
GNA		immo certe. novi ingenium mulierum:

nolunt ubi velis, ubi nolis cupiunt ultro.

THR		bene putas.
GNA	iam dimitto exercitum?	
THR		ubi vis.
GNA		Sanga, ita ut fortis decet

815 milites, domi focique fac vicissim ut memineris.

SAN	iamdudum animus est in patinis.	
GNA		frugi's.

THR   What!

CHR   An Athenian citizen.

THR   (*scornfully*) Wow!

CHR   And my sister.

THR   The barefaced impudence!

CHR   Soldier, I now warn you once and for all not to commit an act of violence on her. (*to Thais*) Thais, I'm going to find our nurse Sophrona to bring her here and show her these tokens.

THR   Are you forbidding me to lay hands on my own girl?

CHR   Yes, I am.

GNA   (*to Thraso*) Do you hear? He's incriminating himself in theft.

CHR   (*to Thraso*) Is that enough for you? (*he exits left to fetch the nurse*)

THR   (*to Thais*) Do you say the same, Thais?

THA   Find someone else to answer you. (*she exits into her house*)

THR   (*to Gnatho*) What do we do now?

GNA   Why not go home? She'll soon be back of her own accord on bended knee.

THR   Do you think so?

GNA   I'm sure of it. I know how women behave. When you want a thing they don't, and contrariwise when you don't they do.

THR   You're right.

GNA   Do I now dismiss the army?

THR   When you like.

GNA   Sanga, do what a true soldier should, and turn your thoughts to hearth and home.

SAN   My mind's been on my pans for some time.

GNA   Good man!

THR   vos me hac sequimini.

ACTUS V

v. i: THAIS. PYTHIAS.

THA pergin, scelesta, mecum perplexe loqui?
     "scio nescio, abiit, audivi, ego non adfui."
     non tu istuc mihi dictura aperte's quidquid est?
820 virgo conscissa veste lacrumans obticet;
     eunuchus abiit. quam ob rem? quid factumst? taces?
PYTH quid tibi ego dicam misera? illum eunuchum negant
     fuisse.
THA   quis fuit igitur?
PYTH   iste Chaerea.
THA qui Chaerea?
PYTH   iste ephebus frater Phaedriae.
825 THA quid ais, venefica?
PYTH   atqui certe comperi.
THA quid is obsecro ad nos? quam ob rem adductust?
PYTH   nescio;
     nisi amasse credo Pamphilam.
THA   hem! misera occidi,
     infelix, siquidem tu istaec vera praedicas.
     num id lacrumat virgo?
PYTH   id opinor.
THA   quid ais, sacrilega?
830 istucine interminata sum hinc abiens tibi?
PYTH quid facerem? ita ut tu iusti, soli creditast.

THR   (*to the whole army*) Follow me. This way. (*he marches off right followed by Gnatho, Sanga, and the rest of the "troops," leaving the stage empty*)

ACT FIVE

Enter THAIS from her house with PYTHIAS.

THA   Do you persist in talking in riddles, you wretch? "I know . . . I don't know . . . he's gone . . . I heard . . . I wasn't there." Won't you tell me in plain words what is going on? The girl's dress is torn, she's weeping, and she won't say a word. The eunuch's gone. Why? What's happened? Answer me.

PYTH Oh dear, what can I say? They say it wasn't the eunuch.

THA   Who was it then?

PYTH That Chaerea.

THA   Which Chaerea?

PYTH That brother of Phaedria's, the ephebe.

THA   What are you saying, you poisonous wretch?

PYTH Well, it's true. I've checked.

THA   What's he got to do with us, for goodness sake? What brought him here?

PYTH I've no idea. I suppose he'd fallen in love with Pamphila.

THA   (*guessing the sequel*) Oh dear, I'm ruined! It's a disaster for me if what you say is true. Is that why the girl's weeping?

PYTH I think so.

THA   Answer me this, you barbarian! Didn't I expressly warn you against this when I left?

PYTH What was I to do? I did what you told me and put him in sole charge of her.

411

THA scelesta, ovem lupo commisti. dispudet
sic mihi data esse verba. quid illuc hominis est?
PYTH era mea, tace, tace, obsecro. salvae sumus:
835 habemus hominem ipsum.
THA ubi is est?
PYTH em ad sinisteram.
viden?
THA video.
PYTH comprendi iube, quantum potest.
THA quid illo faciemus, stulta?
PYTH quid facias, rogas?
vide amabo, si non, quom aspicias, os impudens
videtur. non est? tum quae eius confidentiast!

V. ii: CHAEREA. THAIS. PYTHIAS.

840 CHAE apud Antiphonem uterque, mater et pater,
quasi dedita opera domi erant, ut nullo modo
intro ire possem quin viderent me. interim
dum ante ostium sto, notus mihi quidam obviam
venit. ubi vidi, ego me in pedes quantum queo
845 in angiportum quoddam desertum, inde item
in aliud, inde in aliud: ita miserrumus
fui fugitando ne quis me cognosceret.
sed estne haec Thais quam video? ipsast. haereo
quid faciam. quid mea autem? quid faciet mihi?
850 THA adeamus. bone vir Dore, salve. dic mihi,
aufugistin?
CHAE era, factum.
THA satin id tibi placet?
CHAE non.
THA credin te impune habiturum?

412

THA You wretch, entrusting a lamb to the proverbial wolf! I'm
ashamed to have been deceived like this. What sort of a
man is this?

PYTH (*looking down the street*) My dear mistress, say no more,
I implore you. We're saved. We've got him.

THA Where is he?

PYTH Over there, to the left. Do you see?

THA Yes, I do.

PYTH Have him arrested at once.

THA What could we do with him, you fool?

PYTH What could we do? You ask? Do me a favour, take a look
and see if there isn't impudence written all over his face.
Well, isn't there? And what self-assurance!

Enter CHAEREA *right, still in his eunuch's costume.*

CHAE (*to himself*) Antipho's father and mother were both at
home, as if they'd stayed in on purpose, so there was no
way I could get inside without being seen. While I was
standing outside the door, an acquaintance of mine came
up. When I saw him, I took to my heels as fast as I could
into a deserted alley, and from there to another one, and
then to another. I was desperate in case someone recog-
nised me as I fled. (*seeing Thais*) But is that Thais I see?
It is. I'm stuck what to do. What's it matter, though? What
can she do to me?

THA (*to Pythias*) Let's go up to him. (*to Chaerea*) Good day,
Dorus, my good man. Tell me, did you run away?

CHAE Yes, madam, I did.

THA Are you happy with your conduct?

CHAE No.

THA Do you suppose you'll get away with this?

CHAE   unam hanc noxiam
       amitte. si aliam admisero umquam, occidito.

THA   num meam saevitiam veritus es?

CHAE   non.

THA   quid igitur?

855   CHAE hanc metui ne me criminaretur tibi.

THA   quid feceras?

CHAE   paullum quiddam.

PYTH   eho, "paullum," impudens?
       an paullum hoc esse tibi videtur, virginem
       vitiare civem?

CHAE   conservam esse credidi.

PYTH conservam! vix me contineo quin involem in
860   capillum, monstrum! etiam ultro derisum advenit.

THA   abin hinc, insana?

PYTH   quid ita? vero debeam,
       credo, isti quicquam furcifero si id fecerim,
       praesertim quom se servom fateatur tuom.

THA   missa haec faciamus. non te dignum, Chaerea,
865   fecisti. nam si ego digna hac contumelia
       sum maxume, at tu indignus qui faceres tamen.
       neque edepol quid nunc consili capiam scio
       de virgine istac. ita conturbasti mihi
       rationes omnis ut eam non possim suis
870   ita ut aequom fuerat atque ut studui tradere,
       ut solidum parerem hoc mi beneficium, Chaerea.

CHAE at nunc dehinc spero aeternam inter nos gratiam
       fore, Thais. saepe ex huius modi re quapiam et
       malo principio magna familiaritas
875   conflatast. quid si hoc quispiam voluit deus?

CHAE (*wheedling*) Forgive this one offence. If I ever commit another, you can put me to death.

THA Were you afraid that I would be a cruel mistress?

CHAE No.

THA What, then?

CHAE I was afraid that she (*indicating Pythias*) would tell tales on me.

THA What had you done?

CHAE Nothing very much.

PYTH Hey, nothing very much, you shameless creature? Does it seem to you nothing very much to rape a citizen girl?

CHAE I thought she was a fellow slave.

PYTH A fellow slave! I can scarcely restrain myself from flying at your hair, you monster! (*to Thais*) On top of it all he comes here to mock us.

THA (*to Pythias*) Come off it! You're crazy!

PYTH What do you mean? I'm scarcely going to be held liable if I do anything to this rascal, especially as he's claiming to be your slave.

THA (*changing her tone*) Let's stop this nonsense. (*to Chaerea*) Your conduct was not worthy of you, Chaerea. Even if I thoroughly deserve this outrage, it wasn't right for you to inflict it. Now I've no idea what to do about the girl. You've upset my calculations: I can't hand her over to her family, which would have been the proper thing and which I'd set my heart on doing in order to gain myself some lasting benefit, Chaerea.

CHAE But I hope that from now on there will be an eternal bond of gratitude between us, Thais. Often a great friendship has been forged from an incident of this sort and a bad beginning. What if some god has willed it?

415

THA equidem pol in eam partem accipioque et volo.

CHAE immo ita quaeso. unum hoc scito, contumeliae
me non fecisse causa sed amoris.

THA   scio,
et pol propterea magis nunc ignosco tibi.

880 non adeo inhumano ingenio sum, Chaerea,
neque ita imperita ut quid amor valeat nesciam.

CHAE te quoque iam, Thais, ita me di bene ament, amo.

PYTH tum pol tibi ab istoc, era, cavendum intellego.

CHAE non ausim.

PYTH   nil tibi quicquam credo.

THA   desinas.

885 CHAE nunc ego te in hac re mi oro ut adiutrix sies;
ego me tuae commendo et committo fide;
te mihi patronam capio, Thais, te obsecro.
emoriar si non hanc uxorem duxero.

THA tamen si pater—

CHAE   quid? ah volet, certo scio,

890 civis modo haec sit.

THA   paullulum opperirier
si vis, iam frater ipse hic aderit virginis.
nutricem accersitum iit quae illam aluit parvolam.
in cognoscendo tute ipse aderis, Chaerea.

CHAE ego vero maneo.

THA   vin interea, dum venit,

895 domi opperiamur potius quam hic ante ostium?

CHAE immo percupio.

PYTH   quam tu rem actura, obsecro, es?

THA nam quid ita?

THA Well, heaven knows I'm ready and willing to look at it that way.

CHAE That's good of you. Let me assure you of one thing: I didn't do this to insult you but for love.

THA I know, and for that reason, by heaven, I'm the more ready to forgive you. I'm not so lacking in humanity, Chaerea, or so inexperienced in the ways of the world, that I don't know the power of love.

CHAE I love you too, Thais, as heaven is my witness.

PYTH (*to Thais*) In that case I can see you need to be on your guard against him, madam.

CHAE I wouldn't dare.

PYTH I don't trust you one little bit.

THA (*to Pythias*) That's enough!

CHAE (*to Thais*) I now beg you to give me your support in this matter; I entrust myself to your care and protection; I take you as my patron, Thais; I implore you. I shall die if I don't marry her.

THA But if your father—

CHAE Does what? Oh, he'll consent, I'm sure, provided she's a citizen.

THA If you're willing to wait a moment, the girl's brother will soon be here himself. He's gone to fetch the nurse who took care of her when she was tiny. You shall be present at the recognition, Chaerea.

CHAE Of course I'll stay.

THA Would you rather we waited inside the house for him to come instead of here in front of the door?

CHAE Very much so.

PYTH (*to Thais*) What are you doing, for goodness' sake?

THA What's the matter?

PYTH   rogitas? hunc tu in aedis cogitas
       recipere posthac?

THA   quor non?

PYTH   crede hoc meae fide:
       dabit hic pugnam aliquam denuo.

THA   au tace obsecro.

900 PYTH parum perspexisse eius videre audaciam.

CHAE non faciam, Pythias.

PYTH   non credo, Chaerea,
       nisi si commissum non erit.

CHAE   quin, Pythias,
       tu me servato.

PYTH   neque pol servandum tibi

905   quicquam dare ausim neque te servare. apage te!

THA adest optume ipse frater.

CHAE   perii hercle! obsecro
       abeamus intro, Thais: nolo me in via
       cum hac veste videat.

THA   quam ob rem tandem? an quia pudet?

CHAE id ipsum.

PYTH   id ipsum? virgo vero!

THA   i prae, sequor.
       tu istic mane ut Chremem intro ducas, Pythias.

V. iii: PYTHIAS. CHREMES. SOPHRONA.

910 PYTH quid, quid venire in mentem nunc possit mihi,
       quidnam qui referam sacrilego illi gratiam
       qui hunc supposivit nobis?

CHR   move vero ocius
       te, nutrix.

SOPH   moveo.

CHR   video, sed nil promoves.

PYTH A fine question! Are you proposing to invite him into the house after all this?

THA Why not?

PYTH Take my word for it. He'll cause some further mischief.

THA Oh for goodness' sake, be quiet!

PYTH You don't seem to realise how brazen he is.

CHAE I won't, Pythias.

PYTH I don't believe you, Chaerea, not until it hasn't happened.

CHAE (*mischievously*) Well, why don't you guard me yourself, Pythias?

PYTH I wouldn't dare to give you anything to guard or to guard you. Get away with you!

THA (*looking down the street*) Excellent! Here's her brother.

CHAE God damn it! Let's go inside, I implore you, Thais; I don't want him to see me in the street in these clothes.

THA (*teasing*) Why not, I ask you? Are you bashful?

CHAE (*with exaggerated modesty*) That's it.

PYTH That's it? Spoken like a true virgin!

THA (*to Chaerea*) Go ahead, I'll follow. (*to Pythias*) You stay here, Pythias, and bring Chremes in. (*she follows Chaerea into her house*)

Enter CHREMES left with the nurse SOPHRONA.

PYTH (*to herself*) What plan, what plan can I now dream up? What means to repay the barbarian who foisted this fellow upon us?

CHR (*to the nurse*) Move faster, nurse.

SOPH I *am* moving.

CHR I can see that. But you're not making any progress.

PYTH iamne ostendisti signa nutrici?

CHR   omnia.

915 PYTH amabo, quid ait? cognoscitne?

CHR   ac memoriter.

PYTH probe edepol narras; nam illi faveo virgini.
     ite intro. iamdudum era vos exspectat domi.
     virum bonum eccum Parmenonem incedere
     video. vide ut otiosus it, si dis placet!

920   spero me habere qui hunc meo excruciem modo.
     ibo intro de cognitione ut certum sciam;
     post exibo atque hunc perterrebo sacrilegum.

V. iv: PARMENO. PYTHIAS.

PAR reviso quidnam Chaerea hic rerum gerat.
     quod si astu rem tractavit, di vostram fidem,

925   quantam et quam veram laudem capiet Parmeno!
     nam ut omittam quod ei amorem difficillumum et
     carissumum, a meretrice avara virginem
     quam amabat, eam confeci sine molestia
     sine sumptu et sine dispendio. tum hoc alterum

930   (id verost quod ego mi puto palmarium),
     me repperisse quo modo adulescentulus
     meretricum ingenia et mores posset noscere
     mature, ut quom cognorit perpetuo oderit.
     quae dum foris sunt nil videtur mundius

935   nec magis compositum quicquam nec magis elegans,
     quae cum amatore quom cenant ligurriunt.
     harum videre illuviem sordes inopiam,
     quam inhonestae solae sint domi atque avidae cibi,

PYTH *(to Chremes)* Have you already shown the nurse the tokens?

CHR All of them.

PYTH What does she say, darling? Does she recognise them?

CHR Yes; she remembers them well.

PYTH Excellent news, by heaven! I'm fond of the girl. You two go inside. My mistress has been at home expecting you for a while. *(looking down the street, as Chremes and Sophrona exit into Thais' house)* Look, here comes that fine fellow Parmeno, swaggering along. What a leisurely saunter, if you please! I think I've found my own way to torture him. I'll go in and make sure of the recognition. Then I'll come out and terrify the barbarian.

Enter PARMENO *left, looking very pleased with himself.*

PAR *(to himself)* I'm returning to see how Chaerea is getting on. If he's handled the situation cleverly, heaven help us, how much praise will Parmeno receive today and how deservedly! Not to mention that I've secured for him without trouble and without cost or outlay a very difficult and very expensive love affair, since the girl he loved belonged to a greedy courtesan; there's the other point— and I reckon this to be my master stroke— that I've found a way for a young lad to discover the character and habits of courtesans in good time, so that having discovered them he will hate them forever. So long as they're out in public, there's nothing more refined, more composed, more elegant, as they pick daintily at their food while dining with a lover. But to see their filth, squalor, and poverty, and how repulsive they are when they are alone at home and how greedy they are for food, how

quo pacto ex iure hesterno panem atrum vorent,
940   nosse omnia haec salus est adulescentulis.
PYTH ego pol te pro istis dictis et factis, scelus,
    ulciscar, ut ne impune in nos illuseris.

    pro deum fidem! facinus foedum! o infelicem adulescen-
      tulum!
    o scelestum Parmenonem qui istum huc adduxit!
PAR   quid est?
945 PYTH miseret me. itaque ut ne viderem misera huc effugi foras
    quae futura exempla dicunt in illum indigna.
PAR   o Iuppiter,
    quae illaec turbast? numnam ego perii? adibo. quid istuc,
      Pythias?
    quid ais? in quem exempla fient?
PYTH   rogitas, audacissume?
    perdidisti istum quem adduxti pro eunucho adulescentu-
      lum,
950   dum studes dare verba nobis.
PAR   quid ita? aut quid factumst? cedo.
PYTH dicam. virginem istam, Thaidi hodie quae dono datast,
    scis eam hinc civem esse? et fratrem eius esse apprime
      nobilem?
PAR nescio.
PYTH   atqui sic inventast. eam istic vitiavit miser.
    ille ubi id rescivit factum frater violentissimus—
955 PAR quidnam fecit?
PYTH   —colligavit primum eum miseris modis—
PAR colligavit?
PYTH   —atque equidem orante ut ne id faceret Thaide.

they devour stale bread dipped in yesterday's soup—to
know all this is the salvation of young lads.

PYTH (*aside, having emerged silently from the house during
Parmeno's monologue*) I'll punish you, by heaven, you
villain, for those words and deeds of yours; you won't get
away with making fools of us. (*aloud, for Parmeno's bene-
fit*) Heaven help us! What a foul deed! Oh the ill-fated
young man! Oh that wicked Parmeno who brought him
here!

PAR (*aside*) What's this?

PYTH I'm sorry for him, and so I rushed out here in misery so as
not to see the shocking punishment they say's coming to
him.

PAR By Jupiter, what's this commotion? Is this the end of me?
I'll go up to her. (*approaching Pythias*) What is all this
about, Pythias? What are you saying? Who's going to be
punished?

PYTH Well may you ask, you brazen creature! You've ruined the
young man you brought here in place of the eunuch
when you were trying to make fools of us.

PAR How so? What's happened? Tell me.

PYTH I will. The girl who was given to Thais today as a pres-
ent—do you know she's an Athenian citizen? And her
brother's from one of the best families?

PAR I don't know about that.

PYTH Well, she's been recognised as one. And he raped her, the
wretch. When the brother discovered this, being a man
of violent disposition—

PAR What did he do?

PYTH —he first tied him up in a horrible way—

PAR Tied him up?

PYTH —even though Thais was begging him not to—

423

PAR quid ais?

PYTH   nunc minatur porro sese id quod moechis solet,
quod ego numquam vidi fieri neque velim.

PAR   qua audacia
tantum facinus audet?

PYTH   quid ita "tantum"?

PAR   an non tibi hoc maxumumst?

960   quis homo pro moecho umquam vidit in domo meretri-
cia
prendi quemquam?

PYTH   nescio.

PAR   at ne hoc nesciatis, Pythias,
dico, edico vobis nostrum esse illum erilem filium.

PYTH   hem!
obsecro, an is est?

PAR   ne quam in illum Thais vim fieri sinat.
atque adeo autem quor non egomet intro eo?

PYTH   vide, Parmeno,

965   quid agas, ne neque illi prosis et tu pereas. nam hoc
putant
quidquid factumst ex te esse ortum.

PAR   quid igitur faciam miser?
quidve incipiam? ecce autem, video rure redeuntem
senem.

---

⁴⁰ Terence uses the Greek term (μοιχός), which applies to a man
(whether married or not) who has sexual relations with a free female de-
pendent of another man, so that Chaerea can be seen as an "adulterer"
in this case. In Athenian law, the husband or son or father or brother of
an adulteress was permitted to kill her lover if caught in the act; the

PAR   What are you saying?

PYTH —and moreover is now threatening to do what they do to
      adulterers,[40] a thing I've never seen and wouldn't wish to
      see.

PAR   How can he have the audacity to do such a terrible deed?

PYTH How do you mean "terrible"?

PAR   Can you think of anything more terrible? Who ever saw
      anyone arrested for adultery in a courtesan's house?[41]

PYTH (*mockingly echoing Parmeno's previous remark*) I don't
      know about that.

PAR   Well, in case you don't know about *this*, Pythias, I hereby
      declare that this is our master's son.

PYTH (*still mocking*) Oh, for goodness' sake! Is it?

PAR   So Thais had better not permit any act of violence against
      him. But why don't I go inside myself?

PYTH Mind what you're doing, Parmeno. You may not do him
      any good and you may destroy yourself. They think this
      whole business was instigated by you.

PAR   Oh dear! So what am I to do? Where can I start? (*looking
      down the street*) But look, here's the old master returning

---

legal situation in the Roman Republic is not so clear. Apart from death,
there were various other traditional penalties for adulterers, including
depilation of the pubic hair with hot ash or the insertion of a radish or
mullet into the anus. But the reference here is probably to castration:
the final scene of Plautus' *The Swaggering Soldier* has a cook flour-
ishing a knife and threatening to castrate the soldier there for adultery,
and Plautus makes other allusions to this punishment.

[41] Athenian law specifically excluded relations with women in
brothels from the charge of μοιχεία.

dicam huic an non dicam? dicam hercle, etsi mihi mag-
   num malum
scio paratum. sed necessest, huic ut subveniat.

PYTH   sapis.
970   ego abeo intro. tu isti narra omne ordine ut factum siet.

V. v: SENEX. PARMENO.

SEN   ex meo propinquo rure hoc capio commodi:
neque agri neque urbis odium me umquam percipit.
ubi satias coepit fieri commuto locum.
sed estne ille noster Parmeno? et certe ipsus est.
975   quem praestolare, Parmeno, hic ante ostium?
PAR   quis homost? ehem! salvom te advenire, ere, gaudeo.
SEN   quem praestolare?
PAR   perii! lingua haeret metu.
SEN   hem!
quid est? quid trepidas? satine salve? dic mihi.
PAR   ere, primum te arbitrari id quod res est velim.
980   quidquid huius factumst, culpa non factumst mea.
SEN   quid?
PAR   recte sane interrogasti. oportuit
rem praenarrasse me. emit quendam Phaedria
eunuchum quem dono huic daret.
SEN   quoi?
PAR   Thaidi.
SEN   emit? perii hercle! quanti?
PAR   viginti minis.

---

[968] an non ⟨dicam⟩? *Bentley,* an non *codd.*
[970] omne ordine *Faernus,* omnem ordinem *codd.*

---

[42] At line 169 twenty minas was the combined price of the eunuch
and the Ethiopian slave girl.

426

from the farm. Shall I tell him or not tell him? I'll tell
him, by god, even though I know it'll mean a thrashing
for me. But I must; the lad needs his help.

PYTH That's sensible of you. I'm off inside. You tell him the
whole story from start to finish. (*she exits into Thais'
house, leaving Parmeno on stage alone*)

Enter the FATHER *left from the direction of the farm.*

FATH (*to himself*) There's this advantage in having my farm
so close: I never get tired of either the country or the
town. When boredom begins to set in, I change location.
(*seeing Parmeno at Thais' door*) But is that our slave
Parmeno? I'm sure it is. (*to Parmeno*) Who are you wait-
ing for here, Parmeno, outside this door?

PAR Who's that? Oh hello, master! I'm glad to see you safely
back.

FATH (*ignoring the welcome*) Who are you waiting for?

PAR (*aside*) Damn it! My tongue's paralysed with fear!

FATH Hey! What's the matter? Why are you trembling? Is
everything all right? Tell me.

PAR Master, first of all I want you to know the facts of the situ-
ation. Whatever's been done in this, it's not my fault.

FATH What?

PAR You were quite right to ask. I should have told you before.
Phaedria bought a eunuch to give as a present to her.
(*pointing to Thais' house*)

FATH To who?

PAR Thais.

FATH Bought one? God damn it! For how much?

PAR Twenty minas.[42]

427

985	SEN	actumst.
	PAR	tum quandam fidicinam amat hic Chaerea.
	SEN	hem! quid? amat? an scit iam ille quid meretrix siet?
		an in astu venit? aliud ex alio malum!
	PAR	ere, ne me spectes. me impulsore haec non facit.
	SEN	omitte de te dicere. ego te, furcifer,
990		si vivo—! sed istuc quidquid est primum expedi.
	PAR	is pro illo eunucho ad Thaidem hanc deductus est.
	SEN	pro eunuchon?
	PAR	sic est. hunc pro moecho postea
		comprendere intus et constrinxere.
	SEN	occidi!
	PAR	audaciam meretricum specta.
	SEN	num quid est
995		aliud mali damnive quod non dixeris
		relicuom?
	PAR	tantumst.
	SEN	cesso huc intro rumpere?
	PAR	non dubiumst quin mi magnum ex hac re sit malum;
		nisi, quia necessus fuit hoc facere, id gaudeo
		propter me hisce aliquid esse eventurum mali.
1000		nam iamdiu aliquam causam quaerebat senex
		quam ob rem insigne aliquid faceret eis; nunc repperit.

V. vi: PYTHIAS. PARMENO.

PYTH numquam edepol quicquam iamdiu quod mage vellem
    evenire
    mi evenit quam quod modo senex intro ad nos venit
    errans.

FATH I'm finished!

PAR On top of that, Chaerea's in love with a music girl in there (*indicating Thais' house*).

FATH What? Really? In love? Does he know what a courtesan is at his age? Has he come into town? It's one thing after another.

PAR Don't look at me, master. It wasn't me that put him up to it.

FATH Stop talking about yourself. As sure as I live, you rascal, I'll—But first explain what exactly is going on.

PAR He was delivered to Thais here in place of the eunuch.

FATH In place of the eunuch?

PAR That's right. Then they arrested him as an adulterer and tied him up.

FATH Damnation!

PAR Observe the impudence of the women.

FATH Is there some other disgrace or damage that you've left unmentioned?

PAR That's all.

FATH Why don't I burst in on them? (*he exits into Thais' house*)

PAR (*to himself*) There's no doubt that I'll get a mighty thrashing out of this, though, since I had to do it, I'm delighted I'm going to cause these women some trouble. The old man has long been looking for an excuse to do something drastic to them. Now he's found one.

Enter PYTHIAS *from Thais' house, convulsed with laughter.*

PYTH (*to herself*) Heaven knows nothing's happened to me for a long time that I could have wanted more than this: the old man coming into the house just now with the wrong

429

mihi solae ridiculo fuit quae quid timeret scibam.
1005 PAR quid hoc autemst?
PYTH nunc id prodeo ut conveniam Parmenonem.
sed ubi, obsecro, est?
PAR me quaerit haec.
PYTH atque eccum video. adibo.
PAR quid est, inepta? quid tibi vis? quid rides? pergin?
PYTH perii!
defessa iam sum misera te ridendo.
PAR quid ita?
PYTH rogitas?
numquam pol hominem stultiorem vidi nec videbo. ah!
1010 non possum satis narrare quos ludos praebueris intus.
at etiam primo callidum et disertum credidi hominem.
quid? ilicone credere ea quae dixi oportuit te?
an paenitebat flagiti te auctore quod fecisset
adulescens, ni miserum insuper etiam patri indicares?
1015 nam quid illi credis animi tum fuisse, ubi vestem vidit
illam esse eum indutum pater? quid est? iam scis te
perisse?
PAR hem! quid dixisti, pessuma? an mentita's? etiam rides?
itan lepidum tibi visumst, scelus, nos irridere?
PYTH nimium.
PAR siquidem istuc impune habueris—
PYTH verum?
PAR reddam hercle.
PYTH credo.
1020 sed in diem istuc, Parmeno, est fortasse quod minare.
tu iam pendebis qui stultum adulescentulum nobilitas

idea in his head. I was the only one who saw the funny
side. I knew what he was afraid of.

PAR (*aside*) What on earth's this?

PYTH Now I'm coming out to find Parmeno. But where is he,
for goodness' sake?

PAR (*aside*) She's looking for me.

PYTH There he is. (*still laughing*) I'll go up to him.

PAR What is it, you silly girl? What are you up to? Why are you
laughing? Can't you stop?

PYTH This is killing me! Oh dear me, I've worn myself out
laughing at you.

PAR How so?

PYTH You ask? Heaven knows I've never seen a more stupid
fellow, and never shall. Oh! I can't begin to tell you what
amusement you gave us in there. Yet once I even be-
lieved you a clever capable sort of a fellow. Well then,
should you have believed what I told you on the spot?
Weren't you satisfied with persuading the young man to
commit an outrage, unless on top of that you also gave
him away to his father? What do you think his feelings
were when his father saw him dressed in those clothes?
(*Parmeno makes a gesture of despair*) What's the matter?
(*still laughing*) Do you now realise you're done for?

PAR Hey! What did you tell me, you wretch? Did you make it
all up? Are you still laughing? Did you think it was clever
to make fun of me, you villain?

PYTH Very much so.

PAR If you get away with this, I'll—

PYTH Will you really?

PAR I'll pay you back, by god.

PYTH No doubt. But this is a threat, perhaps, Parmeno, for
some day in the future. More immediately you are going

431

flagitiis et eundem indicas. uterque in te exempla edent.

PAR   nullus sum!

PYTH   hic pro illo munere tibi honos est habitus. abeo.

PAR   egomet meo indicio miser quasi sorex hodie perii.

V. vii: GNATHO. THRASO. (PARMENO.)

1025 GNA   quid nunc? qua spe aut quo consilio huc imus? quid
        coeptas, Thraso?

THR   egone? ut Thaidi me dedam et faciam quod iubeat.

GNA   quid est?

THR   qui minus quam Hercules servivit Omphalae?

GNA   exemplum placet.
        utinam tibi commitigari videam sandalio caput!
        sed fores crepuerunt ab ea.

THR   perii! quid hoc autemst mali?

1030   hunc ego numquam videram etiam. quidnam hic pro-
        perans prosilit?

V. viii: CHAEREA. PARMENO. GNATHO. THRASO.

CHAE   o populares, ecquis me vivit hodie fortunatior?
        nemo hercle quisquam. nam in me plane di potestatem
        suam
        omnem ostendere, quoi tam subito tot congruerint com-
        moda.

PAR   quid hic laetus est?

---

[43] Donatus explains that the shrew squeaks loudly while eating and so betrays itself to captors even in the dark.

[44] Omphale was a Lydian queen to whom Hercules was bonded as a slave in expiation of the murder of Iphitus, a prince from Oechalia in Euboea. Lucian refers to a painting which showed Omphale beating Hercules over the head with a slipper (*How History Should Be Writtten* 10, *Dialogue of the Gods* 13.2).

[45] See *The Woman of Andros* note 40.

THE EUNUCH

to be strung up for getting the foolish young lad into disgrace and then giving him away to his father. Both of them will make an example of you.

PAR I'm done for!

PYTH It's the reward that you get for your present. I'm off. (*she exits into Thais' house*)

PAR I've destroyed myself today with my own squeaking, just like the proverbial shrew.[43] (*he stands aside as Gnatho and Thraso approach*)

Enter GNATHO and THRASO right from the direction of Thraso's house.

GNA What now? What are we hoping or planning to achieve by coming here? What are you up to, Thraso?

THR Me? To surrender to Thais and do whatever she commands.

GNA What?

THR Why not? Hercules was a slave to Omphale.

GNA A fine precedent! (*aside*) I'd love to see her soften up your head with her slipper![44] (*aloud*) But I hear her door.[45]

THR (*as Chaerea emerges from the house*) Damn it! What the hell's this? I've never seen this fellow before. Why is he bursting out in such a hurry?

Enter CHAEREA from Thais' house in a state of elation.

CHAE Fellow countrymen, is there anyone alive today more fortunate than me? Nobody at all. The gods have clearly manifested all their powers in my case; so many blessings have been heaped upon me so unexpectedly.

PAR (*aside*) What's he so joyful about?

CHAE   o Parmeno mi, o mearum voluptatum omnium
1035   inventor, inceptor, perfector, scis me in quibus sim gau-
        diis?
        scis Pamphilam meam inventam civem?
PAR   audivi.
CHAE   scis sponsam mihi?
PAR   bene, ita me di ament, factum!
GNA   audin tu hic quid ait?
CHAE   tum autem Phaedriae
        meo fratri gaudeo esse amorem omnem in tranquillo.
        unast domus.
        Thais patri se commendavit in clientelam et fidem;
1040   nobis dedit se.
PAR   fratris igitur Thais totast?
CHAE   scilicet.
PAR   iam hoc aliud est quod gaudeamus: miles pelletur foras.
CHAE   tu frater ubiubist fac quam primum haec audiat.
PAR   visam domum.
THR   num quid, Gnatho, tu dubitas quin ego nunc perpetuo
        perierim?
GNA   sine dubio, opinor.
CHAE   quid commemorem primum aut laudem maxume?
1045   illumne qui mi dedit consilium ut facerem, an me qui id
        ausu' sim
        incipere, an fortunam collaudem quae gubernatrix fuit,
        quae tot res tantas tam opportune in unum conclusit
        diem,
        an mei patris festivitatem et facilitatem? o Iuppiter,
        serva, obsecro, haec bona nobis!

CHAE (*seeing Parmeno*) Parmeno, my dear fellow, the deviser, the initiator, the perfecter of all my delights, do you know how happy I am? Do you know my Pamphila has been found to be a citizen?

PAR (*without enthusiasm*) I've heard so.

CHAE Do you know she's engaged to me?

PAR (*realising the significance of this for himself*) Heaven help me, splendid news!

GNA (*aside to Thraso*) Do you hear what he says?

CHAE And then I'm delighted for my brother Phaedria, whose whole affair is in calm waters. We're one family. Thais has entrusted herself to my father's care and protection. She's thrown in her lot with us.

PAR So Thais is wholly your brother's?

CHAE Of course.

PAR Then there's another cause for rejoicing: the soldier will be thrown out.

CHAE Make sure my brother hears the news as soon as possible, wherever he is.

PAR I'll see if he's at home. (*he exits into his house*)

THR (*aside to Gnatho*) Can you have any doubt that this is the end of me for ever?

GNA (*aside to Thraso*) None at all, if you ask me.

CHAE (*to himself*) Who deserves to be named first or praised the most? The one who suggested the plan of action, or myself who dared to carry it out? Or should I praise Fortune the helmswoman who has packed so many favours into a single day? Or my father for his good humour and generosity? Oh Jupiter, I beseech you, preserve these blessings for us.

V. ix: PHAEDRIA. CHAEREA. THRASO. GNATHO.

PHAE   di vostram fidem! incredibilia

1050   Parmeno modo quae narravit! sed ubist frater?

CHAE   praesto adest.

PHAE gaudeo.

CHAE   satis credo. nil est Thaide hac, frater, tua
dignius quod ametur. ita nostrae omnist fautrix familiae.

PHAE   hui!
mihi illam laudas?

THR   perii! quanto minus speist, tanto magis amo.
obsecro, Gnatho, in te spes est.

GNA   quid vis faciam?

THR   perfice hoc

1055   precibus pretio ut haeream in parte aliqua tandem apud
           Thaidem.

GNA difficilest.

THR   si quid collubuit, novi te. hoc si effeceris,
quodvis donum praemium a me optato: id optatum aufe-
res.

GNA itane?

THR   sic erit.

GNA   si efficio hoc, postulo ut mihi tua domus
te praesente absente pateat, invocato ut sit locus

1060   semper.

THR   do fidem futurum.

GNA   accingar.

PHAE   quem ego hic audio?
o Thraso.

THR   salvete.

PHAE   tu fortasse quae facta hic sient
nescis.

Enter PHAEDRIA *from his house.*

PHAE (*to himself*) Heaven help us! What Parmeno has just told me is unbelievable. But where's my brother?

CHAE Here, at your service.

PHAE I'm delighted.

CHAE I'm sure you are. There is nobody more worthy of love than your Thais, brother. She's such a supporter of our whole family.

PHAE What! Are you praising her to *me?*

THR (*aside to Gnatho*) Damn it. The less my hope, the more I'm in love. I implore you, Gnatho: my hopes lie in you.

GNA What do you want me to do?

THR Contrive somehow by persuasion or bribery for me to retain some footing with Thais.

GNA It's difficult.

THR If you set your heart on something, I know what you can do. If you achieve this, ask me for any gift you like as a reward; you'll get what you ask.

GNA Really?

THR Really.

GNA If I achieve it, my condition is that your house should always be open to me whether you are at home or not, that there should always be a place for me even without an invitation.

THR I give you my word.

GNA I'll gird myself for action. (*they approach Phaedria and Chaerea*)

PHAE (*to Chaerea*) Who's that speaking? Oh, Thraso!

THR Good day to you both.

PHAE Perhaps you're not aware what has been happening here?

437

THR		scio.
PHAE		quor te ergo in his ego conspicor regionibus?
THR	vobis fretus.	
PHAE		scin quam fretus? miles, edico tibi,

si te in platea offendero hac post umquam, quod dicas mihi

1065   "alium quaerebam, iter hac habui," periisti.

GNA   heia! haud sic decet.

PHAE dictumst.

THR   non cognosco vostrum tam superbum—

PHAE   sic ago.

GNA prius audite paucis; quod quom dixero, si placuerit, facitote.

CHAE   audiamus.

GNA   tu concede paullum istuc, Thraso.

principio ego vos ambos credere hoc mihi vehementer velim,

1070   me huius quidquid facio id facere maxume causa mea;

verum si idem vobis prodest, vos non facere inscitiast.

PHAE quid id est?

GNA   militem rivalem ego recipiundum censeo.

PHAE   hem!

recipiundum?

GNA   cogita modo. tu hercle cum illa, Phaedria,

ut lubenter vivis (etenim bene lubenter victitas),

1075   quod des paullumst et necessest multum accipere Thai-
dem;

ut tuo amori suppeditari possit sine sumptu tuo ad

omnia haec, magis opportunus nec magis ex usu tuo

1063 scin . . . periisti *Phaedriae dat* Σ, *Chaereae* A
1066 sic ago *Phaedriae dat* Σ, *Chaereae* A

THR I am.

PHAE Why then do I see you still in this vicinity?

THR I'm in your hands.

PHAE Do you know how much so? Soldier, I hereby inform you that, if I ever again find you in this street, even if you say "I was looking for someone else; I had to come this way," it's the end of you.

GNA (*to Phaedria*) Come on now! That's no way to talk!

PHAE I've told you.

THR This arrogance is not like you.

PHAE That's the way it is.

GNA Listen to me a minute first, and, if you like what I say, do it.

CHAE (*to Phaedria*) Let's hear him.

GNA (*to Thraso*) You stand aside a little over there, Thraso. (*to Phaedria and Chaerea as Thraso moves out of earshot*) First, I very much want you both to understand that what I'm doing here I'm doing principally for my own sake. But if it benefits you at the same time, it would be foolish of you not to do it.

PHAE What is it?

GNA I propose that you accept the soldier as a rival.

PHAE What! Accept him?

GNA Just think. Much as you enjoy living with her, Phaedria— and you do enjoy living it up with her—god knows you've little to give her, and Thais needs many gifts. If you want the demands of your love affair to be supplied without any expense on your part, there is nobody more convenient or more useful. First of all, he has the means to

---

1068 audiamus *Phaedriae dat* Σ, *Chaereae* A
1076 suppeditari A¹, suppeditare A²Σ *Don.*

nemost. principio et habet quod det et dat nemo largius.
fatuos est, insulsus, tardus, stertit noctes et dies,
1080   neque istum metuas ne amet mulier. facile pellas ubi ve-
        lis.

PHAE quid agimus?

GNA   praeterea hoc etiam, quod ego vel primum puto,
    accipit homo nemo melius prorsus neque prolixius.

CHAE mirum ni illoc homine quoquo pacto opust.

PHAE   idem ego arbitror.

GNA recte facitis. unum etiam hoc vos oro, ut me in vostrum
    gregem
1085   recipiatis. satis diu hoc iam saxum vorso.

PHAE   recipimus.

CHAE ac lubenter.

GNA   at ego pro istoc, Phaedria, et tu, Chaerea,
    hunc comedendum vobis propino et deridendum.

CHAE   placet.

PHAE dignus est.

GNA   Thraso, ubi vis accede.

THR   obsecro te, quid agimus?

GNA quid? isti te ignorabant. postquam eis mores ostendi tuos
1090   et collaudavi secundum facta et virtutes tuas,
    impetravi.

THR   bene fecisti; gratiam habeo maxumam.
    numquam etiam fui usquam quin me omnes amarent
    plurumum.

1083 *sic A; personas invertit* Σ
1086 ac lubenter *Chaereae dat* Σ, *Phaedriae continuat* A

440

give, and nobody gives more generously. He's stupid,
crass, a dimwit, who snores night and day; so you needn't
worry that the woman will fall in love with him. You can
easily throw him out when you want to.

PHAE (*to Chaerea*) What do we do?

GNA Besides, and in my opinion this is quite the most impor-
tant thing, there's nobody in the world who entertains
better or more lavishly than he does.

CHAE (*to Phaedria*) It seems as if we need the fellow, whichever
way you look at it.

PHAE I think so too.

GNA You're doing the right thing. I have just one more
request, that you accept me into your circle. I've been
rolling this stone uphill long enough.[46]

PHAE We accept you.

CHAE And willingly.

GNA In return for this, Phaedria, and you Chaerea, I offer you
Thraso to feast upon and to make fun of.

CHAE I like the idea.

PHAE It's what he deserves.

GNA (*to Thraso*) Come over here, when you're ready.

THR (*coming over*) For goodness' sake, how are we doing?

GNA How? These people didn't know you. Once I revealed to
them your true character and praised you in keeping with
your deeds and virtues, I won them over.

THR Well done! I'm most grateful. (*complacently*) I've never
yet been anywhere where I didn't win people's hearts.

---

[46] A proverbial phrase for an impossible task, derived from the pun-
ishment of Sisyphus, who was compelled in Hades to roll a rock up a
hill, from which it always rolled down again. In this context *saxum* is also
a term of abuse, alluding to Thraso's stupidity.

GNA dixin ego in hoc esse vobis Atticam elegantiam?
PHAE nil praeter promissumst. ite hac.
Ω   vos valete et plaudite.

1094 ite hac *Phaedriae continuat* A, *Gnathoni dat* Σ

GNA   (*to Phaedria and Chaerea*) Didn't I tell you that he had real Attic charm?

PHAE   (*with heavy irony*) It's exactly as you promised. (*pointing towards Thais' house*) Come this way.

ALL   (*to the audience*) Farewell, and give us your applause.[47]

---

[47] See *The Woman of Andros* note 55.

METRICAL ANALYSIS

Andria

1–174 iamb. sen.
175–179 mutatis modis canticum
    175 iamb. oct.
    176 iamb. dim.
    177 iamb. oct.
    178–179 troch. sept.
180–214 iamb. oct. (nisi 196–198 iamb. sen.)
215–224 iamb. sen. (plus 225 iamb. oct., 226 iamb. sen., 227
   iamb. oct.)
228–233 troch. sept.
234–239 iamb. oct.
240–253 mutatis modis canticum
    240 iamb. dim.
    241–242 troch. sept.
    243 iamb. oct.
    244 iamb. dim.
    245 troch. oct.
    246 troch. dim. cat.
    247 troch. oct.
    248–251 troch. sept.
    252 iamb. dim.
    253 iamb. oct.

254–260 troch. sept.

261–269 iamb. oct.

270–298 iamb. sen. (plus 299–300 iamb. sept.)

301–308 mutatis modis canticum

    301 troch. oct.

    302 troch. sept.

    303–304 iamb. oct.

    305 troch. oct.

    306 troch. sept.

    307 troch. oct.

    308 troch. sept.

309–316 iamb. oct. (plus 317 troch. sept., 318 iamb. sen.)

319–383 troch. sept.

384–393 iamb. sen.

394–403 iamb. oct.

404–480 iamb. sen.

481–486 canticum lyricum

    481–484 bacch. tetr.

    485 iamb. dim. cat.

    486 iamb. sen.

487–509 iamb. oct. (nisi 497–498 iamb. sen., 506 ut vid. iamb. sept.)

510–523 troch. sept. (nisi 517 troch. dim. cat.)

524–532 iamb. sen.

533–536 iamb. oct. (plus 537 iamb. dim.)

538–574 iamb. sen.

575–581 iamb. sept.

582–604 iamb. oct.

605–609 mutatis modis canticum

    605 troch. dim. cat.

    606 troch. sept.

    607–608 troch. oct.

609 troch. sept.
610–620 iamb. oct.
621–624 troch. sept.
625–638 canticum lyricum
    625 dact. tetr.
    626–634 cret. tetr.
    635 cret. tetr. sync.
    636 iamb. dim.
    637 cret. dim.
    638 cret. dim. augm.
639–649 troch. sept. (nisi 641–642 iamb. oct.)
650–654 iamb. oct.
655–681 iamb. sen. (nisi 663–664 iamb. oct.; plus 682–683 iamb. oct.)
684–715 iamb. sept.
716–819 iamb. sen.
820–860 troch. sept.
861–865 iamb. oct. (nisi 864 troch. sept.)
866–895 iamb. sen.
896–928 troch. sept.
929–958 iamb. oct.
959–981 troch. sept.

Heauton

1–174 iamb. sen.
175–180 mutatis modis canticum
    175 troch. oct.
    176 troch. sept.
    177 troch. oct.
    178 troch. dim. cat.
    179–180 troch. sept.

181–241 iamb. oct. (nisi 187 troch. sept.)
242–256 troch. sept.
257–264 iamb. oct.
265–311 iamb. sen.
312–339 troch. sept.
340–380 iamb. sen.
381–397 troch. sept.
398–404 iamb. oct.
405–561 iamb. sen.
562–590 mutatis modis canticum
    562–563 troch. oct.
    564 troch. sept.
    565 iamb. oct.
    566 iamb. dim.
    567–569 troch. oct.
    570 troch. sept.
    571 iamb. oct.
    572 troch. oct.
    573 troch. sept.
    574–578 iamb. oct.
    579 troch. sept.
    580–582 troch. oct.
    583–584 troch. sept.
    585–588 iamb. oct.
    589–590 iamb. sen.
591–613 troch. sept.
614–622 iamb. oct.
623–667 troch. sept.
668–678 iamb. oct.
679–707 iamb. sept. (plus 708 iamb. sen.)
709–722 troch. sept
723–748 iamb. sept.

749–873 iamb. sen.
874–907 troch. sept.
908–939 iamb. sen.
940–979 troch. sept.
980–999 iamb. oct.
1000–1019 mutatis modis canticum
    1000–1002 iamb. sept.
    1003 iamb. oct.
    1004 iamb. dim.
    1005–1012 iamb. oct.
    1013–1016 troch. sept.
    1017–1018 iamb. oct.
    1019 iamb. dim.
1020–1067 troch. sept.

Eunuchus

1–206 iamb. sen.
207–224 mutatis modis canticum
    207 troch. oct.
    208 troch. sept.
    209 iamb. dim.
    210–211 troch. sept.
    212 iamb. oct.
    213 iamb. dim.
    214 troch. sept.
    215 iamb. dim.
    216–217 troch. oct.
    218 troch. sept.
    219–223 iamb. oct.
    224 troch. sept.
225–254 troch. sept.

255–291 iamb. sept.
293–306 mutatis modis canticum
    293–297 iamb. oct.
    298 troch. sept.
    299 iamb. dim.
    300 iamb. sen.
    301 iamb. dim.
    302–303 iamb. oct.
    304 troch. oct.
    305 troch. dim.
    306 troch. sept.
307–319 iamb. oct. (plus 320 iamb. sen., 321–322 iamb. sept.)
323–351 iamb. sen.
352–366 troch. sept.
367–390 iamb. oct.
391–538 iamb. sen.
539–548 iamb. sept.
549–561 mutatis modis canticum
    549–550 troch. sept.
    551–552 iamb. sept.
    553–556 iamb. oct.
    557 iamb. sept.
    558–559 troch. oct.
    560 troch. sept.
    561 iamb. sept.
562–591 iamb. oct.
592–614 iamb. sept.
615–622 mutatis modis canticum
    615 troch. oct.
    616 troch. sept.
    617 iamb. oct.
    618–620 troch. oct.

621 troch. sept.
622 iamb. oct.
623–628 troch. sept.
629–642 iamb. sen.
643–658 mutatis modis canticum
    643–644 troch. oct.
    645 troch. sept.
    646 iamb. oct.
    647 iamb. dim.
    648 iamb. oct.
    649 troch. sept.
    650 iamb. oct.
    651 troch. sept.
    652 iamb. dim.
    653 iamb. oct.
    654 troch. oct.
    655 troch. sept.
    656–657 iamb. oct.
    658 iamb. sen.
659–667 iamb. oct.
668–702 iamb. sen.
703–726 troch. sept.
727–737 iamb. oct. (plus 738 iamb. sen.)
739–746 troch. oct.
747–754 mutatis modis canticum
    747 troch. dim.
    748 troch. oct.
    749 troch. sept.
    750 iamb. oct.
    751–752 troch. sept.
    753–754 iamb. sept.
755–770 troch. sept.

451

771–787 iamb. oct.
788–816 troch. sept.
817–942 iamb. sen.
943–970 troch. sept.
971–1001 iamb. sen.
1002–1024 iamb. sept.
1025–1030 troch. sept.
1031–1049 iamb. oct.
1050–1094 troch. sept.

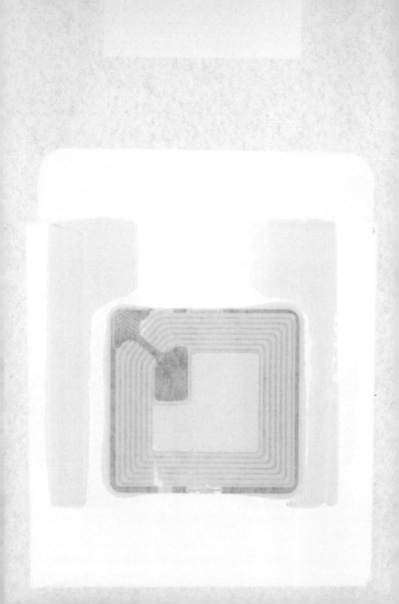

LUTHERAN THEOLOGICAL SOUTHERN SEMINARY

3 5898 00120 3625

PA 6756 .A1 B36 2001 v.'
Terence.
Terence

LINEBERGER
MEMORIAL LIBRARY
LUTHERAN THEOLOGICAL
SOUTHERN SEMINARY
COLUMBIA, SOUTH CAROLINA 29203

DEMCO